BLACK NERD PROBLEMS

BLACK NERD PROBLEMS

WILLIAM EVANS
AND OMAR HOLMON

G

GALLERY BOOKS

NEW YORK   LONDON   TORONTO   SYDNEY   NEW DELHI

G

Gallery Books
An Imprint of Simon & Schuster, Inc.
1230 Avenue of the Americas
New York, NY 10020

First Gallery Books hardcover edition September 2021

GALLERY BOOKS and colophon are registered
trademarks of Simon & Schuster, Inc.

For information about special discounts for bulk purchases,
please contact Simon & Schuster Special Sales at 1-866-506-1949
or business@simonandschuster.com.

The Simon & Schuster Speakers Bureau can bring authors
to your live event. For more information or to book an event,
contact the Simon & Schuster Speakers Bureau at 1-866-248-3049
or visit our website at www.simonspeakers.com.

Interior design by Michelle Marchese

Manufactured in the United States of America

10 9 8 7 6 5 4 3 2 1

Library of Congress Cataloging-in-Publication Data has been applied for.

ISBN 978-1-9821-5023-5
ISBN 978-1-9821-5025-9 (ebook)

To Maes Hughes, T'Chaka, Neji, Ted Kord,
Jean Grey fifty-leven times, Mufasa, Poussey Washington, Sasha
Blouse, them ninjas Madara took out with the paper bomb, and all
the heroes who couldn't make it to see the release of this book.
None of this is possible without your sacrifice.

Contents

CONTENTS

CONTENTS

Intro: From the Top

WILLIAM: Listen, when Omar and I met on the mean streets of Madison, Wisconsin, doing the grimy shit called poetry slams back in 2008, we didn't know we would end up writing a book together. Man, I didn't even like this muthafucka's stage name. True anime rivalry/friendship shit, man. We slammed against each other, we watched each other get bullshit scores or win crowns. And then we started talkin' nerd shit. All the nerd shit.

OMAR: Through nerd shit all connections are possible. In 2013 we brought you Black Nerd Problems, the website. Eight years of memes, live tweets, *Game of Thrones* recaps, and the hard pop culture ESPN-level analysis that cyber streets needed. It all led to this Black-ass nerdy-ass book. Originally, we told Simon & Schuster we wanted this shit published on papyrus. We doing this for the old-school printing press. Y'all want that Old English back? Y'all want that Shakespeare back? Well, that's too damn bad 'cause this right here written in Wakandan (we'll do a loose translation for those unfamiliar).

WILLIAM: Nah, we writing this shit like a manga, the rest of this shit you gotta read right to left, fam. [I'm joking, don't do shit. Omar and I can't speak nothing but English and Black-ass English. I've been watching subbed anime for years and I couldn't speak a sentence of Japanese with a *Naruto* Rasengan to my head.]

Seriously though, what Black Nerd Problems has taught me is how wide-ranging our nerddom can be. I didn't start reading comics till 2006. I didn't start watching anime on the regular until I edited someone else's Black Nerd Problems piece. Omar been talkin' about *Hajime no Ippo* like it's his Quran or some shit, and I love him, but I STILL ain't seen a second of that joint. But I will defend that shit to my dying breath. You: "Man, sports anime is okay." Me: "That's cuz you ain't hip to *Hajime*, bruh!" And that's the point of this book, yo. You may not catch every reference, every *jutsu*, every filler arc, but we trying to make sure you know we felt that shit.

OMAR: And isn't that the heart of being a nerd? **Naruto* flutes chime in* That feeling of excitement and passion for a show, book, or character that you fucks with and then wanting to share that among friends or even strangers, hoping they feel the same thing you do? *Morpheus from *The Matrix* voice* Isn't that worth nerding out over? Isn't that worth fighting for, for Black nerds and nerds of color to come together and share that joy? We thought so.

Re-Definition: Nerd Isn't a Person, It's a Spectrum

OMAR HOLMON,
aka Noah Webster's Ghostwriter

BEFORE WE CAN get into this real rap raw nerd essays and content, it's important to understand what we as authors mean when we refer to the term *nerd*. How we define the word may be different than how the reader defines it. So allow me to get my TED Talk monologue on to break the definition of the word *nerd* down by how it has come to be defined in dictionaries. *takes off my regular square-framed glasses and puts on my public-speaking PowerPoint presentation tortoiseshell-framed glasses*

The online *Merriam-Webster* dictionary defines a nerd as an "unstylish, unattractive, or socially inept person; *especially*: one slavishly devoted to intellectual or academic pursuits."

Dictionary.com defines a nerd as "1. a person considered to be socially awkward, boring, unstylish, etc.; 2. an intelligent but single-minded person obsessed with a nonsocial hobby or pursuit: *a computer nerd.*"

As words evolve, they go through semantic change or, more fittingly, semantic progression. Semantic progression occurs when the modern meaning of a word is entirely different from its original meaning. Watch the breakdown: *dope*, as a noun, used to just refer to a "stupid" person (1850s); later on in time it became a reference to drugs (1880–1900s), but as an adjective it can refer to something as good or great (1980s). You can think of countless other words that you've seen evolve via idioms and slang, which varies across cultures and ethnicities. One word that hasn't officially (as of me writing this in 2020) evolved in the dictionary is the term *nerd*.

Now, you may be reading this and thinking, "Where's this goin'? Who gives a fuck? Why did he switch glasses when he was already wearing glasses?" Well, if you're reading this book (that clearly says *Black Nerd Problems* on it) or just "glimpsing through it," *Jeff Foxworthy voice* *youuuuu* might be a ~~redneck~~ nerd. Regardless, hear me out and watch how I flip this shit.

The only saving grace between both online dictionaries' descriptions is their second definitions for the term: "one slavishly devoted to intellectual or academic pursuits" and "an intelligent but single-minded person obsessed with a nonsocial hobby." Growing up in the 2000s from my teen to college years, I came to understand the term and had the term broken down to me as "a person that knows a little bit about a lot of things," whereas a geek knows a lot about one specific thing. For me, and I want to say for a lot us that identify as nerds, this is a commonplace interpretation of the word, but as far as I know, I haven't ever seen that reflected on paper regarding the word in an "official" definition.

I stated all that to say this: it's been a long time since the term *nerd* came in the context of a jock vs. an academic, or the popular high school quarterback pushing a scrawny kid into a locker, or the "mean girls" knocking books out of someone's hands. Now in 2020, it ain't really the *Revenge of the Nerds* movie setting for the context of the word—I'm hard-pressed to say if it ever was . . . and thank god 'cause even in that movie about underdog "nerds" trying to get their revenge, it's full of misogyny and racial ste-reotypes. Speaking of stereotypes, media representation gotta be factored in the description for a nerd as well, right? A nerd is usually a male (which is usually sexist), typically white (which is typically racist), scrawny or fat (but in the derogatory fatphobic way), that's (lest we forget) into some obscure hobby/thing no one else cares about. [Sidebar: If you're reading this and wanting to say Steve Urkel from *Family Matters* as a breaking of the mold by being the first mainstream Black nerd, I question why Urkel, who debuted in 1989, gets that credit and not Dwayne Wayne from *A Different World*, who was a fucking mathematician and debuted two years before Urkel. Dwayne Wayne and Steve Urkel were both nerds, the only difference was Urkel played heavily on the exaggerated stereotypes of a nerd. So, is a nerd only recog-nized as a nerd when it comes with a full package of stereotypes? Never mind that the nerdy character Roger "Raj" Thomas from *What's Happening!!* debuted in 1976. Wouldn't he be both their OG? But I digress . . .]

Okay, so we got the origin/etymology of *nerd* down, right? Boom. Now dead all that. With the way the term has evolved and how it's been incorporated in mainstream media, *nerd* is much more than a singular person, it's a spectrum. *Nerd* has evolved more so into being a fan of a genre. That genre doesn't have to just be comic books, movies. Sneakerheads are fans of sneakers and know them in explicit detail. They could be considered nerds. Hip-hop heads who know their entire history of the music genre can be considered nerds. Academic nerds. Cooking-show nerds. Sports fans are mos def nerds by being able to recount a player's performance statistics like an RPG character. The list goes on. If you enjoy something, anything you want, if it excites you and you want other people to know of it and enjoy it, then you're a fan of it, which also means you're a fucking nerd for it. That sounds beautiful and inclusive on paper, doesn't it? Sounds great on paper . . . Here's the problem. To be a nerd means being part of a subculture. A cultural group or collective within a much larger culture that doesn't adhere to the status quo, beliefs, or interests of the larger culture. If you're a Black or POC nerd, then you're in a subculture within a subculture (*Inception* shit). The problem is being a part of this subculture means you're part of a minority, which then becomes attached to the identity of being a nerd.

So, when nerd shit starts becoming trendy, a divide occurs, with those nerds now being in an era where this thing only a few loved becomes loved by even more folks. This hobby that was part of the minority is now enjoyed by the majority. So, what happens when what you fan out for isn't the obscure cool thing only a few know about anymore? It's like having a favorite band or artist that was low-key for a long time suddenly blow up with a hit single. Its fan base widens and now they've got a larger reach. There's that feeling of having been there riding for them before they sold out, as the cliché goes. As if everyone enjoying or having access to them now somehow dilutes the enjoyment for those there from the beginning. You know exactly what I'm talking about. Watch the breakdown: We get big-budget superhero movies yearly now. They've become the new Spaghetti Westerns. These superhero movies bring more folks to comic books, comic books become more common reading material and are even seen as a more mainstream-adjacent hobby and not seen as "just for kids." Nerds that fucked with comics when it wasn't associated with cool or trendy then feel like "It wasn't accepted like that when I was coming up. Now that it is, how do I fit in?" Therein lies the problem.

Individually, that nerd is no longer part of a small underdog group; they become part of a larger group that likes comic books now. It's like going from the Resistance to joining the Empire. There's this fear of losing that cool subculture-minority identity that they've come to identify themselves by. So, in order to hold on to identity, you see folks using all the knowledge they've acquired as a litmus test for others to see who was there from the beginning like them or knows as much as them. Now when someone comes into this group liking comics but doesn't know Professor X's Social Security number stated in a back issue from thirty years ago, then they're "not a true fan" or "not a real nerd" or, if they're a woman, a "fake geek girl." All this from a fear of a loss of identity. See how fear is the path to the dark side? Fear leads to anger. Anger leads to hate. Hate leads to ~~suffering~~ gatekeeping. Nerds gatekeeping other nerds to see if they're "nerdy" enough for the nerdy club looks like Anakin Skywalker cuttin' down them Jedi younglings. You're hurtin' the cause instead of helping it, fam.

If the definition of *nerd* needs to go through semantic progression and the term *nerd* has evolved into a spectrum instead of just an individual, then the individuals that adhere to this spectrum must become more malleable and welcoming to all portions of said spectrum in order to make the definition true. I don't think *nerd* as a subculture is a thing of the past or a Force ghost now. The progression of *nerd* as a subculture shouldn't be feared, especially when *nerd* as a spectrum contains various multitudes and hues. I mean, think of the word *nerd* like the Pokémon Pikachu: we've gained so much experience over the years, it's time for that fucker to evolve into a Raichu. However, if due to the fear of a loss of identity folks keep gatekeeping the term as if it's a title to be earned instead of a realization one comes to across a spectrum of genres, then the definition of *nerd* will remain as it has been over the years, a Pikachu. Yeah, it's cute, convenient, and comfortable, but with what we know now and all this experience, the definition of the word could take that next step and evolve into so much more . . . like motherfucking Raichu or a hue in a vast nerdy mutherfucking spectrum.

It's Time We Stop Pretending That Simba Wasn't Garbage in *The Lion King*

WILLIAM EVANS,
aka Diversity Consultant to Pride Rock

SAY WHAT YOU will about Disney movies (and there's plenty), but you can't be out here in these streets acting like Disney ain't got hits. They've been servicing the young, the old, the old with youngins, and everyone in between for more than seventy-five years, fam. But the banger? The one that make you call up the fine gender-nonconforming gal/guy lion on a Friday night and ask if you trying to Disney and chill is *The Lion King*. Ain't even close, folks. Not even. *Lion King* is exactly that, king of the gotdamn Pride Rock, and to this day, it still tops my chart.

But even as we come to give praise to one of the best that ever done it, we have to set some baselines first. One: Rafiki was reincarnated as a brotha in Atlanta named Darius. Two: "Can You Feel the Love Tonight" is one verse and a couple of lyrical choices away from being borderline risqué for a G-rated film. And three: Simba, the beloved protagonist of the film, is straight up landfill. Trash. Rubbage. Election 2020. Whatever you want to call it, man. Every time I see a clip of Simba whipping his premature mane back and forth, I want to yell at the TV, "But YOU AIN'T THAT NICE, B, *vigorous hand clap* YOU AIN'T THAT NICE."

I know, Simba is an American icon. Like a Kardashian. Or the Confederate flag. But I ain't convinced, man. Simba made some calls that just don't sit right on my spirit. I recently watched *The Lion King* with my daughter, thinking that I was about to enjoy one of the best movies of all time while watching my daughter enjoy the majesty of this film for the first time. Man, listen. As soon as Rafiki lifted your dude up to the heavens and the whole hood bowed, it all came rushing back to me, like wait . . . they bowing down for who now? Elephants lowering their tusks for the softest cub in the Pride Lands?

But let's be fair, I guess, it's pretty hard to follow Mufasa. It's basically like when Bad Boy tried to replace Biggie with Shyne and then that shady shit went down in the club and Shyne caught ten years in prison for it. I mean, he did have one hit, at least. Simba's "I Just Can't Wait to Be King" should've been "I Just Can't Wait to Book This Passport Out the Pride Lands when Scar, aka Marlo, Moves In on My Corners." But we should've known, man. We should've known when this dude hopped his ass on the back of an ostrich, smiling like Drake in a gentlemen's club while singing in C major. You can't be king like that, fam. King Robert Baratheon woulda never been caught doing some dumb shit like that, yo.

And Mufasa one of the realest to ever do it, I get that. Mufasa was like every Black parent who had gained the respect of his neighborhood and workplace but still couldn't keep his son from doing some dumb shit. Man, that scene when they walking back from the elephant graveyard with Mufasa way in front and Simba and Nala way in back reminded your boy of many a ride home when I was sitting in the back of the Dodge, silent as fuck, watching steam rising off my pop's head. But even Mufasa was gentle when he proved the point and wrestled away that anger with his cub. Then Mufasa was like, "Simba . . . Look at the stars. The great kings of the past look down on us from those stars. Whenever you feeling cocky, just remember these cats was the real deal and therefore exposing how garbage you really are."

For real, man, Simba was the son of the king. This dude ain't have no chores, stayed getting into shit and never taking responsibility for his actions. Basically Simba is the lion version of privilege and affluenza. I know Scar set that shit up to merk Mufasa, but Simba was the catalyst, man. Scar was like the dude in *Carlito's Way*, offering Guajiro a Coke in the cooler like, "Nah, man, it's just in the bottom, you just have to reach down for it." Sheeeeyet. Simba straight up fell for the Wu, the 36 Chambers, and the Gambinos.

Y'all gonna have to give me a moment, I don't think I've ever written about the death of Mufasa. I know it messes with the whole story, but Mufasa ain't have to go out like that, man. I mean, this is Disney, ayebody's mom gets buried before the intro credits hit, but dead Disney dads? That hits different for the brand. How you gonna give us *Hamlet* where we actually liked the king before he got rocked? You can't be killin' heroes and grand patriarchs like that on-screen, fam. Nah, Optimus Prime did that, so hopefully, you won't have to go through that. The hood might never forgive Disney for putting Mufasa out on the street, dead as all hell in the canyon like that. Also, when's the last time Disney just made you watch a dead body for, like, five minutes. I'm like, gotdamn, get my man Mufasa a white sheet or some shit.

Yes, I'm still salty about Simba bouncing like that. I get that dude fled the hyenas because they were about to have a lion two piece and a biscuit. But when Simba came to see his pop's not breathing, he gotta own that shit. Dude fled the Pride Lands like he had warrants. Involuntary manslaughter, to be clear. You know how Malia Obama took a gap year? Simba basically took a gap adolescence and left the hood in tatters. Simba wasn't concerned what was going down with his mom? Nala? He left Nala behind like Princess Leia chained up in the Cantina with Scar the Hutt. His mom a widow and a captive now. She had to be thinking about her son leaving her behind like, "But fuck me though, right?"

Scar basically brought crack to the hood in his absence, but Simba out here singing "*no worries*" with two stoners backpacking across Europe. So Nala having to come find his ass is the "we ran out of money, can you wire us some cash, but the butler gotta show up themselves to take your ass home" phase. He hit grown-up Nala with "Hakuna matata" and Nala hit him with "If you don't get that punk-ass free love bullshit the fuck up out my face, lion . . . Lions in the hood dying and you out here quoting a gotdamn meerkat? The fuck happened to you?" Dude needed guidance from his dead father just to get off his ass, fam. Mufasa was like, "Remember who you are." And I'm like, yeah, Simba 'bout to remember he a punk ass that dipped out on his fam over some survivor's guilt shit.

Here's a list of the best Disney heroes:

1. Mulan
2. Aladdin
3. Moana
4. Elsa
24. The mice in *Cinderella*
48. Lilo
136. Mulan's daddy's sword
. . .
. . .
. . .
378. Simba

I'm sure y'all want to give credit to Simba for coming back and claiming the kingdom, but he could've overpowered Scar's weak ass a lot earlier, like when he grew his big-boy paws, plus the Pride Lands was looking like Walter White's old home after folks found out he was Heisenberg since he been gone. I'm not saying Simba can't live, man, he just shouldn't be out here enjoying all this birthright and privilege at the expense of the realest lion in these streets getting 86'd in the middle of the plains like that. Then all the animals in the kingdom bowed to him like nothing changed! Like he didn't leave them on Dune with the sandworms and shit for years. Y'all need to look into some representative government, man. I don't think this is workin' for the everyday animals of the Pride Lands. Just remember that the next time "Circle of Life" start knockin' on your TV, you ain't got to take that knee for Simba's coronation, man. He ain't earned it, fam.

Raising the Avatar:
No One Woman of Color
Should Have All Them Haters

WILLIAM EVANS,
aka Korra's Earthbending Second Cousin
on Her Mama's Side

I DON'T ARGUE with strangers on the internet anymore. I know, there are rules to this fake discourse shit and I'm breaking them. But I can't summon the care like I used to. I'm old, I blame my knees. But there's a giant asterisk next to that statement for what I just can't let go unchecked in my corners of the interwebs. I will still fight people who:

- Use the wrong Black celebrity photo in a tweet because they think we all look alike
- Claim that they got bullied because they liked nerdy stuff when there's an 80 percent chance they were a gatekeeper and elicited their own scorn
- Throw dirt on Avatar Korra's name

I could maybe tolerate the first two, but Korra slander is non-negotiable. Yeah, I know, *The Last Airbender* is a superior animated show. There's a lot of reasons for that, but we ain't got time. Yes, you love you a lovable pacifist in Aang cuz cute and cuddly dudes that avoid conflict even when the fate of the world is at stake is your happy place. It's okay, I once tried to convince myself that Jay Electronica had a better verse on "Control" than Kendrick Lamar. We're all allowed to be wrong from time to time. Here's what's important though, my benders. Korra never stopped fighting for y'all. The fight was for her too, make no mistake. But she never dodged a fight and never bended herself toward an ambiguous verdict. You gotta respect it.

For me personally, there are two eras of *The Legend of Korra*: before the birth of my daughter and after.

BEFORE

If you're a fan of the Avatar universe and not just an old-guard patriarch that enjoys animated shows, then enjoying Korra should be a no-brainer. The Avatar is immensely powerful, brash. Cocky and stubborn. But still wide-eyed and susceptible to wonder. Still open to experiences and people different than her. A driving force of wanting to defend the helpless with a sense of moral justice. I just described one of the most common archetypes of an all-powerful protagonist in your favorite fiction story. Except Avatar Korra is a teenaged girl and no one girl should have all that power. Am I right? Who the fuck she think she is? All this bending without permission.

There are only two arguments against the character that is Korra (leaving the third one out cuz we not giving homophobic fans more air than this aside), but they are pretty easily debunked. If you don't like Korra because she is cocky as hell, I'd like to remind people that Korra knew she was the Avatar as a toddler because she could bend three elements from the jump, as opposed to the electoral college having to come inform her. A lot of y'all use every Twitter meme possible to post a picture of yourself next to a benign accomplishment. The hell do you think you would do as a five-year-old bending three elements? The people that hate Korra for this reason are the people that want to humble twenty-seven-year-old $100M athletes who pretend their abilities are ho-hum. Come on now.

The second is about her "losing" the Avatar line. Which is a thing. Written into the show. Kind of like how Aang sacrificed the Avatar state so he could come defend Katara and end up getting his shit rocked. But him being healed was a thing. Written into a show. Y'all gotta learn plots, man.

My point for all of that being, um, sexism? We don't grade men characters with the same scrutiny. The unlikable political woman clause. This is important, but important for me personally. Mostly because I have a daughter.

AFTER

When my daughter was five or six, our TV options were pretty predictable. *Bubble Guppies. Dora the Explorer.* Pretty much anything in the Nick Jr. or Disney Junior catalog. On a lazy weekend, desperate to climb out of the sing-along toddler hellscape, I gambled that she might like *The Legend of Korra*. I put it on without telling her anything about it, but the fact that it was a cartoon with a young girl for the main character was enough to get us started and hold her attention.

But it worked. At the time, book three of *Korra* had just begun, so I was in full *Korra* fandom. But something changed after that weekend. Over the course of ten days, the three of us watched the entirety of books one and two (my wife seeing book two for the first time, but already being a fan of the first one). I probably would've stopped after however far into the catalog we traveled on that first day, but suddenly, my daughter's typical requests for *Doc McStuffins* or *Pocoyo* (excellent animation if you're not hip) were replaced with

"Daddy, I want to watch Korra. Daddy, what happened to Korra?" What kind of father would I be to deny her that?

There was a practical hypothesis for why she wanted to keep watching *Korra*. Maybe it was the new shiny thing. Maybe it was much more than that. For people that shrug their shoulders or roll their eyes when it comes to representation on TV, my daughter is a pretty good test study. She will watch or indulge just about anything that is aimed at her age demographic, but she consistently veers toward characters that look closer to people of color, like Dora or Princess Elena. You know, people that look like her. She had all *Doc McStuffins* everything, but the reality is almost all kids had all *Doc McStuffins* everything at the time because she's that great. But there's a big difference between the lovable pigtailed girl who can talk to her toys and the confident, boastful teenager/young adult who harnesses all the physical power in the world, but has to learn how to navigate the world diplomatically. I want Doc to be my daughter's best friend. I want Korra to be the woman my daughter aspires to.

With a series' worth of recaps and more, I'm not exaggerating when I say that I've spent close to forty thousand words on *The Legend of Korra* and the character of Avatar Korra already. This isn't a chapter (exclusively) about how awesome Korra is (to paraphrase Bolin, I already know how awesome Korra is . . . she's awesome). This is a chapter about how my daughter once tackled me, kneeled on my chest, and yelled, "I'm the Avatar, you gotta deal with it!" This is a chapter about her looking over my shoulder while I was editing a *Legend of Korra* recap and then asking me to put her hair in three ponytails and roll her sleeves up past her shoulders to show her muscles like Korra does. My daughter didn't just want to do the things that Korra did on TV because she was a superhero, just like the way that boys run around showing their open palm to people after watching Iron Man. She sees herself in Korra in a fashion she hasn't with other characters on TV before.

It's been a joke among my friends for a while, but I often feel like I'm raising the Avatar. My daughter is smart and gifted in her physical attributes. She already seems to be good at about everything we throw at her. She's also bossy, headstrong, and impulsive. What she will be allowed to have, which Korra was allowed to have (and most TV characters don't), is a real emotional arc that charts maturity and resourcefulness. I really look forward to years down the road, where I might have the opportunity to revisit *The Legend of Korra* with my daughter when she can understand many of the more mature themes at work in the show, the likes of which manage to elude its critics from time to time as well.

Characters like Avatar Korra are a bridge between the cute and cuddly Doc McStuffins and the complicated young adult characters like Elida from *Vagrant Queen*. Korra is a character that can remind my daughter of her own power and also of the way the world will react to her. I heard a boy at school tell my daughter that she was better at playing dodgeball than him only because she had "big girl muscles." I know, we ain't got time to unpack all of that.

And before you ask: yes, yes he was.

But her response was that Korra has muscles too. And it's possible she would've had another example to reach for quickly and with so much validation behind it, but I'm not entirely sure.

And that's the point about representation. It isn't always about us putting up billboards that say, "We need people of color represented because we want people of color represented." It's often about how those marks of validation sit in our subconscious, or how we avoid talking ourselves out of the gifts that people would seek to weaponize against us.

The Legend of Korra has run its course as far as new episodes go, and despite all the ways that Nickelodeon tried to cripple its own product, it wrapped up the series on its own terms and in the most beautiful way possible as Korra and Asami walked off into the sunset (or spirit realm, if you will) together. But my connection to that world, that vision of maturation and rebirth and that untouchable protagonist, is something that won't fade away so easily for me. When my daughter was much younger we emulated Korra in so many ways. In the bath, we splashed each other and called it waterbending. When spring rolled around, we planted the garden and dug into the earth like badger moles. This was her lesson in earthbending. A few years later, when the winter snows came, she wanted to help me prep the fireplace. When I let her light it and the soft whoosh came from the new fire, she surprised me when she said, "You finally let me firebend!" Whistling, or airbending, is taking the longest. Like Korra, it doesn't really fit her personality much, but that doesn't mean she doesn't want to master it. So we're working on it, still. Daughters deserve to have all the available tools at their disposal. The world depends on it.

You Can't Win When Escapism Won't Let You Escape

OMAR HOLMON,
aka Harry Houdini's WiFi Password

KNOW THE GREAT thing about being a nerd? When the world gets crazy, there's an avenue of different media you can use to escape it. Pick your pop culture poison. Video games, comic books, movies, television, novels—there's a plethora to choose from in order to get away and recharge. I'm currently saying this as a Black male and writing this on June 11, 2020. Nearly three months after police kicked in the door on Breonna Taylor, Black EMT, and killed her in her own home while she was sleeping. Two weeks after George Floyd, a Black man, had an officer kneeling on his neck for eight minutes and forty-six seconds, leading to his death. There was no video of what happened to Breonna, but there was of what happened to George. As I type, protests are occurring not only all over the United States of America but the world as well, to declare that Black Lives Matter during a global pandemic.

Lemme run that again: around the entire world there are rallies, protests, and marches declaring that Black women, trans women, men, trans men, and children matter while COVID-19 is pulling a *28 Weeks Later*. Racism is so bad it got folks out to protest during a whole pandemic. The entire world is saying, "Stop killing Black folks." I don't exaggerate when I say I never thought I'd live to see this in my time. And yet, there's an entire section of those in power that don't get the message (or don't want to get it), saying, "But . . ." Meanwhile, Twitter becomes the new CNN, a thread of police brutality happening in real time with more than four hundred–plus videos of police brutality at these peaceful protests. I sat there going through the computer screen looking glass, viewing all of these videos for hours on end, night after night. About a day or two later, Will asked me what I was doing amid everything going on. I told 'em about the rabbit hole I was going down. Upon hearing it, he said, "Man, that doesn't sound like self-care to me," and he was right. It wasn't. But that's where the works of fiction I mentioned before come in tho, right? Ehhhhh . . .

Wanna know the rough thing about being a Black nerd? Sometimes you see art imitate life so well that it captures the Black experience in America by accident. The very experience that you turned to fiction to escape from for a moment gets thrown right back in your face inadvertently. The best example of this is Jonathan Hickman's writing in *Avengers*, vol. 5, #37, where the Fantastic Four's Mister Fantastic's daughter, Valeria, gives him a note containing advice for a problem he's facing. The note said, "You can't win. Time to start figuring out how not to lose." I read that quote seven years ago, back in 2013. To this day, I'm still hard-pressed to find another quote that so perfectly describes the Black experience in America to me. I'm not trying to summarize the Black experience down to one key phrase, especially one that sounds so bleak. But it really do be like that living in this country, man. This is a capitalistic society. Capitalism really only exists when ya have someone to shit on. Black folks been the ones taking that hit repeatedly. This, along with racism, contributes to a reality where we can't win, and even though we didn't have any part in creating this system of oppression, the onus is on Black folk to figure out how not to lose. All of which is to say, I hate it here. Still, I don't want to leave this country—not because leaving means they win, but because I was born here. I'd rather be here helping with the progress toward ways where we don't lose completely.

Still, there comes a time when you gotta step back and disconnect from what's goin' on. Rightfully so too, because escapism isn't a bad thing. You're giving yourself time to get better or just freedom. The problem is it's hard to do that James Harden step-back from race-related issues when you see instances of art imitating life and you're Black 24/7/365. When you're a Black nerd, there's certain things that you can read or see that resonate so much that once again, it snaps you out of what was supposed to be an escape and right back into what you were trying to escape from.

For example, I decided to get back into *Spider-Man* on PS4 to finish the "City That Never Sleeps" storyline. It was alarming how close to home the game hit with what's happening in real time with COVID-19 and the protests. In the story, there's a virus released that becomes a pandemic. One mission has you run into a Black Sable agent named David Obademi that's trying to get clinical masks out to the public and supplies to the war-torn country. Listen, I came here to get away from COVID-19's clutches, but this game making me remember there's a whole-ass pandemic goin' on outside no person is safe from in the real world still. When we first meet David, he's getting jumped by the corrupt members of a private military force. I automatically thought back to that Twitter-thread rabbit hole where police officers were destroying protestors' food and medical supplies. Art be imitating life way too hard at times, man.

There's another part in this storyline where Peter Parker talks to fellow Spidey Miles Morales and prepares him for Spider-Man training. Peter has Miles studying mathematical equations and physics to understand everything that goes into how using web-shooters and web-slinging as Spider-Man works. There's a point in the game where Miles uncovers the web-shooters Peter has made for him and they have this interaction:

> **MILES:** I can see that the nozzle size and shape is the same as your other ones.
> **PETER:** Yeah, so?
> **MILES:** Well, according to Hooke's Law elastic force is linear with distance, given all factors are equal. But you and I aren't equal.

Peter then realizes Miles is right, that the differences in pounds between them can affect so many things like tensile strength and web-fluid consumption. Miles, knowing this, figures out a 0.7-millimeter adjustment to the nozzle diameter will even things out.

I'm not sure if this conversation between Miles and Peter was a subtle reference toward racial equity, but it was damn well the first thing that my mind jumped to. Peter, being the only Spider-Man for so long, assumed he was the default and what worked for him should work for Miles. However, they aren't the same person. Therefore, those differences hinder Miles instead of help. This simple line of dialogue says so much . . . and if people in positions of power or with platforms in the real world were more like Peter Parker when called on shit, it'd be a better place. It could all be so simple, couldn't it?

Funny enough, there's another comic book quote from Jonathan Hickman that inadvertently touches on the Black experience. In *New Avengers*, vol. 3, #20 (2013), the Black Panther T'Challa is fighting against the Rider but saying they don't need to fight. T'Challa believes their issue can be worked out. Mind you, the issue was their planets/universes clashing together. One universe had to go so that the other could survive. The Rider tells him there's no need for platitudes, this fight between them was inevitable, so why lie? T'Challa, now agreeing, has a dagger appear in each hand provided by his suit and says, "Very well . . . No more lies. There will be death here today." It's such a hard-hitting line that sticks with me. So much so, it pops into my mind every time I see a post online about police killing a Black person. There's this moment of pause before I get in depth to the details of the matter for more information about the victim and how they were killed. Each time I take that leap into all that fucking hurt, I think, "Very well . . . No lies. There will be death here today," preparing myself for the reality of what I am about to encounter or engage with.

I hear the phrase while I'm scrolling through all the videos of Black folks the media puts out on display being brutalized by police whether they be on the news channel or on social media to raise awareness. Just the phrasing of that quote hits me at my core. It makes me think about how a regular day gets interrupted with images of a dead Black person on display or moments before their death. As if to say that good day you were just having was a false image. That good day you were having is irrelevant now or it was a lie, because this death, this unnecessary loss of Black life, this preventable loss of Black life, is still happening. "No lies. There will be death here today" reads to me in regard to social media platforms as "There will be a Black death on your timeline today, there will be a Black death in your news feed today, there will be a Black death here today." If there isn't, consider it nothing more than luck. Wild, right? Often it feels like no matter where you go, even in imagination, you can't escape the sight or the thought of Black loss.

sighs heavy as fuck I be wanting to get my self-care on, man. I swear. It's just so hard when the fiction you consume unexpectedly hits you with a reminder of what's going on in real time inadvertently. Don't get me wrong. There is escapism for Black people. There are other routes to disconnect. I just find it ironic that, as a Black nerd, when art imitates the Black experience in life even inadvertently, it hits so different when it's a phrase that exemplifies the struggle. The fucking roughest parts of that struggle. The parts where the best Black folk can do to survive is not lose from this position we've been put in where we can't win.

Into the Spider-Verse Got Three Moments Better Than the Best Moment of Your Favorite Comic Book Movie Not Named *Into the Spider-Verse*

WILLIAM EVANS,
aka Spider with the Webs and the Drip

ART IS SUBJECTIVE. Everyone has a preference. Some people think anime is high art. Some people think the opera is trash. The debate about what art and art forms we love and love less are the beautiful foundations of what makes life worth living and show the uniqueness of people and what they enjoy. Unless we're talking about *Into the Spider-Verse*. Cuz that shit perfect. This is an objective critique. You might think, "William, I enjoy a good superhero story, but perfect?"

Yes. You're wrong. I don't even know what you just said in your head while reading this, but you're wrong. Go argue with your momma.

And now that we have established a scientific baseline for perfection, I have an aside. I picked three moments cuz I ain't trying to exhaust y'all. Even perfection can be a fatiguing element in this much abundance. We can talk about the animation, point-blank

27

period. Or we can talk about the callback to the comic book origin stories ("Okay, let's do this one last time," a Spider-Person says for the fourth time). The Biggie transition that introduces Uncle Aaron. The comic book thought panels, including the ever-increasing volume of Miles's inside his own head. MILES FUCKING MORALES. The voice acting of the whole crew.

But let's also be very honest. You came to a book called *Black Nerd Problems*, so let's not mince words. This is the Blackest super-hero shit since the first *Blade*, yo. Miles shouting out Brooklyn while they tag a wall off a subway route in his unlaced Jordans?!? What?! You ain't supposed to see this shit with a budget like this! You put Mahershala Ali, Brian Tyree Henry, and Shameik Moore all on the same track? Is this movie catching bullets? With its teeth? Spider, please. But I digress.

There are three moments that are just straight up untouchable with no qualifier for me. And that shit is throughput of our Spider-Heroes. Moving in chronological order, we gotta start with the greatest.

BLOND PETER PARKER HAS ENTERED THE MUTHAFUCKIN' CHAT

I don't besmirch new Spider-Man fans. The ones riding that Miles wave into the fandom. The ones that saw a Puerto Rican and Black web-slinger and thought, "NOW I'm a Marvel fan." I welcome you with open arms. We have buttons and coffee mugs for you. But let's also be very clear. Peter Parker been the best of us for a long fuck-ing time. And the legend has never been as strong as when Miles stumbles upon his fight against Fisk and his time-shifting doomsday device. A couple things of note about this scene:

One, before Peter saves Miles, he was beating the brakes off of Green Goblin. Like, mad that you paid $80 for pay-per-view when the fight lasted two rounds type of ass-whuppin'. I'm not "blaming" Miles for what transpired next. All I'm sayin' is Peter blew a halftime lead cuz he was saving Miles while his enemies were on the court in the third quarter getting free buckets. And two, the jokes. Don't. Stop. There's a lot of people that talk about superheroes being inherently fascist. I think it's a good point made by people that are decaying like Sunday-morning roadkill on the inside. I typically qualify that with *white* superheroes might be fascist. Obsessed with accumulating power and removing the agency of everyday folks. But the reason they call your boy your friendly neighborhood Spider-Man is cuz he's here for the people, yo. The most humble of superheroes. And humility is great, but also boring as hell if you ain't got the jokes to go with it. I'm an Ohio kid. I don't know how New Yorkers feel about it, but when Peter tells the Green Goblin that he can't allow Fisk to open a portal cuz Brooklyn can't be sucked into a black hole (Staten Island maybe, but not Brooklyn), it made me damn near squeal.

And then he saves Miles from falling a really, really far way down. The moment between them is so damn short but still perfect. The web giveth and the web taketh away. Peter isn't threatened to know there's another person like him out there. He doesn't do the "gotta learn the hard way like me" tough talk. He tells Miles that he'll have to show him the ropes, ya know, once he destroys the big machine over his shoulder that could wreck the space-time continuum. What follows is THE sequence. Well, maybe not THE sequence cuz that comes up later. But THE (1) sequence for the first part of the movie. It only lasts about eleven seconds, but Peter vaults away, lands on a skinny scaffolding, tiptoes along its edge, jump flips up to a rotating carbine, web-sticks one hand to a higher carbine and rides the elevator up, and jumps off the top of that while web-slinging to slingshot himself to the ceiling, where he sticks and makes his way toward the control panel.

So true story: My homie and coauthor Omar and I saw this movie on the same night, but he was in New York, I was in Ohio.

And we both, in our separate theaters, watched that sequence and thought, "My god, Peter Parker is the fuckin' GOAT." I don't even think it's up for debate, yo. I don't know who checkin' him. Y'all can debate M.J. and LeBron. Have fun. Superheroes? I think that debate is over.

WHAT'S. UP. DANGER?

I got any *Breaking Bad* fans in here? What's the Venn diagram for folks that watched Walter White take over the New Mexico meth business and the folks that watch animated comic book films with Black folks? Anyways, there's the iconic scene in *Breaking Bad* when Skyler White sees the walls closing in on her and her husband, Walt. Powerful men are coming to kill them and she pleads for Walt to finally end this charade and go to the police. But Skyler doesn't actually know who Walt is or what Walt has done. And perhaps this is the moment when Walt realizes who he actually is. Skyler says Walt should "admit you're in danger." And Walter counters, "I am not in danger, Skyler. I am the danger. A guy opens his door and gets shot and you think that of me? No, I am the one who knocks."

So like, take that scene, keep the word *danger*, and take the venom from over nine thousand down to zero. And oh, make it Black. THEN you have the "What's Up Danger?" moment. Let's also be clear, this is the best moment on this list, but we going chronological (and it sets up the last moment, you guessed it, perfectly). This is not only the best moment in the movie, it's the best "superhero realizes who they are and what they're capable of" moment in history. Like, including time measured in BC. That's Before Clark Kent. Blasphemers.

You can start this moment when the track starts playing, but you gotta go back further than that. To the whole Spider-Crew deciding that Miles just ain't ready for the prime time and that past-his-prime brunette Peter B. Parker would turn on the collider to enable everyone to go home. Which would kill him. This shit crushing, yo. PBP was the one trying to sell Miles as the real deal to the whole team, but he has to admit to himself and to Miles that he was projecting and that Miles isn't actually ready. The shot from outside Miles's window as PBP breaks it down to him, with the rest of the Spider-Crew clinging to the wall listening, but out of Miles's view, breaks my heart every time (every time being about 742 at the time of me writing this, by the way). PBP webs Miles to his chair after Miles can't perform under pressure and we're left with our hero, helplessly asking, "When will I know I'm ready?" and PBP's words: "You won't. It's a leap of faith." And then the impossible Brian Tyree Henry as Miles's father, Jefferson, visits his dorm. It's the combo of being left behind and his father telling him how limitless his talent is. Internalizing all those things in succession: the rejection, the abandonment, the loss, and then his father picking him back up exactly when he needed it. Then the chair he's strapped to isn't a dead end as much as a trial. We see that cold blue coursing through his veins and then, ya know, the venom blasts happen and set him free. The chair, the webbing, our expectations, all get obliterated. And then the beat drops.

All praise to Black Caviar and Blackway for giving us this song. And Black people. Praise to Black people in general since we're here. But back to that leap of faith. Look at the material! The efficiency of this moment. Miles approaches the shed and already got the bio unlock on his arrival. Aunt May being the Pennyworth to Miles's Spider-Man. The voices of his parents and mentors guiding him. Customizing the Spider-Suit with his paints. The squeak of the Jordans on the windows of corporate America before the leap. Why are you reading this when you could be watching this shit right now?! But the leap itself is fucking poetry. Miles makes the jump (and of course we get the inverted fall with Miles rising into the sky), but Miles turning his fear and helplessness into agency THE THING.

He goes from falling and flailing for forty stories to the purposeful nosedive gaining speed before he shoots the web-shooters to the top of the building. BUT WE AIN'T DONE. Miles going from swinging to the ground, where his momentum is pulling him, to sprinting through traffic, the parkour of the truck, the drawstring of your boy's hoodie flapping as he runs across Wall Street's face in the Jays. It's . . . It's almost too much. I need a minute. Several. I'll catch y'all in the next session. But still. Best coming-of-age moment. EVA.

NO MORE SPIDER-MAN DYING EVER AGAIN

Listen, you can't pull off the most beautiful vault with tight flips and spins and not stick the landing. *Into the Spider-Verse* stuck the landing like it was driving a nail into the damn ground. Before we get to THE (1) part, you can't talk about this endgame without making note of the real shit:

First, when Miles comes back and gives Doc Oct the phantom punch, the whole Spider-Gang is revitalized with the out-of-nowhere but completely in character drop from PBP saying, "I love you! I am so proud of you! Do I want kids?" (Let me answer that for you, PBP: I dunno, fam. Kids are amazing, mostly because they are not yet corrupted humans. But I haven't slept in ten years, there aren't nearly enough family or unisex bathrooms out there in the early years, and don't even get me started on how expensive preserving human life is. I'm just saying, don't make any snap decisions.)

Second, this movie is all about things coming full circle. The way Miles and Peter are webbing away from the ceiling while talking is the final form of their earlier escape through the woods from Alchemax. *Thwip* and release. *Thwip* and release. And then, of course, there's Miles stealing the goober from PBP. Remember earlier in the film when Miles had PBP tied up, trying to figure out why he watched Peter Parker die, but here was Peter in his uncle Aaron's apartment? But while Miles is working through it, PBP gets free and tells Miles, "Watch the hands." Well, Miles is a grown-ass Spider-Man now. And he returns that "watch the hands" in kind. Then Miles duplicates the traversal from Peter Parker at the beginning to deactivate the collider. If you've forgotten, please go back to the first section of this essay, but the short version is SPIDER-MAN IS THE GOAT, THE WHOLE GOAT, AND NOTHING BUT THE GOAT, SO HELP ME SPIDEY SENSE.

Aiight, I've stalled long enough and the tears already coming, so let me just get to this shit. Peter done sent everyone home but PBP and Fisk has had it. PBP rushes off to take on Fisk but Miles is like, "Nah, b. Your fight is over." And then THE LINE from PBP:

"I can't let Spider-Man die."

Look, no disrespect to Olympians everywhere, but ain't no torch passing like this, my dude. There's no "you could be Spider-Man one day." No "you will step into the shoes of this universe's Spider-Man." Nah. NAH. You are Spider-Man. PBP got nothing left to teach him, man, the glow up is complete. And of course, the validation from Miles back to PBP despite all his insecurities: "Neither can I." I'd say that shit gave me goose bumps, but this is Marvel's world, so I'll say my Spidey sense go crazy every time I watch that part. And that moment ends with the student becoming the master, down to the sweep kick and the leap of faith for PBP.

Didn't I tell you this shit was perfect? I mean, I made my case and I didn't need the shoulder touch callback. The shoulder touch, yo! Anyways. You might have your faves that don't come from *Into the Spider-Verse*. But this is America, I respect your right to be dead-ass wrong.

I Hate It Here: *Food Wars* Would Be the Most Annoying Anime to Live In

OMAR HOLMON,
aka Stove Top Contessa

HERE'S A QUESTION: What fictional universe would you wanna live in? Yeah, these are the hard-hitting questions we're here to ask, dammit. It's a tough choice, ain't it? You gotta consider which genre suits you best as well as other factors. For example, I love comic books but I would never live in the Marvel Comics or Marvel Cinematic Universe. You see all the collateral damage they did in New York?! That's where I reside, man! I'm not trying to look out the window to see Thor and the Hulk fighting supervillains on my block so now I gotta wait to go to the corner store. Got me complaining the whole time 'bout them always fighting down here but they never over in Williamsburg knocking folks through brownstones and into Priuses. I wouldn't wanna live in the *Star Wars* universe either because I'd be beyond fed up if I was with the Sith or the Resistance. Fam, the Sith had a lead on the Jedi/the Resistance for how many years and still managed to lose? Don't get me started on the Resistance—they got rocked and had their numbers dwindle so much that by the time of *Rise of Skywalker* everyone that was doing admin work for the Resistance now on the front lines. The fuck does Ahmed from accounting know about shooting a blaster gun?

For my money, I'd pick an anime universe to live in. Only problem is, which one? Anime shows can literally be about anything from sci-fi to sports or fantasy to music. I am tempted to say that the anime *Naruto* is the universe I'd take residence in. *Naruto* is a show about a lil abandoned boy named Naruto Uzumaki that becomes a ninja in order to one day get chosen to be Hokage of the Hidden Leaf Village (the title of the strongest ninja that protects everyone in the village) so the villagers that shunned him will then embrace him. As Naruto grows up, we see him fighting to reform the whole ninja system and bring peace to all the nations with ninja villages. *Naruto* is really a beautiful story that talks about how important bonds and friendships are to keep people on the right path or bring them back to the light no matter how lost in the darkness they are. I just know that personally, my one big problem is that if I am livin' in that universe, I am not going to be as compassionate as Naruto Uzumaki is.

Naruto out here sympathizing with some of the folks who were legit ready to kill him on a ninja mission. Yet, through the sheer power of friendship (after throwing a few hands), he turns enemies into friends. Me? We can be friends after they're six feet in the fucking ground. I'm sorry, I'm not sitting here listening to a "why we should be friends" speech accompanied by a sad-ass flashback to my enemy's childhood. Forgive me if I don't wanna see where this person that's been trying to kill me for the past two twenty-minute episodes is coming from. Naruto would arrive to help me as a reinforcement and be attempting to pull at their heartstrings, but just as they began to see the error of their ways, I'd Shawn Michaels superkick their head off their shoulders because I didn't read the room to realize we were at an unwritten cease-fire. Now I'm frus-

WILLIAM EVANS AND OMAR HOLMON

trated, arguing with Naruto like, "Oh, I'm fucking sorry, that ninja tried to kill me not five minutes ago before you showed up. My bad not realizing you were trying to have a heart-to-heart sit-down with them in the middle of a damn fight."

Look, Naruto got his name in the title of the show, so he gon' be all right. I ain't got that type of plot armor, so I'ma have to kill these enemies that step to me. Then there's how Naruto handled things with his rival/"best friend" Sasuke Uchiha. Man, Sasuke left the Hidden Leaf Village to seek power from Orochimaru, a ninja enemy of the state, then Sasuke worked for Akatsuki, a terrorist ninja organization, and on top of that he attacked a meeting of all the head village leaders then killed Danzo, the Hidden Leaf Village's stand-in leader (who honestly had that smoke coming). Your ninja was out here wylin'! Naruto's friends had a legit intervention with him to tell him that they were going to take Sasuke the fuck out. Not out clothes shopping, house shopping, or for drinks followed by dinner. They were planning on killing that man. Naruto said that Sasuke was his responsibility, that he'd handle him.

Fam, I woulda already been en route to find Sasuke and beat his ass. I'd have beat his ass not with kindness or the power of friendship but with these damn bare hands, 'cause he out here making our village look bad and fucking our money up. Listen, I love a heart-to-heart moment followed by a flashback to relate to a character as well, but some characters just need their asses beat. That boy Sasuke? Yeah, he needed an ass-whupping way earlier than when he got it from Naruto. I'd have let Sasuke choose between getting the brakes beat off 'em or the floral arrangements for his funeral service.

Hmm, maybe I don't have the temperament to live in the *Naruto* universe. I'd still consider taking up residence there. I'll tell you what anime I wouldn't be caught dead in. There's no way I'd ever step in the *Food Wars* anime universe without being held at gunpoint. *Food Wars*, or *Food Wars! Shokugeki no Soma*, is a really good fictional anime cooking show. The chefs are all young students attending a school where they learn and battle against/with one another. The show breaks down a lot of actual chemistry that goes into real-life cooking with the dishes they are creating—why certain seasonings react with each other, which ingredients complement one another to bring out flavor, the way a meat is cut giving it a different taste. Living in this anime universe should be a foodie's dream, right? Not me. I don't wanna live in the *Food Wars* universe, because every time the chefs serve a dish, everyone that eats it gets transported to Freaknik '91.

I'ma let the non-Black folks reading this take the time to google Freaknik. Go ahead. See what I'm talking about? Yeah, now imagine that happening but in your mouth. In *Food Wars*, the dishes these chefs make get judges talkin' like they on an episode of HBO's *Real Sex* when describing the flavors. They legit go Skinemax talking about how the seasonings, sweetness, savoriness (savory-ness? savor-i? . . . Sir Mix-a-Lot?), etc., complements the dish. After all that is said, and the judges, customer, or whoever is eating the dish can't take it anymore, this shit gets into *Booty Talk 19* territory as they hit a cutscene where these people's clothes literally start flying off like the Ecstasy pill just hit. These folks out here orgasming over food, man. That's what they're implying.

Sometimes it's just a cutscene of either people moaning or their clothes legit flying off. All over the screen we got women hittin' their O face as the spotlight hits their unmentionables that we are now mentioning. Men got their genitalia glowing, which leads me to believe they essentially bustin' on themselves 'cause their pants clearly flew off prior. Oh, they giving you all the erotic softcore fan service in *Food Wars*. I just know I can't with that shit. Now let's be clear, I'm not saying that I can't live in the *Food Wars* universe because I'm a prude or sexually repressed. I keep it '95 Adina Howard in the morning and in the evening. I'm just saying the trade-off for eating out-of-this-world food being erotic fan service with each bite is going to be mad extra after a few days. Sure, it's cool the first time I eat an upside-down pineapple cake and I gotta excuse myself to go switch into a spare set of pants. That's dope. I get close to that feeling in real life whenever my wife makes butter chicken and garlic naan. I get it.

So, if eating that fruit and Bavarian cream verrine makes you make a mess on yourself, more power to you. I'm happy for you. I'm right there with you. But let's not act like that shit wouldn't have moments where it'd be weird or annoying as fuck. If I'm meeting up with a friend and they're asking me how everything's going, I'm really not trying to talk about how the death of my mother still haunts me as they're reenacting the diner scene from *When Harry Met Sally*.

ME: It's just hard, you know?
FRIEND: YES! YES! I KNOW, SO HARD! OH, I KNOW!
ME: All right, let's talk about this after you're done with
   your frittata.
FRIEND: KEEP GOING! KEEP GOING!
ME: I . . . I really don't want t—
FRIEND: THE FLAVORS KEEP GOING!
ME: Annnnnd you're not talking to me. Cool. Cool . . .
   cool.
FRIEND: *now nude and catching their breath* Whew . . .
   Yeah, man, moving on is har—
ME: Nope! Not gon' act like that didn't happen, especially
   since you kept eye contact going the entire time.

That shit would be very weird among catching up with friends. Don't even get me started about catching up with family. That shit would be extremely awkward. I cannot stop thinking about that. You know what else I think about? Do folks just be out here busting in restaurants while eating food with other customers around? Is that just the norm? I'm just imagining that it must really be hard to even have a conversation when the man at table 3, right in my peripheral vision, is putting nipple clamps on before he dives into his Gotcha! Pork Roast. You know damn well people would take it that fucking far. That's the shit the anime isn't showing us. Hey, maybe it's just me, but that's what I think about. Like trying to have a date night with my wife and the couple at table 5 climaxing at just the sound of the mac and cheese being mixed and poured onto their plates. You get where I'm coming from? You ain't going to be hearing a damn thing the person you're dining with is saying over the sound of folks climaxing. Not to mention, how I expect to see servers wiping EVERYTHING down once customers are done eating.

Hey, maybe I'm the crazy one here. Maybe the dream is to be in a universe where the food is so delicious an orgy is considered a bunch of people getting together for brunch, swinging is considered everyone ordering off the shared-plate menu, and an open relationship is saying, "You've GOT to try this," while reaching over to have someone eat off your fork while your partner is aware and totally comfortable with what's occurring. Maybe I'm the weird one for not wanting to have my laundry bill skyrocket from busting each time I have a peach cobbler. I'm just saying, I don't wanna have to keep hydrating after every bite of the hanger steak I ordered. *Food Wars* is a great anime, but I know the cost of living in that universe is one I don't have enough change of clothes to afford.

Y'all Gotta Chill with the Slander and Let Batman Cook

WILLIAM EVANS,
aka Commissioner Jamaal Gordon

I KNOW IT'S my fault for taking the bait. Twitter ain't real life, but folks have gotten real comfortable on there. Quote tweeting to dunk on takes they don't like. Twenty-part tweet threads to nowhere. And talking shit about Batman. I'm fed up on that last one. Batman ain't did nothing to nobody but mind his business and do some moon-lighting in a Kevlar suit that might resemble a nocturnal character. Okay, that's probably not true. For Batman to be Batman, he gotta mind his business, your business, the slum you came up in's business. But like the Deacon from *The Wire* says, a good churchman is always up in everybody's shit. Okay, Bruce probably ain't attending church since his parents' service. You know what, let's just say Batman been getting punted the last few years for clout and I'm tired of it. I know he gets every new DC comic. I know you can't make a DC movie or TV franchise without the Bat being involved. The brand is that strong, y'all. He's lightweight a progressive hero if y'all give that man a chance.

LET'S TALK PAPER

First off, I already know what y'all thinking. Billionaires shouldn't exist. The way my politics are set up, I'm inclined to agree with you. So maybe this is a terrible start . . .

But let me say this, there's a lot of billionaire-ass behavior Bruce Wayne doesn't rock with that I appreciate. Bruce ain't out here buying up development properties and selling them to his elite friends. Bruce saw that gentrification train roll past Wayne Manor and was like, "I'm good, I'll walk." Could Bruce be doing more with his money for the city of Gotham? The perpetually dark and gray-ass Gotham? I mean, yeah, probably. Funding the orphanage is literally the least he could do. I don't know what the GDP of Gotham is, but it's hard to imagine he couldn't Andrew Yang that shit and fund the legislation of a universal income.

Still, Bruce ain't out here consolidating wealth. The money is a curse, yo. He inherited that shit like bad vision. He not even trying to make more money. Your boy cares about justice, not dividends. You ever see Bruce out here advocating for a tax cut? You ever see Bruce trying to put a golf course where a low-income neighborhood once stood? I don't know what the tax codes be like in Gotham, but I feel like Bruce is willing to pay his fair share. And it's not like he has a disdain for poor people. He has a disdain for EVERYBODY. It's not like he out here funding terrible politicians. He learned his lesson with Two-Face and said never again.

BATMAN SAID FUCK (MOST OF) THE POLICE

While we talking money, you ain't never gonna see Bruce Wayne or Batman out here on some Blue Lives Matter or Thin Blue Line bullshit. He hates them muthafuckas the most! Forget Gotham for a second—you know how few murders get solved every year? You literally have a 40 percent chance of getting away with murder, folks. Like, please reset your expectations of what law enforcement actually does for a minute. And they couldn't find the killers of the richest people in the city? Batman been knowing they worthless. The Gotham PD is a corrupt unit of blowhards who shoot first and ask questions of the crime boss controlling them later. Batman got the best tech in the world, but his home police force still out here with the same equipment from 1974. Is it Defund the Police in Gotham? Probably not. But Bruce could've made them bastards supercops and he was like, "Nah. I got a cape, we gonna be aiight."

Batman shows up at a crime scene and talks to exactly one muthafucka. He don't even like Gordon that much either cuz he never says goodbye, he just leaves that dude on read constantly. And when the riots start up in Gotham cuz Harvey Bullock shot a kid in the back, where Batman gonna be? It ain't bustin' up protestors. My dude gonna be up on the gargoyle fifty stories above the street. My dude don't mess with law-abiding citizens like that. Besides, you know Riddler out there plotting some shit, he gotta make time.

I AM HERE ONCE AGAIN TO TALK TO YOU ABOUT PRIVILEGE

Let's keep this shit real simple. That's a white billionaire dressing up as a bat patrolling the city. First off, let's not kink shame my dude. Imagine what you would be wearing if you had "fuck you" money and it made you feel powerful. Second, until we get more brave writers out there (with staying power), Batman just gonna be white, just gonna be white, just gonna be white. This is where we at. So yeah, he probably gets away with so much more shit than someone from a marginalized community would. But here's what I know: Ain't no complaints about Bruce being inappropriate at Wayne Enterprises. There's no lawsuits against Bruce for promoting a toxic work environment. This may be because Bruce is almost never there cuz, again, HE DON'T REALLY CARE ABOUT NONE OF THIS

MONOPOLY SHIT. But the fact remains, Bruce ain't throwing his influence around for terrible power dynamic shit.

I also want to take a look at Batman's rogues' gallery. You might know the most popular ones: Penguin, Riddler, Killer Croc, Poison Ivy, Scarecrow, Clayface, Two-Face, Mr. Freeze, the Joker. You notice anything? Y'all better let him bring these white terrorists to justice. Batman ain't out here targeting folks from marginalized communities, man. I mean, that mostly cuz comic books been really monolithic forever and Black people hardly existed there. But a win is a win, I make no apologies. I'm lightweight like, them bastards are crazy as fuck, let them stay white, to be honest. We got enough stereotypes to combat, we don't need crazy comic book villain added to the list. What you gonna do, make the Mad Hatter into Headpiece? Or Mad Lids & Timbs? He just gonna have a bunch of New York Yankees hats in different colors? I'll pass. Yeah, I know Bane is out there being his brilliant and brawny Mexican self. But he broke Batman's back, yo. What else you want from the Bat? I didn't say he was perfect and he wasn't gonna want vengeance every once in a while. I know Bane is an addict and there are a lot of ways to show more empathy toward dude when he out here terrorizing the streets. But again. Broke. His. Back.

After that, finding other people of color that Batman gets into scuffles with is very hard. You know how many rungs on the ladder you gotta climb down before you get to Bronze Tiger? Which of course is racist as hell. He's from the era of comics where if a character wasn't white, you had to explicitly state that in their name. You could maybe count Ra's al Ghul, but there's mutual respect there and Ra's is basically a king of a foreign land. Batman ain't exactly "beating up" on him. And sometimes Deadshot has been either written, animated, or cast as a Black person . . . but dude is a sniper. And Batman is clearly about this gun control in these streets.

STOP THE (GUN) VIOLENCE

I originally wanted to say Batman don't do that ultraviolence, but you gotta qualify that with *gun* violence, cuz Batman will still whup someone's ass, quite mercilessly in fact. But Bruce been radicalized by his parents' death and he don't mess with them ballistics like that. So Batman doesn't use guns and he doesn't kill people (look, work with me here, he don't kill people directly or on purpose). Listen, Twitter, you can't have it both ways. You can't be mad about the lack of de-escalation techniques and use of lethal means against suspects and also get on Batman, cuz these folks get arrested and are out of Arkham a month later to terrorize the city again. Batman is justice, not the broken-ass justice system. What you want dude to do, start putting folks into exile? Y'all want lobotomies, Nurse Ratched?! Y'all better holla at the Gotham City district attorney and stop giving Batman grief about this.

If there's a critique about Bruce Wayne and the potential of his political power, it's that he could be pushing for tighter gun laws. But one, Bruce don't trust a fucking soul in Gotham, so that corruption got him not believing in nobody with power. And two, a lot of Batman's rogues been spreading the mayhem in a lot of ways without the literal gun in hand. Batman done seen some things. He might hate guns because of what happened to his parents, but he realizes there's some other shit out there. Have you seen Victor Zsasz with a knife? Poison Ivy killing folks with hibiscus? You got me fucked up. Like, please, Gotham, pass some background checks. But that ain't solving all your problems.

I'LL TAKE THE COWL, FAM

The most damning thing about Batman is the real-world evidence that more present and active policing on a community actually increases the chance of violence in those communities. There's national studies that show the increased likeliness that people with no previous criminal record who have interactions with police are much more likely to commit a crime than those who haven't. You got a Memphis study that shows crime reducing proportional to the decrease in police presence. And Memphis gave us Three 6 Mafia, ain't none of them putting up riddles all over the city with folks in death traps. So by proxy, the reason that Batman has such an extensive group of villains wreaking havoc on Gotham is because Batman himself is beating villains' ass in Gotham. And listen . . . I got no answers for you. What you want Batman to do, break one rib instead of four on a villain? You want him to drop the gruff voice and pick up an Obama cadence when trying to get someone to reveal the location of the person they kidnapped? You don't take the brush out of Michelangelo's hand. You don't take the coke out of Pusha T's flow. Let Batman cook.

All I'm saying is being on top makes you an easy target, and folks taking shots at Batman all day and tomorrow. I don't trust billionaires, and the way he takes in children to be his wards and then turns them into vigilantes is . . . concerning. But we all need some help, right? Not even Batman can do it all alone. Even Batman needs a support system. And a cheering section.

Okay, he's rich and white and operates with impunity. He's probably fine.

What Happens to a New Fictional Black Character Deferred?

OMAR HOLMON,
aka A Raisin in the Cinnabon

THE HARDEST THING about being a Black nerd is the patience. Enjoying a story, waiting to see people that look like you appear in it, and then hoping that they'll have more than a supporting role. This dilemma runs rampant in DC and Marvel comic books when it comes to Black/POC heroes or characters. A good fix for that has been an approach that Marvel Comics has taken with a few long-standing heroes like Wolverine, Captain Marvel, and Nova for example, having POC teens that have been created to take up their mantles. It is a dope idea but not a permanent tactic for representation, because the problem becomes previous heroes and characters of color with long-standing history or a fan base being abandoned.

Whenever "create new Black or POC characters" is offered as a solution for expanding representation and diversity, I instantly think of the Black characters that were created by Marvel and DC Comics alike, just for this purpose. Those characters are nowhere to be seen today. I'ma expand on that more in a bit. The problem with this assembly line of creating more and more new characters is that we end up with an abundant number of diverse characters with potential that become stuck in comic book limbo. Comic book limbo is basically the Upside Down from *Stranger Things*, where characters hang out in obscurity. What I'm getting at is if you grew up as a person of color and a comic book fan, you had no idea when you were going to see your favorite character again.

For instance, Marvel Comics put out a book called *The Crew* by Christopher Priest back in 2003. There was a biracial (Black and Jewish) member named Kasper Cole in the group who debuted in 2002. Kasper had impersonated the Black Panther in a solo series for a time before getting his own identity as a hero, then becoming the White Tiger and joining the Crew's series. I rocked with Kasper Cole heavy. When *The Crew* ended, Kasper Cole wasn't seen again until he had a small cameo sitting at a hero's funeral in *Captain America: Sam Wilson*, vol. 1, #10, thirteen years after his last appearance.

These characters aren't just missing in action for a short while. They're straight missing in fiction for decades. They become raisins in the sun: presented for the moment, then left to dry out. There are so many characters of color created to have their stories told once. I can sound off on a bunch of characters I grew up with (by grew up with I mean been scouring for shreds of cameos and appearances still to this day) and haven't heard from in years. Let's get into it.

Orpheus (Gavin King) was created to be the Black Batman by Alex Simmons and Dwayne Turner in 2001. Gavin King was a Gotham kid that traveled the world and came back to help out in the city. His whole stance was Black people needed to see themselves out there fighting crime as well, and Batman couldn't be everything to everyone. Fam, King was my dude, woke as fuck, using disguises to get information from police, working as a TV producer by day. And my man. Was. Hilarious. He was part of a six-person crew that was "small but elite." I'm talking so nice that the computer expert for the hero community, Oracle (at the time Barbara Gordon, aka Batgirl), couldn't gather or hack any information on him. Gavin's people blocked her at every turn. He even told that shit to Batman too ("Oracle is nice, but my people are good too, bruh") and then asked if Robin was around 'cause he knew a partner that wanted some pointers from him. I looked for this dude in every Batman and Bat family title after his debut in *Orpheus Rising*. Son didn't appear till like a year later in an issue of *Birds of Prey*, then maybe once more before he was killed off in *Batman: War Games*. Yeah, a new character that got his story cut off after a year, fam. We didn't get any expansion into the organization he was involved with that trained him or the other mystery men connected to Orpheus.

Empress (Anita Fite) showed up in the pages of the *Young Justice* comic book and she was flourishing as the creation of Peter David and Todd Nauck. Young Justice was a team for the teen heroes that had Robin, Superboy, and Wonder Girl on its roster. Empress was a new member but had her own character development and backstory: her father, Donald Fite, was an agent of a clandestine organization with his partner, Ishido Maad, Anita's godfather. Anita even had her own villain, the Baron Agua Sin Gaaz, who killed her mother then later her father. When that happened, every teen hero in the DC Universe answered the call to ride with her and attack Zandia, where Agua Sin Gaaz was ducking the 187. Anita's story is fucking wild. She remains one of the most underused characters in the DC Universe. She hit the scene with a unique set of mystical powers and her dual-bladed emperor's stick, plus she had the flyest outfit. It had burgundy-colored boots, sash, gloves, and mask. The rest of the fit was like a scale-mail armor like Captain America's original look, except for Empress the scale was colored gold. Her mask had an opening for her autumn-colored hair to stick out too. Ughhh, I loved it! Anita was well rounded, facing adversity being the new team member and getting treated a type of way from the member she "replaced" and working through it, death, vengeance, and even dating a de-aged Lobo/Slobo. Anita is a character still in her prime but stuck in comic book limbo since her last appearance in issue #38 of *Super Girl* in 2008.

Jakeem Thunder (Jakeem Johnny Williams) was the only reason I read *Justice Society of America* back in the 2000s. Created by Grant Morrison, Mark Millar, and Paul Ryan in 1998, Jakeem was a standoffish kid known for cursing, having an attitude, and being anti-authority. Oh, plus he had control over a magical sprite named Ylzkz that can grant his every wish. However, the wish had to be very specific because the sprite's power worked extremely literally. This meant Jakeem wielded top-level power, but all he ever wanted was a friend, and Ylzkz became his best friend. When Jakeem's power was stolen by the Ultra-Humanite villain to take over and reshape the world, Jakeem spent months as part of a resistance team to regain his powers in order to set the world back to normal. This mission took months and caused him to mature very quickly. Once Jakeem got further character development, we saw more of his backstory: his mother died of cancer, his father didn't know he was born, and he was raised by his aunt but often left alone like a latchkey kid. We saw the effect of Jakeem's power but never full scale what he could do with mastery over it. We got a young Black boy wielding his own magical genie. Jakeem appearances have always been sporadic in issues of *Justice Society*. Jakeem's longest tenure being gone was from his last appearance in 2010 until recently in *Teen Titans*, vol. 6, #38, in 2020 (in a supporting role).

Don't think for a moment that the list stops there. Back in 2002, there was an issue of *Superman* (vol. 2, #179) that introduced a Black hero named Muhammad X that Superman ran into in Harlem. The story centers around Muhammad X stating, "Superman doesn't come up to Harlem," and Clark pondering if there isn't enough people of color superheroes being seen or recognized, or that he's actually hurting the Black community by helping. It's a comic issue on race, but whose story are we talking 'bout here though? Muhammad X's story? If it's his story, then why is he only in four pages? This new Black character was made, but we ain't hearing further into his side of the issue. Not fully, at least, or what brought him to his belief. Nah, this is for Superman's development. Superman is told by Lois Lane that he's the most color-blind person she knows. He talks to members of the Justice League about why there aren't more Black heroes on the roster, asks the younger heroes who their favorite heroes are and why. When Superman runs into Muhammad X a second time, he tells him, "I can't change the color of my skin . . . what I try to do is something far more difficult . . . to be a human being. And hopefully, someday, we'll see each other only in that way." As he flies away, Muhammad X says, "Yeah, well . . . I guess that's how you sleep at night."

That issue took place in 2002; it's now about nineteen years later and that is the only appearance of Muhammad X. In 2011 there was supposed to be a story about Superman coming to the aid of Sharif, a hero that was a follower of Islam that was receiving pushback from the people (Americans) he's trying to help. It was supposed to happen in *Superman* #712. Sharif was on the cover for the issue. That story didn't drop and was replaced with a filler story instead. A spokesperson for DC Comics said, "DC Comics determined that the previously solicited story did not work within the 'Grounded' storyline." The "Grounded" storyline was about Superman walking across the United States in search of the real America. Bruh, if you want the real America, it ain't gonna get any realer than Islamophobia (don't worry racism, we see you too).

You can't tell us we need new heroes for our stories to be told when the heroes already exist and aren't getting an opportunity to be in the story because they get killed off (Ryan Choi, James Rhodes), sidelined (Eli Bradley, Crimson Avenger II), or shut down before they even have a chance. Meanwhile, we're just waiting and hoping they appear again somewhere. Which is why it's so important in film when a person of color is the best actor for the job and gets cast for a historically white role. The average comic book reader has likely never heard of anyone I've listed thus far; none of these characters are ever going to have a film to call their own if they're even lucky enough to make it to television (shout-out to Icon and Rocket on *Young Justice*). Don't get me wrong, when Riri Williams came on the scene, reverse engineered Tony Stark's Iron Man armor, then took over his comic book series as the main character (Tony died), that shit was incredible. However, Tony Stark came back to life, and Riri Williams got her own series and identity as Iron Heart. See, there is a pattern when the new hero of color comes in on a legacy slot. The status quo changes only for a few years (two to three at most).

Peter Parker was dead for years in Ultimate Universe when Miles Morales took over, then came back to life (as the title was ending, mind you). Miles was no longer the only Spider-Man, then got moved to the main Marvel Universe (Marvel's 616 Universe) and now serves as the second Spider-Man. Sam Wilson was Captain America while Steve Rogers was aged up and out of commission. Steve Rogers got his youth restored, shared the title of Captain America with Sam, then like clockwork, Sam just went back to his former heroic identity, the Falcon. Now, Kamala Khan is a unique case. She became the new Ms. Marvel, but her legacy slot is safe because there is no one to contest it since the former Ms. Marvel, Carol Danvers, became Captain Marvel. So luckily, Kamala will never be demoted from the title of Ms. Marvel and gets to exist as the sole one of that mantle. This isn't me complaining, I'm just pointing out a pattern a white consumer may not be aware of while their favorite character has three separate titles to flood the market with their story.

In comic book reboots or revamps, recognizable heroes get revamped or have a person of color successor. This does stretch over into movies as well. We've seen Marvel and DC Comics cast heroes, villains, and supporting characters that are white in comics as people of color. Zendaya as M.J. in *Spider-Man: Homecoming* and *Far from Home*, Vondie Curtis-Hall as news reporter Ben Urich in *Daredevil* on Netflix, Samuel L. Jackson as Nick Fury, and Zoë Kravitz in the upcoming *Batman* movie. Making fictional characters white is not a time-honored tradition that should be set in stone. Y'all remember when Amandla Stenberg portrayed Rue in *The Hunger Games*? There was a lot of internet backlash over Rue being cast as Black even tho in the Hunger Games books she is described as having "dark brown skin and eyes."

I'll never forget when I saw this tweet saying, "Kk call me racist but when I found out rue was black her death wasn't as sad. #ihatemyself"—a fanboy Twitter gem.

You can say, "But Rue isn't real," but if that's what a certain corner of the internet thinks about a fictional Black girl being killed, I can only imagine how they felt about the news of Black women like Sandra Bland, Korryn Gaines, and Jessica Williams or Black trans women like Mya Hall being killed. They probably still felt nothing because when you're Black and you die it's just not as sad. Yeah, I'm going to disagree with that section of the internet like a sixteenth-century judge slamming a gavel down shouting, "Hear ye! Hear ye!" trying to get the court back to order.

Black/POC characters and stories matter to me in real life as well as in fiction. Which is why I want to see stories of characters of color that have been around longer in Marvel Comics and DC Comics instead of an assembly line of new characters being added into the elephant graveyard that is comic book limbo after a quick supporting role appearance or being pushed to the side for not "selling well." Listen, if Matt Fraction and David Aja can work their magic to make *Hawkeye* (the Avenger that the internet clowns every so often) one of the most top-tier comic book series ever put out by Marvel Comics, then anything is possible for characters with the right creative team backing them. There is no excuse. I want to see all the Black characters in comic book limbo get new creative teams (preferably of color) to tell fresh stories with them. I want to see those once-new POC characters that everyone has forgotten about fleshed out and spotlighted more. I'm in my mid-thirties, man, I can't keep spending decades hoping to see characters of color I've been interested in get taken off the bench because I may not have that many years left. I'm just saying, there's a whole roster of heroes riding the pine waiting for that shine.

Two Dope Boys and a Comic Book: The Superhero Fade Heard Round the Multiverse

WILLIAM & OMAR,
aka The #1 Pop Culture Color Commentating Tag Team

BEFORE CHADWICK BOSEMAN made box office waves as the live-action Black Panther in February 2018, writer Jonathan Hickman's *Avengers* #40 dropped on January 14, 2015, showing T'Challa the Black Panther making big power moves. All you need to know to start with is T'Challa has had beef with Namor the Sub-Mariner (one of Marvel's on-again, off-again antiheroes) ever since he flooded Wakanda. T'Challa had to put his grievance aside in order to work with Namor—he reminded Namor that their beef was tabled for now, however, "Every breath you take is mercy from me." In *Avengers* #40, T'Challa kicks over the table and makes good on his promise as he draws out the blade his father had bestowed upon him and places it right where it belongs: three feet deep into Namor's chest cavity.

Which brings us to our conversation where neither of us could stop talking about the Avengers-on-Avengers crime in these Marvel streets. We decided to document our conversation in order to show how exciting comic books and great storytelling can be.

WILLIAM: Off the top, let us pay our respects and pour out some salt water for the ankle-winged, super-V-neck king of the Atlantic.

OMAR: Aquaman said the funeral arrangements for Namor will be held at Joe's Crab Shack off Fourth Avenue and Smith Street. B.Y.O.B. (Bring. Your. Own. Butter.)

WILLIAM: So let's back up, cuz the fam been waiting for this shit since Namor gave the greatest city on Earth the "Noah Ultimatum" in *Avengers vs. X-Men*. People been waiting on him to catch those bars like *Walking Dead* fans were wishing walker outbreaks on Andrea.

OMAR: Namor been too comfortable in Marvel post-fuckboy acts. He then proceeded to have Wakanda attacked AGAIN. Yo, his Atlantean/white privilege was showing its whole ass. Meanwhile, T'Challa was listening to "Ghost of Christopher Wallace" as his dad told him, "You best clap that boi."

WILLIAM: Bruh, we gotta give the Lord and Savior Jonathan Hickman some credit, Da Gawd told us two years ago, in issue #2 of *New Avengers*, this shit was coming. This was his *Black Dynamite* "I threw that shit before I walked in the room" moment.

OMAR: I'm wondering how he proposed this to Marvel. Hickman: "Sooo you know your boy Namor, one of ya oldest characters, arguably the first mutant? . . . Yeah, him. T'Challa gon' make him bait for Shark Week in this run." Marvel: "You can't do—" Hickman: "Shh—shh—shhhhhh. But I did and I will."

WILLIAM: I really hope that twenty minutes before the Marvel movie announcements, that there was one called *The Atlantean King* and Hickman picked up a phone, dialed a number like, "Hey. Yeah, it's Jonathan. No, don't worry about the greeting, you didn't know it was me. Anyways, that Namor movie? Yeah, uh-huh. Well, you might want to pull that one. You can hint at that shit later, but I got other plans. I know you got graphics already and a date. I'm just telling you it ain't gonna happen."

OMAR: Here's the thing about this too . . . who hates that it had to be Namor? For real? Who hates that it had to be him? NO ONE, BOO BOO! NOT. ONE. BODY.

WILLIAM: Naw, I mean, he had one of the hardest moments in this run when he stood up as a representative of our Earth-616 and told them heroes from Earth-4290001 it was time to pass the sticks, but who out there rockin' #NamorWasRight shirts today?

OMAR: Namor is going to be remembered entirely for how he died (for however long that is). He always said he did what had to be done, which may be true, but that shit caught up with him.

WILLIAM: Yeah, let's get into what actually happened in *Avengers* #40 one time, before Namor got a bellyful of that Sleepytime tea. How dope was the passing back and forth of the King's Blade? I appreciate Hickman sticking to the Chekhov's gun theory where if you show a King's Blade in the first act, you gotta jam it into a muthafucka and push him off a platform down to an exploding Earth in the third.

OMAR: The play on the phrase that kept being repeated, "It's a blade for a king." I kept thinking as in possession, but in actuality it could be interpreted as a weapon for killing a king to crank that regicide.

WILLIAM: Jaime Lannister, favorite son of Wakanda. Though Shuri don't play that shit.

OMAR: We never get to see it, but I wish we saw the scene with T'Challa explaining this plan to Black Bolt and Black Bolt agreeing. Black Bolt arrived with T'Challa as part of the game plan as well, so this had to be in play for dummmmb long.

WILLIAM: Yooooooooo, when Black Bolt jumped on the track, that was Kendrick walking into the street on the "Nosetalgia" video with Pusha T. Black Bolt anchored the record like André 3000 circa 2013.

OMAR: Black Bolt been waaiiiiiitin' to put Namor in his place. He hit him with the Mariah Carey, then looked at T'Challa like, "Hey, man, what you waiting on? WE GOTS TO GO!"

WILLIAM: Black Bolt hit Namor with that Aretha and then bounced knowing Maximus was on that planet too. Or did he? Black Bolt was cool with merkin' his brother? I dunno, I guess we don't know what went down when the Cabal came in eight months ago and said, "Fuck yo couch," but still. He just put his kin on the exploding Summer Jam screen.

OMAR: We've seen murder happen throughout Marvel, but I can't recall one where we seen a hero merkin' another hero (both of whom are Avengers, no less). You know Steve Rogers gon' say some American judicial-ass shit to T'Challa on this.

WILLIAM: And T'Challa gonna tell Steve to kiss his kingly Black ass. Wakanda figured out how to disable guns years ago, you think

T'Challa can't figure out how to deactivate the nutrients in Rogers's Metamucil? Sheeyet, Steve's old ass better have a Coke, an EKG, and a smile, and shut the fuck up.

OMAR: T'Challa is nowhere in the wrong for this. After all that was done to Wakanda, after T'Challa decided not to kill a whole other planet in order for our Earth-616 universe to survive, just to have Namor walk over, reset the router in order to blow Earth-4290001 the fuck up. Namor really said, "Fuck all your moral compass, monologues, and bystander-at-the-switch dilemmas, I got shit to do today." T'Challa is in no way wrong for his actions in the least.

WILLIAM: T'Challa just #PutTheBladeWhereItBelongs, fam. That's it. If this were Florida and he was the White Tiger, this would be covered under Stand Your Ground laws. He had to do it, man, he had Biggie, Pac, Big L, J Dilla, and all the Panther gods telling him he needed to get this shit done.

OMAR: *Cornel West hit 'em up on the phone, said, "What you waitin' on?" / Assata Shakur hit 'em up with a tweet, said, "What you waitin' on?" / Chuck D send a text every hour on the dot sayin' / "When you gon' drop Namor, hero? You taking long."*

WILLIAM: Yeah, man, feels so good for Black Panther to get back on this *Murda Muzik.* Don't ever say Da Gawd don't make good on his promises. T'Challa, first Avenger to catch a body in 2015. The leadership we need and deserve in the two-dime, dime-nickel.

OMAR: This is an act in which T'Challa is letting Marvel Universe know what Namor figured out way too late, that: *"You're talking to* *the Vibranium-wearin', African king–reppin', limelight-stealin', tech-dealin', limousine-ridin', jet-flyin' son of a gun. And I'm having a hard time holding these Vibranium claws down."*

NOW GIMME A BODY BAG AND A RIC FLAIR WOOOOOOOOOO!

My Theory on How Black Folks' Black Card Actually Works

OMAR HOLMON,
aka Capricorn with a Real Nigga Rising

I'M WRITING THIS after having just finished watching *The Wire* and it feels like I just got done with a marathon. I've always joked about being the shame of my friends for not having known of it when it was big back in the early 2000s—what I never really analyzed, however, is that whenever I stated that I wasn't aware of the show, my Black friends would joke about my Black Card being revoked or having it be up for renewal, which led me to a weird realization: Have you ever noticed how there is no breakdown for what defines the Black Card?

I'm talking about how it works, what truly makes up the mechanics of the card itself . . . There is no pie chart whatsoever. The Black Card is referred to in passing among us as this totem that each Black person acquires at birth. Unless you're biracial, in which case some might (incorrectly) say that you have to earn it. Listen, this isn't a wolf ticket I'm buying or selling, because that's just segregation among each other. A lighter complexion doesn't mean you need to get put on a waiting list, because that one-drop rule was made just for the occasion of keeping passing folk out. Trust that discrimination will find your ass REGARDLESS. Being biracial doesn't stop you from claiming that Black Card as your birthright.

Fact is, that's mostly what we know of the Black Card, isn't it? That it's our birthright, right? And in order to maintain it the rules state that one must keep it real, one hunned, and Black. Now the question comes in "keeping it real": Does it mean to yourself, your culture, or both simultaneously? Do the needs of Black culture outweigh the deed to who you are? And how does this all get measured on your Black Card? That's the tricky part. For example, grits are Black as fuck, right? That's a given. Blackest night of my life was eating catfish and grits in Harlem while listening to Tupac's "Ambitionz az a Ridah" playin' in the background. Personally, I don't like grits, but my sister fucking LOVES 'em (she is Black and Indian). Does that take away from my Blackness? Does her Blackness outweigh mine? Does me knowing the vernacular for and the location of "the kitchen" redeem my Black Card for a stamp of approval?

Now how about the side of the Black Card where the needs of the culture outweigh your own? It isn't until recent years that I realized the time spent with my father was him raising me as a Black militant-as-fuck person from day one. We weren't talking basketball, soul music, or movies. Every single second of my time spent with that man was filled with Black history, not just in America—I'm talking worldwide. In hindsight it seems that to my father this excessive amount of knowledge and culture outweighed everything else. My father wanted his child, his Black child, to know these facts about the Black people and culture that we stemmed from. Possessing this knowledge of Black culture and history was worth more than my need for what I thought father-son bonding looked like.

See, some envision the Black Card as a punch card where unlocking certain things (for example, knowing the location of "the kitchen" or the lyrics to a song in *The Wiz*) earns a stamp of approval on the card. I never saw it as that. To me, it's this badge that you're given, right? The Black Card is always with you and materializes whenever you level up. It informs you of your clearance grade. To me, nothing is ever deducted from you (because the world does that for us daily), but you can only level up with experience points. And the knowledge that acts as your experience and is used to level you up isn't up for scrutiny, because I may not gain the experience points of having seen the show *Oz*, but I know who Imhotep is, that he is regarded as the father of medicine, a poet, and a polymath, and I can quote him. Does not viewing *Oz* (fiction) outweigh that knowledge (nonfiction)?

The way I view the Black Card's experience system is like a video game: if you didn't complete the *Oz* TV series viewing mission, then you don't get the experience points that *Oz* provides or have *Oz* as an unlocked achievement. Simple, right? It gets more complex when you identify with subcultures. For instance, I identify as a nerd. There is no Nerd Card per se, but in this subculture, you have to prove how much of a nerd you are as a way of flexing your authenticity because someone will test you.

To be a Black nerd is to be in a subculture within a subculture. It's ironic, as diversity has been scarce creator-wise and character-wise for the longest time within certain realms of nerddom, yet to prove I am a nerd, I must be extremely versed in my field of expertise (comic books), the majority of which for the longest time were created by and marketed for cisgender white males. But I gotta be knowledgeable on *Star Wars* (which had like five Black people in the galaxy [insert clone troopers argument here], but whatever) or *Star Trek* in order to prove my nerd cred (I ain't even 'bout that space adventure life like that), even though growing up this was seen as a conflict of interest with my Black Card. Why? Well, as Donald Glover said about being a Black nerd in his *Weirdo* stand-up special,

"That shit was illegal until like 2003." Which is to say, these portions of pop culture weren't associated with having Black fans.

My "nerd cred" is always going to have to be a skill tree set attached to my Black Card. They can't be separated. I made a nerd clutch his pearls when I told him I never saw *Tron*. He said, "Are you serious? You gotta see *Tron*!" I said, "Man, the fuck I look like watching *Tron* on VHS in 2015, bruh? Fuck *Tron*, there weren't any digital Black people or people of color up in that watered-down *Ghost in the Shell*–ass game. You know what nerd shit from the '80s I was fucking with comin' up? *The Last Dragon*. Oh, you never heard of it? I'M NOT SURPRISED. Knew your ass ain't got the glow." You gon' try and run my nerd cred, you best select what Game Over title you want as the backdrop at your funeral, 'cause NOT ON MY WATCH.

I'm more prone to get defensive when anyone wants to discredit my nerd. "You're not a nerd" is a slap in the face, because you don't know the shit I been through repping this subculture in the streets before this shit became chic and cool, muhfucka. I earned these stripes. Now when another Black person says, "I'ma have to check your Black Card," or threatens that you'll have it revoked, it's all in jest, a way of saying that you've been caught slipping on something you should be hip to because Black culture has embraced and cosigned it. Obviously there are some that may mean that statement maliciously, I don't gloss over that or pretend it doesn't occur. I can recall numerous occasions when I was younger and mentioned how I didn't own Jordans or follow basketball and a white kid commenting, "You're not really Black," as if they were the authority on the matter, which they honestly have no right to say, especially when they're a stranger or a friend of a friend. The initial instinct when this occurs, with me, at least, has always been, "And who the fuck are you to tell me about being Black?" It'd be at this point they'd say they were just kidding, but it'd be too late because I wasn't, so now this conversation about why they felt comfortable enough to say such a thing to me but not expect a response. Perhaps it's a mark of being the "safe" Black guy and not dangerous or tough. Odds are if you are Black and come off as nerdy in a way that some white folk perceive as unconventional for Black people, then you have heard the "you're not Black" critique or the ever inescapable "I'm Blacker than you are."

I was in South Africa visiting my then girlfriend and had a white dude say to me, as a joke because I'm American, "I'm more African than you are." Now obviously it was said in jest, but the bite was still the same because what do we say about the relationship between the truth and jest? Y'all know it. The most frustrating part was that I'm literally in one of the fifty-four sovereign countries located on the continent I've been told to go back to a number of times in my life, and even here I'm "not Black enough." Of course I could've pointed out that being a citizen of South Africa via colonization (vintage gentrification) is way different than being African/ Black and torn from your home, but you gotta pick your battles, so fuck me, right? (Plus I looked up and saw Mufasa telling me, "I know. I know . . . Just let this one go.")

I'll charge that shit to the Black Card 'cause ignorant comments (real life or online) MUST count as experience points. I don't care, I don't care, I don't fucking care. As far as I'm concerned, when Black folk start growing gray hair, that's not age catching up or even stress, that's you physically leveling the fuck up from having to deal with systemic oppression's fuck shit on the regular. I had to listen to a dude who was darker than me explain why he rides for All Lives Matter, the reasoning being that no life is more important than the other and all lives are equal, but HE THEN STATES FOUR SENTENCES LATER IN REGARDS TO POLICE RACIAL PROFILING: "Come on, I'm Blacker than you [Note: He meant complexion-wise]. I know it can happen to me."

Son, by the time I was done explaining how the *too* is implied in Black Lives Matter (too) and walked out of that conversation, I had enough experience points to reach a level that I shouldn't be able to get to till I'm damn near in my fifties AT LEAST. The Black Card isn't a ranking system for how Black you are and will become. No, more than anything it's a fucking gauge for all the shit you've been through, will go through, and have yet to go through in the world.

I semi–used to think there was a +999 cap on the Black Card, that there was some final level where you reach Morgan Freeman–level clearance and then Iram of the Pillars rises from the depths before you, you enter another dimension, and you walk through elaborate halls where eons of Black history, African culture, and scriptures not forgotten but hidden away from the world thrive only for those who have reached the final stage of Blackness, then the ghosts of Toussaint Louverture, Henrietta Lacks, Audre Lorde, and Uncle Phil appear before you as a figure in the distance walks down a spiral staircase in the shadows while slow clapping then steps forward into the light, revealing himself to be none other than Samuel L. Jackson, and he says, "Congratulations, motherfucker, you've reached the ultimate stage of Blackness . . . peak muhfucking Blackness." Peak Blackness knows no final form.

Top Five Dead or Alive:
Tai Lung (*Kung Fu Panda*)

WILLIAM EVANS,
aka Jim Kelly as an Anthropomorphic Fox

FIRST THINGS FIRST, if you don't fuck with kung fu, pandas, or *Kung Fu Panda*, then you chose the wrong book aisle after dark, homie. Speaking ill of any of those things will get you reenacting Ricky's last moments in *Boyz n the Hood*. You can't swing a Pixar employee without hitting a new animated film with talking animals/creatures with top-notch celebrity voice talent, but across all animated studios, *Kung Fu Panda* is still upper echelon, fam. Especially when the Minions got their own film and every year on this Earth promises the potential of another *Ice Age* sequel or spin-off. And if we talkin' *Kung Fu Panda*, we talkin' about some against-all-odds, martial arts deliciousness. Here's the quick and dirty on the plot:

Po is a number one fanboy of the Furious Five, five handpicked martial arts experts from the animal kingdom training in perpetuity just up the block from his pop's noodle shop. On the day that wise Master Oogway, aka Turtle Shell Yoda, is to pick the next Dragon Warrior, the assumption is that one of the five will be chosen. But when Po tries to get that backstage pass to see who will get chosen, his shenanigans lead Oogway to picking him as the Dragon Warrior instead. Your boy ain't kunged a fu in his life. But now he has a destiny to fulfill. Shifu, the master that has personally trained the Furious Five, is, well, furious. But you know how this works. Po has heart, and in animated films heart has like an 80x skill multiplier. He convinces his naysayers and saves the village.

"Save from whom?" you may ask. Well, that's why the fuck we came here in the first place. We talkin' villains, yo. Nothing beats the original. Tai Lung was the truth. Ever see the anime *Fullmetal Alchemist*? Where the protagonist Elric brothers do some taboo shit they had no business doing that cost them body parts and shit? It was the cost for seeing "The Truth." That's the kind of Truth we talkin' about with Tai Lung. As the greatest snow leopard of all time, for *Kung Fu Panda*, you gotta put Tai Lung in the Top Five Dead or Alive.

But if they ever flip sides like Anakin
You'll sell everything includin' the mannequin
They got a new *%&^, now you Jennifer Aniston
—Kanye West, "Gone"

Yo, you know how this dark prophecy shit works. Cat's (literally cat, since dude is a snow leopard) just out here surviving as an orphan, trying to find his place in the world, and also happens to be a once-in-a-lifetime type of talent. Tai Lung was the prodigy but was denied his legacy cuz Oogway saw darkness in him. So yeah, homie was mad he done worked his whole life to be told that some unseen thing made him unworthy. You ever work your whole life for a job you're immensely qualified for, just for the CEO to be like, "Nah," when you up for promotion? I mean, if you're a person of color, I might already know your answer. But you might have the impulse to fuck up the Jade Palace.

But you aren't a master of Leopard Style, so you didn't. Tai Lung was and went into straight "who gon' check me, boo?" mode. Well, Oogway checked him, to answer that last question. Oogway was THE master and he brought Tai Lung down with like a pressure point strike. That shit happened so quick his fitness tracker didn't even pick up the exercise. But that's beside the point. The Rap Game was Dragon Warrior, and Tai Lung still had the hottest mixtape in the street. Maybe we need to look at Shifu and his shoddy leadership. Dude practically raised Tai Lung, but I guess we on some nature vs. nurture shit, huh? Fuck that, free Tai Lung.

> *I swam down shit's creek and came up clean*
> *With a new lease on life like Andy Dufresne*
> —Jay Electronica, "Exhibit A"

Actually, fuck that. Tai Lung gonna free himself. Look, maybe you think it was right to deny Tai Lung his destiny, and maybe you somehow stayed after the intro while not being a huge *Kung Fu Panda* fan. But what I will not take any argument on is that Tai Lung's prison escape from Chor-Ghom is the greatest prison escape of all time. I said that shit and won't take it back. Don't @ me.

Tai Lung was in prison for twenty years, fam. They hit your boy with the Hannibal Lecter for martial arts master vice for twenty years. In his prime? That's like LeBron being in a cast from age nineteen to thirty-nine and still being the most feared player on the court when he's forty. Dude picked his lock with a fuckin' peacock feather and his own tail, cracked his knuckles, rolled his neck, and basically told the whole prison to get right with their god.

Dude was still chained up and dodged not one, not two, not three, but four crossbow bolts, using the last one to free one of his hands. Then, when your boy got free, he threw the crossbow bolts into the wall and straight up platformed that shit like Mega

Man. Your boy was out here running on the walls, telling Prince of Persia to go to hell. They tried to release the flutes on your boy and Ramsay Bolton him with the arrows. Nope. Raised the platform and tried to abandon him in the pit. NOPE. After that (for a while) it was all Taijutsu and he just . . . you know what, dude just whupped everybody's ass. No need for metaphor here, fam, he just took muthafuckas apart like Michael Dell did his first computer.

Then they try to blow up the bridge to prevent his escape. They really out here trying to merk Da Gawd, yo. Tai Lung out here climbing falling rocks until he hits the ceiling where the last explosives are, then returns that shit to sender like Amazon sent him the wrong shirt size. Nah, this shit was next level and four minutes of legend making and legend forging. When he walkin' over the unconscious bodies of all the prison guards, your boy grabs the messenger Zeng by the neck and sends him back to the Jade Palace with a copy of Jay-Z's "Public Service Announcement" with the first bars on a loop: *"Allow me to re-introduce myself . . ."*

> *Magnetic, the flows are athletic*
> *Dimensions are perfected*
> *But the static and kinetic is power*
> —Yasiin Bey, "Casa Bey"

Speaking of when he tossed his demo to Zeng after he broke out of prison, it's the first time we hear Tai Lung's voice, and yes, my ninjas, it's the gawd of vocals and monologues, Al Swearengen himself, Ian McShane. Yo, if you've read just about anything from me, then you know I want Ian McShane to star in every gotdamn thing *Being John Malkovich* style. But he's perfect to voice the most terrifying villain in these kung fu streets. The charismatic and yet menacing demeanor. The matter-of-fact jaguar shade style. The confidence of a predator cat that just wants to watch the world burn. Dude is Mr. Steal Your Technique in the Club. McShane got the vocal range of a fuckin' guided missile and gives Tai Lung all the nuance necessary—from fighting his former master to his ultimate defeat, it's all there.

> *Being feared go farther than any part of me having respect does*
> *So I play to the tune of my own eardrum*
> —Royce da 5'9", "Wait"

Unlike the sequels (which I still fux with but they still ain't 2Pac, nah mean), Tai Lung was a beast because it was all him, yo. He didn't need no fuckin' cannons or all the metal in China. And he didn't need the mastery of the mystic arts like chi to imprison souls to fight for him. Tai Lung was the fuckin' Rock Lee from *Naruto* of *Kung Fu Panda* villains. Just straight up, you can catch these hands and I don't need any backup singers.

Fuck your rhythm section. Fuck your autotune and your sound engineer. Fuck your background vocals and your Super Bowl pyrotechnics. Tai Lung out there with one mic like Nas, spittin' the ill shit a cappella with nothing but a spotlight and the fiercest claws this side of the Ming Dynasty. He should've known he didn't need the Dragon Scroll cuz he been wreckin' the game with nothin' but blood, sweat, and other cats' tears his whole life.

> *They wear them lifetime*
> *They tell they [leopards], Tai did this*
> *Pointin' to their scars like, nah, baby, really Tai did this*
> —Inspired by Nas, "Loco-Motive"

Simply, Tai Lung was the fuckin' illest in combat. I don't care. I don't care. I don't care. I already broke down his prison escape. His next move after the prison break? When he fought the Furious

Five. By himself. Furious Five really thought they were going to prove themselves by sending Tai Lung back to prison, and Tai Lung said, "The only thing getting sent back is this Bob Evans breakfast I ordered cuz it got cold WHILE I BEAT THE BRAKES OFF ALL FIVE OF YOU." He took on the Furious Five like that shit was a warm-up before his 6:00 a.m. CrossFit class. He out here on a rope bridge handing out overtime to five kung fu masters like the Jade Palace was short-staffed and someone needed to make up the hours.

Tigress tried to hit him with "How do you know I'm not the Dragon Warrior?" and Tai Lung hit her back like, "Ain't nobody coming to see you, Otis!" And then after surviving their best effort there, your boy hits them all with the good night juice and leaves them to go tell the village to knock them milk bottles together and come out to play.

Do I even need to get into how Tai Lung put the paws on Master Shifu? How your boy literally broke out the super combo from *Street Fighter* and hit Shifu with the hot nickels? Sheeyet, Tai Lung out here doing the Lord's work with the rage and the technique and nobody could see him . . . until the obligatory ending where the hero (Po) must prevail against the superior foe. Let's not mince words here, I love *Kung Fu Panda*, the movies and the character. But Tai Lung might be the best to ever do it. And Po beat your boy with belly flops and adrenaline fueled by hunger pains. I'm disgusted. But I love it. But also disgusted.

Tai Lung deserved better, man, but this is what his actual destiny was. Not to be the Dragon Warrior, but to be the antagonist in a DreamWorks animated production. Let's pour out a little sake for our snow leopard with the dark future and fast kicks. May he know some peace (but mostly war) in the spirit realm.

Green Lantern Comics Have Low-Key Been Tackling Police Accountability for a Minute

OMAR HOLMON,
aka The Black Friend John Stewart Vents To

IF YOU GAVE me a microphone right now, on the spot, and told me to deliver a dissertation on a topic, odds are I'm going to be talking about DC Comics' *Green Lantern* (Silver Age incarnation), created by John Broome and artist Gil Kane. I can break down each *Green Lantern* from the lore to the characters, the highs, the lows, and when they tell me to cut it short 'cause I'm going overtime, I'd say, "Too bad, 'cause those three hours were just the introduction. The real shit starts now." I've always loved the concept of the Green Lantern. If y'all aren't familiar with the character, lemme give you a quick rundown. Picture this shit. Space is broken down into 3,600 sectors. At the center of the universe is the planet Oa, home of the Guardians of the Universe, also known as Oans. The Guardians are small blue aliens that are old as fuck, the Big Bang was like fireworks goin' off outside their window. They're the peacekeepers of the universe. The Guardians created the Green Lantern Corps to be their ambassadors, so to speak, throughout the universe and they are armed with power rings.

73

Power rings are one of the (if not *the*) most powerful items/weapons in the universe. A power ring allows its wearer to make whatever they can imagine exist as a solid-light construct that the user wills into taking shape in reality. The only limit is the user's own imagination, willpower, occasional battery recharge, and a yellow impurity that makes the ring not work on anything yellow (this we're gon' circle back to). Every Green Lantern uses the ring uniquely, but they all follow the same rules. The laws/principles that Green Lanterns abide by are as follows:

1   The protection of life and liberty within the assigned sector.
2   Following the orders of the Guardians without question.
3   Noninterference with a planet's culture, political structure, or its population's collective will.
4   Acting within local laws and obeying the local authority within reason. (Presumably, the Guardians' orders can overrule this when necessary.)
5   Taking no action against anyone or anything until they are proven to be a threat against life and liberty.
6   Refusing to use the equipment, resources, or authority of the Corps for personal gain.
7   Showing respect for and cooperating with other members of the Corps and the Guardians.
8   Showing respect for life, which includes restraint of force unless there is no reasonable alternative.
9   Giving top priority to the greatest danger in the assigned sector.
10   Upholding the honor of the Corps.

Mind you, revisions can be made to these laws. How does one become a Green Lantern? Glad you asked. You get selected by having the ability to overcome great fear. When a Green Lantern dies, their ring goes off to find another inhabitant of that specific sector of space to take up the mantle. Test pilot Hal Jordan became the first earthling to become a Green Lantern. The aliens chosen to be Green Lanterns all come from different walks of life: queens (Iolande), warriors (Boodikka), doctors (Soranik Natu), pacifists (Jessica Cruz), lawyers (Malet Dasim). When they are chosen by the ring, they become part of an institution that is billions of years old. I loved this concept so much and the stories of the Green Lanterns that their lantern insignia was my very first tattoo. The tattoo is an homage to my favorite Green Lantern, John Stewart. John Stewart is a Black architect from Detroit who questioned authority as opposed to his predecessor, Hal Jordan, who always challenged authority. Hal Jordan is someone who usually sees things in black and white, whereas John Stewart is the type of person who sees the gray areas.

John Stewart made his debut 1972. In 2004, John Stewart got a retcon (a revision) added to his origin story stating that he was a former marine sniper before becoming an architect. The retcon added a new layer to the character that I appreciated, because it gave John incredible moments. There's one comic panel where John uses his power ring to create a sniper rifle construct. Due to John's architectural background, we see every nut, bolt, and piece coming together to create the rifle as if it's an architectural blueprint right before he hits an enemy sniper nearly three galaxies away. That shit looked so fucking cold. I loved that my favorite character was getting more shine but also worried that this marine origin retcon gave a very pro-military message. Especially since Hal Jordan already had a military background as an air force combat pilot. Thankfully, even with the military background, John Stewart was still written and seen as a mediator first, then a soldier. Especially when he became the leader of the Green Lantern Corps, which was important to me.

Earlier, I called Green Lanterns ambassadors, but in the comics they're more synonymous with being militarized intergalactic law enforcers. Still, every alien species interprets their Green Lantern's role differently. On Earth, Green Lanterns are referred to as space police or cops. However, in the real world of the United States of America, policing's history has roots originating in catching slaves in the South. Meanwhile up north, police were people hired to protect property and shipping goods. From their incarnation to present day, police officers have been brutalizing, incarcerating, and killing Black folk. The comparison of Green Lanterns with police made me worry that the series could be considered a sci-fi version of copaganda. Thankfully, throughout the multiple volumes of *Green Lantern* comics, they were DC Comics' first series to really address race, poverty, and religion and provide commentary or ideology of what a combination of humanitarianism and law enforcement could be. It was this realization that lemme breathe a sigh of relief that I can fuck with the Green Lanterns guilt-free because the biggest difference between them and police is that they're written as people who actually serve their community and are held accountable when they abuse their power.

There's long been a discussion of how police are called for things that are outside of their jurisdiction and are expected to handle small-scale cases with people that they aren't trained or equipped to handle. That's not even getting into how their training is only like, what, six to eight months? While law enforcement in other countries go through years of training, especially in de-escalation, and fewer people are killed by law enforcement. There's a tweet from a friend of mine, CB Rucker, that puts into perspective the use of policing in the United States: "Replace 'cop' with 'mu'fucka with a gun' and you'll see how stupid our use of police is. The neighbors are too loud, so we call a mu'fucka with a gun to get them to turn down the noise? There's a Black person you don't know present, so you call a mu'fucka with a gun? See how insane this shit is. That's our 'answer' to shit."

Switching gears from comics to live-action series for a moment, HBO's live-action TV series *Watchmen* displayed an accountability to the police's use of guns perfectly and subtly in its first episode. In the second opening scene, an officer pulls over a driver and sees memorabilia that indicates the driver is part of a local white supremacist terrorist group. The officer then goes to his police car, calls the situation in to his headquarters, and asks permission that his gun be unlocked from its holster in the car. This is such a subtle nod to show that in that world, even police have to abide by strict gun control procedures. This scene immediately stood out to me. I feel it is something not shown in cop shows often. In the *Green Lantern* comics, they tackled an inverse of this situation. Ever since the Green Lantern Corps's incarnation, a Green Lantern's power ring wasn't allowed to use lethal force. When the Corps was involved in a war against the Sinestro Corps, the Guardians of the Universe, their superiors, allowed them the use of lethal force for the first time ever. After the war, there was a conversation among the Green Lantern Corps members that resulted in some members refusing to use lethal force. Almost immediately we see the first occurrence of abuse of lethal force take place. Some Green Lanterns were bringing the body of their fallen comrade back to his family. They arrived to see their comrade's family dead. Their killer was Amon Sur, an intergalactic terrorist. Amon Sur was waiting for the Green Lanterns to arrive so that he could surrender and news of what he did would spread. That alien got killed on the fucking spot by a Green Lantern named Laira.

Laira was charged with murder. Even her teammates told their fellow corpsmen it was murder, not justice, as everyone debated about it. Laira stood trial for her actions. Her ring had recorded and logged her actions for all to see, and she was stripped of her Green Lantern "badge" and power ring. Open-and-fucking-shut case. As it should be. Laira's story always makes me think about how in the United States a lot of people thought body cams on officers would make a difference to curb police brutality. Surely, if we see what they see and are doing, then officers can be held accountable. That thought stays in my head, since body cams on officers really gave us nothing more than a front-row seat to the deaths of unarmed Black people. I mean, that's when the cameras were even turned on or kept on during alter-cations. Body cams made Black deaths viral and a form of public execution, and these police officers were still not held accountable.

We watched Black children killed, Black men shot or choked out to death, Black women literally being assaulted by police. There's footage of an officer from Miami holding a Black pregnant mother down, knee on her shoulder, and tasing her stomach. Even with footage, a lot of these officers were given time off with pay or fired, but not many convicted or even going to trial. It got made clear very quickly that even seeing isn't believing for white America. There's no coming back from that. You may wonder, "How is video evidence still not enough?" Trust, I'm over here wondering the same damn thing, man. Folks thought the problem of "well, we weren't there so we don't know what happened"/"he said, she said" would be fixed by body cams. How ironic that now you can go on your news feed and see that horror live, in color, and still know there's a slim chance those officers responsible will be held accountable. Which brings me to think about the upper administration of police lying their asses off or burying evidence. There's no bigger picture with the police for peace. They let folks get fired at times, but those people get rehired in a different department with those stains on the record fully visible. What part of the reform is that? I couldn't tell ya, but I can tell ya what part of the racism that is. The systemic part.

There are countless instances where officers were not only lying to help each other but hiding evidence where they could have prevented the death of someone in custody. Instead, they stood there and did nothing. We've witnessed so many instances that didn't require force whatsoever and ended with a Black person's name as a hashtag to give light to their death. Ironically enough, a Green Lantern named Sojourner Mullein, created by N. K. Jemisin and artist Jamal Campbell and the first (Earth) Black woman to become a Green Lantern, dealt with a similar issue. She joined the military and police force in hopes of changing things. When she witnessed her partner beating a person with the end of their gun, she froze in shock. When Sojourner testified against her partner she was fired. She was fired for doing the right thing. In the real world this shit doesn't happen often, because the police protect one another and their actions, no matter how heinous. Now maybe you're reading this and know one cop that did do the right thing. That's one outta how many thousands/millions of officers abusing power, keeping up this systemic structure of oppression? Again, I do not believe there is a way to reform this shit, fam.

I don't believe that "it's only a few bad apples" ruining it for everyone. We're not talking 'bout bad apples ruining an apple crumble pie. We talking 'bout a lot of muthafuckas that have access to a gun and authority getting away with killing Black people. Before becoming one of my favorite wrestlers, Mustafa Ali spent four years as a police officer. Ali said he became an officer because he wanted to promote change from within. I'll never forget seeing him talk about how Black folks were targeted for arrest and incarceration and the profit that comes due to the design of the criminal justice system. He said that shit on the WWE (World Wrestling Entertainment) Network and in a *Sports Illustrated* interview, citing that what he saw as an officer is a big part of why he supports the Black Lives Matter stance and movement. I bring that "change from within" idea up as it's hard for one person to change an entire structure built on racism.

You may get tired of me saying this, but you guessed it! There's an example of this in the *Green Lantern* comics as well! A Green Lantern named Thaal Sinestro was considered the greatest of all time until it was discovered he used his power to act as a dictator on his home world Korugar. When the Korugarian citizens revolted, Sinestro was found out and punished by the Guardians of the Universe. A rebel leader named Katma Tui was chosen as the replacement Green Lantern for Sinestro. However, the damage was already done. The Korugarians had spent so long under Sinestro's rule that now, for them, the Green Lantern symbol was akin to a Nazi swastika. They didn't want Katma there as a Green Lantern. Katma left her planet, essentially abolishing Green Lanterns as a presence there for more than forty years till her replacement was selected. She became a legend in the Green Lantern Corps, but to her people she's called Katma Tui, "the Lost."

We've seen in real-life history how one person, Hitler, corrupted a peaceful symbol used across many cultures, especially in India, for thousands of years and turned it into a symbol that inflicts terror toward a group of people. The symbol's original meaning doesn't change, but for the Jewish community, the bastardized version will always represent a symbol of terror. In regard to policing, when you're Black and hear that *woop-woop* siren call and see them flashing red and blue lights, your body hits that fight-or-flight response waiting for the officer to come up to your car window, and based on their mood, you don't know if you're going to make it to your destination or a jail cell alive. With Katma Tui's tale, we see that even when people try to change the image of an institution and that institution employs one of the folks that called for a change, the communities and people harassed by the institution aren't going to just forgive that shit.

Whew, I've been shitting on copaganda and cops for a good minute now. I will say that there is media out there aside from

Green Lantern comics that to an extent does the work of social commentary on police as well. *Brooklyn Nine-Nine* is a TV show about a diverse cast of cops at a fictional precinct set in Brooklyn. Throughout the show we see the officers of the Nine-Nine being both police in a comedy as well as providing commentary on police and police issues. The show addresses the shortcomings of the law, the officers, or even society through humor. It's usually in quick beats and happened more so later on into the series. The show is still copaganda, but this shit is legit funny as fuck but can flip the switch when necessary for the more serious moments. There's one episode where one of the main characters, Lieutenant Terry Jeffords, is out of uniform and gets racially profiled by an officer near his home. When he goes to file a complaint, it gets denied by his superior, Captain Raymond Holt, who is also Black. Holt tells Terry he wants him to pick his battles. This complaint could alter Terry's career as an officer, which would inhibit him from getting promoted to a position where he could change things. Terry ain't trying to hear that. Later on, Holt apologizes to Terry after coming to the realization that as a Black gay officer in the '80s, the advice he offered was how he had to do things. Now Holt was in a position to be the change he wanted to see in the police force and would stand by Terry's complaint.

There's a bunch of serious scenes like this mixed into *Brooklyn Nine-Nine*'s comedy. As of now, the show has been renewed for an eighth season. The problem is how will it address what's happened with police brutality, numerous protests, and calls for the abolishment of police that have occurred in 2020? It has to touch on these topics without the show leaning even more into copaganda and being apologetic/sympathetic to cops' perspective. It's not an easy task, but the show positioned itself in this lane of being woke cops. Not tackling it would be a disservice to its fan base. Members of the cast have been vocal that they must find a way to address today's climate in their upcoming season as well. I gotta give 'em credit for being 'bout keeping the same energy for social commentary that they came in with. I fuck with the *Green Lantern* comics series because they've kept the same energy providing commenting on social issues for years.

The stories and tales of the Green Lantern Corps give me the escapism I look for without any heavy copaganda or police sympathy. Reading about this intergalactic peacekeeping organization that abides by the rules of respecting every alien's culture, religion, and customs when they step into communities foreign to them provides comfort in fiction. I don't get or see that comfort when I think of the police in the real world due to their actions, track record in Black communities, and murder rate of Black and Brown people. I've said it repeatedly, I can't fathom an institution with these racist practices getting reformed when they don't even hold officers that abuse their power accountable. Accountability is such an easy thing in these *Green Lantern* works of fiction. There's no reason it can't be as applicable in the real world in regard to cops, but it isn't. Maybe that's what actually kept me reading the series for so long. In these *Green Lantern* stories, I get to see the accountability and justice of these peacekeepers sworn to protect their section of a galaxy. Whereas in the United States of America, a person sworn to protect a community abuses their power on video and gets to punch in to work the next day to do it again.

The 2000s and 2010s Golden Era of TV Gave Us a Lot of Great Television and Made Me So Damn Tired

WILLIAM EVANS,
aka DJ Tony Baritone

IF WE'RE KEEPING it buck, this era kind of started in the late '90s when *Oz* dropped on HBO. *Oz* was different, yo. *Oz* didn't adopt the darkness, it was born into it. Molded by it. Whatever show you thought was gritty before *Oz*, head to the back of the line and try again. If you don't know the origin story, Oz was the nickname for the Oswald State Correctional Facility. This was a level 4 maximum (read: the "worst of the worst") prison where your boy Ernie Hudson, who never got his real *Ghostbusters* shine, is the warden. In a plot that must keep prison reform activists up at night if they ever watched this, we spend time in "Emerald City": a ward of the prison where the unit manager Tim McManus tries to focus much more on rehabilitation and reform over punishment and retribution. In a very cynical way, that shit is an abject failure in the end. Folks getting murdered ayeday. Racial groups get more entrenched instead of harmonization (everyone's beloved J. K. Simmons was a neo-Nazi leader, y'all), the prison guards become compromised in the most outsized way (what up, Edie Falco!), and they gotta shut the whole thing down.

Oz is important for a number of reasons, not just limited to a crazy lineup of "before they were mega TV stars" performers on the show, but in showing how far and grown-up TV was ready to be. Yeah, we've had premium channel programming for a long time, but this was appointment TV where they encountered (often messily) real moral dilemmas that weren't very black-and-white. We can debate the quality of the show (actually, the end of the show is an absolute train wreck, debate ya family on that), but the influence is undeniable. *Oz*'s questioning of morality and never really having a moral center made *The Sopranos*, which started two years later, possible on the network. *Oz* is the first show I can remember that had the "time check" test, where so much wild and crazy-ass shit would happen, with the drama on twelve, and I'd look at the clock and be like, "Wait, we still have another half hour of this?! Impossible."

Oz may have laid the groundwork, but *The Sopranos* built the damn house with a bunch of rooms and a long-ass winding driveway down from a hill in New Jersey. Now we're talking about prestige TV and, specifically, starting the HBO drama dynasty that lasted for more than a decade. *The Sopranos* set a standard for so many things like the black hat protagonist in Tony Soprano, the mega spotlight on the auteur showrunner in David Chase, and finally the investment and opinion of everyone in how to best stick the landing of your show. *The Sopranos* still stands up, by the way, watching parts of that series more than twenty years later. Gandolfini is still a marvel. The world is still full and fleshed out. And Black folks are still called "mulignan." Wait, what? Yeah . . .

There's a throughput of this golden era of TV so many of us fell in love with. It starts with a man. A white man. A wonderfully acted white man. He has a compromised moral compass. He might just be a bad guy, but he's our bad guy. But that guy, that white guy, is the sun with which everyone is stuck in his gravitational pull. It's not a bad way to make a TV show. But during that decade plus, it was damn near the only way.

There's a whole discourse about legions of white dudes taking the "wrong lessons" from Tony Soprano and Walter White and Don Draper, but yo . . . I'm bored with that take. You're bored with that take. Cuz like, an entitled dude that thinks being an asshole is how to make people love you didn't need someone with superior genetics like Jon Hamm to affirm that for him. But what's interesting is how this formula wasn't really explored outside of white men during this time. They all had white wives that were their foils most often.

[Side note: Can we get a fucking apology to folks like Anna Gunn (Skyler White) and January Jones (Betty Draper) who took so much internet abuse because they were the omega to sometimes legit evil dudes? Like the projection was strong with that one, fellas. Remember that episode of *Justice League Unlimited* when Lex Luthor and the Flash body swapped and the Flash (in Luthor's body) left the bathroom without washing his hands and justified not exercising basic hygiene by saying, "Because I'm EEEEVIL"? That, Skyler White haters, that's what y'all sound like. Anyways . . .]

While it can be argued that the success of *Oz* made HBO a concrete landing spot for *The Sopranos*, the true spiritual successor for *Oz* would have to be *The Wire*. With some of the overlapping characters (Lance Reddick DA GAWD and J. D. Williams most notably) and a plot featuring the street warfare of Baltimore's drug trade, the shows, although tonally different, feel like they could exist in the same universe. The other notable reason they are similar? Black people. Of the golden age shows that followed *Oz*, *The Wire* was one of the few ensemble cast shows where the perspective changed depending on the plot and that fought hard not to center a character. Season one of *The Wire* begins with Detective Jimmy McNulty's crusade to take down the drug trade in the city but quickly expands to show how he is just a cog in the machine. Both within the world of the show and as a performer on the show itself. Because of its structure, there is the *Wire* effect now, where folks are on the lookout for *Wire* cast alums, because so many were given time to shine. A lot of actors on high-profile shows find work after their big show ends, but the reverence and following that the actors on *The Wire* draw are a testament to the screen time they were allotted.

This is how I came to define that era of TV once I had a little distance, the success of shows that mostly left Black folks off the roster. Where Black people were props and story arcs but rarely part of the overall importance of the show. There's an argument to be made for *Boardwalk Empire*, specifically season four, which might have been the Blackest season of television that year, but even then, we're talking about well into the 2010s. And even more glaring in the popular format of shows at the time, where were the single Black protagonist dramas? Where was the Black antihero with their own orbit, where they manipulated the world around them for their own selfish desires with a spouse that became hated by the viewing public because they possessed some semblance of a moral compass?

[You'll notice my gender neutrality here, because the lack of Black protagonists in this genre of TV making was barely represented more by women. For HBO's part, *Sex and the City* was still running, but you also had *Buffy*, *Gilmore Girls*, *Alias*, *Desperate Housewives* . . . okay, maybe we're not talking about prestige TV as much with those last couple, but still . . . The 2010s would give a much larger rise to Black women protagonists—not overwhelmingly, but substantially more racially diverse than the previous decade had been.]

Looking back on those shows, what further exacerbates the lack of Black inclusion is the way Black characters are subjected in the narrative. Basically to show how great or shitty the protagonist is. Dr. House making racially insensitive remarks shows you how edgy or against societal niceties he is. Which means he's a great doctor because he doesn't think like other people. Charlie, the "body man" for the president in *The West Wing*, is given about five minutes of screen time to discuss the fact that he's Black, but the president being oblivious to that as a possible issue generously projects his acceptance of a diverse coalition. Or most pessimistically shows he "doesn't see color." And I guess *Battlestar Galactica* just showed us that there are very few Black people in the future. Past. Whatever, *Galactica* pissed itself in the end.

The 2000s and 2010s are still my favorite era of straight up TV making. The stories were unique. The acting often top notch. But I was a spectator a lot more than a participant. When folks showed up that looked like me, they were often a means to an end, or the ridicule they had to endure was the point of their existence. The golden era isn't as golden when you realize how little the best shows diverged from themselves. But in the words of Omar Little, you with it because "it's all in the game, yo. It's all in the game."

Craig of the Creek:
When We See Us

OMAR HOLMON,
aka Running Round the House Smelling Like Outside

I WITNESSED A milestone life moment while watching WWE programming one night. I was in my sister's living room, casually viewing the cruiserweight division dubbed 205 Live as T. J. Perkins was wrestling. Perkins was doing an array of *lucha libre* moves before stopping to do his signature taunt where he holsters his hands as if they were guns. Shit looked so smooth as the camera zoomed in on him. I'd seen him do this hundreds of times, but what made this time special was when I heard, "Hey, he looks like me," out of nowhere. I moved the ottoman toward me to see my nephew, who was seven at the time, looking up from his Beyblades to TJP on the television. I told him, "That's 'cause he's Filipino."

My nephew said, "So, he's Asian like me?"

"Yep. You know there's a wrestler here named Mustafa Ali, he's Pakistani but also Indian like you. He looks even more like you. His friend Cedric Alexander is on this show too, he's Black like me and like you are too."

I could see the gears turning in my nephew's mind. He grew up in Singapore with my sister, who is Black, Indian, and light-skinned, and a father who is Sri Lankan and dark-skinned. When he was a baby, I made up a song to sing him called "Ethnically Ambiguous Baby" as a joke, knowing that he was going to be this Brown biracial kid hearing "So, what are you?" throughout life. Here we were six years later where he's a Brown kid seeing this wrestler that doesn't have his exact complexion but instantly recognizing that they share similar features and hearing about these other wrestlers that are the same race as him. While he was contemplating all this information, the first thing I thought was "Lemme see if I can get him interested in New Japan Pro Wrestling wrestlers as well so I can have someone to watch this stuff with." My second thought was "How fortunate is my nephew, in 2017, to be able to see himself on television at seven years old." Looking back, I realized that growing up, I never had this moment that my nephew was experiencing. It wasn't until 2018, where at thirty-three years old I saw this show on Cartoon Network called *Craig of the Creek* and truly saw a Black character that I instantly resonated with on sight.

If you're not up on *Craig of the Creek*, lemme learn you real quick. It's an animated show that follows Craig Williams, a nine-year-old Black boy middle child living his life in the Maryland suburbs of Herkleton with his all-Black everything family and playing with his friends Kelsey and J.P. at a creek near where they live. Craig enjoys exploring uncharted areas of the creek, Kelsey sees herself as a warrior and carries a sword made out of PVC pipe, and J.P. is the optimistic, imaginative, unpredictable member of the trio. Craig's family and friends are the main focus and then there's the creek. The creek is broken up into different territories where different types of kids hang out. There's a group of kids with bikes called the 10 Speeds that hangs out at Ramp City, an area of man-made hills of the creek. The horse girls, a bunch of girls that act like horses, hang out in the meadow of the creek. The sewer kids are in pool and beach attire running round in the sewer labyrinth. There's an area for everyone from the anime kids to the paintball kids. They're all mapped out by Craig, he's essentially the cartographer of the creek or "Map Boy," as he calls himself. There is either a kid or a group of kids for everyone watching the show to relate to. What I love the most is when you see a group of children or people on the show, there's always a Black person or person of color. Before *Craig of the Creek* even got a second season, I knew this show would be the greatest cartoon of all time.

That's some bold shit to say, but lemme break it down. When we talk "greatest of all time," for me, I do it by eras. In this case, there are cartoons we will always look back at fondly 'cause of nostalgia, but when we talking GOAT tier, it's only fair they ranked within their time and there are some exceptions to the rule. *Craig of the Creek* will be an exception to that rule because of three key animated GOATs that came before it: *Adventure Time*, a fantasy-genre cartoon that had elements of role-playing video games; *Steven Universe*, a space-adventure-type show where a majority of main and supporting characters were either women or coded as women; and *We Bare Bears*, a story about three anthropomorphic bears as adoptive brothers trying to fit into human society. These shows really paved the way in a big way for these cartoons disguised as kid shows that are actually for adults too. *Adventure Time* tackled trauma, consent, and friendship. *Steven Universe* took that baton and tackled gender issues, had nonbinary gender–conforming representations, showed women in power, and wrote the book on handling queer-coded characters. *We Bare Bears* said, "Bet. What we gon' do is have this show about bears but the majority of humans you see in the background will be people of color. We gon' draw Black men and women with actual detailed Black hair and features and we gon' showcase Asian folks accurate as fuck, as well as other cultures too." *Craig of the Creek* is god-tier status, because the shows that preceded it raised the bar, and by going the extra mile to really represent different cultures, backgrounds, and identities like the shows before it, and by adding its own personality into the mix, *Craig of the Creek* been doing salmon ladder pull-ups with that bar ever since. This show is an amalgam of all that these shows tackled and broke down for the point of view of kids.

The show handles things for the point of view of kids brilliantly. A game of four square on the blacktop feels like an anime battle to the kids playing. We see the kids doing *Dragon Ball Z* Super Saiyan–type power ups, which we witness visually through their eyes. *Craig of the Creek* has numerous homages like this to anime and other genres of pop culture nonstop each episode, but that ain't even half the trill! It tackles and addresses real-world shit too. You know how people say, "Well, how am I supposed to explain gay people to my kid?"—well, *Craig of the Creek* did that shit simple as fuck. In the "Ferret Quest" episode, everyone splits up to catch a ferret. Craig makes a female ferret sock puppet to lure the real ferret in. J.P. says, "But what if he crushes on guy ferrets?" They then create a male ferret sock puppet (with a six-pack), and when the ferret still doesn't show up they realize they should represent all ferrets. They then create various sock puppet ferrets. Boom. Simple as fucking that. We see kids on the show introduce themselves and others with their preferred pronouns and hear certain characters referred to as they/them. They literally touch so many bases with this show. I tune in to see what they could possibly do this time around. How much better can this show truly get from here?

Which brings me to the "Under the Overpass" episode, where Craig, Kelsey, J.P., and Kit (who runs the Trading Tree store) are in a raft exploring the uncharted part of their creek that flows into the next town over, Herkleton Mills, to get honeysuckle flowers for

Kit's store. When they return under the overpass that the creek flows through, this Black kid with long locs in a poncho gets the drop on them. Yo, this kid takes out a bow and proceeds to get busy. We see Kelsey, the fighting warrior of the group, swinging her sword to knock his arrows back while in the raft and she gets grazed across the face with an arrow, and we see a magenta mark on her cheek. Kelsey sniffs it and says, "Scented marker? HE'S TRACKING US!" That shit killed me. Of course a kid ain't going to be shooting actual arrows, so he made kid-friendly trick arrows. The archer kid then sinks their raft with an arrow that was a bundle of pencils and warns them to never return to the overpass.

I tell you I ran that whole scene back repeatedly for weeks. I was amazed because I fucking love archery. The first time I held a bow and arrow was in a day camp in fourth grade. I fell in love with it instantly. Look, I'm the guy making the case that Hawkeye deserves his spot on the Avengers. That's how hard I go for archery. It's my favorite physical hobby to do. Whenever I'm visiting friends or going overseas, my favorite thing to do is find an archery range and just shoot arrows. I like seeing the different stances and forms instructors use to shoot. I was in South Africa at an archery range learning from an instructor who said the best way to shoot was to have the bow in front of you and pull the drawstring back till it touches the tip of your nose then shoot. This is my shit, man; archery feels and even looks like it requires such grace and finesse. I never imagined I'd get to see a Black cartoon character that was nasty as fuck with the bow. A lil Black boy that loves archery. It's such an obscure/underrated skill, right? Plus, I've never seen a Black archer on television before. We later find out his name is the Green Poncho, which is an homage to DC Comics' archer-themed super-hero Oliver Queen, aka the Green Arrow.

Man, I sat ready to find out more about this kid week in and week out, waiting for him to show up. This shit took me back to Saturday-morning cartoons, hoping to see that dope-ass character and his story again. My favorite part of watching *Craig of the Creek* became waiting for the Green Poncho to appear in episodes and learning more about his storyline involving the kids from the other side of the creek. Remember how I said there's a kid for everyone on the show? I realized right the fuck there that Green Poncho is my kid. He's an archer on his vigilante shit that's, again, clearly a nod to the archer superhero Green Arrow and even Hawkeye from Marvel Comics. Watching the show, I never even realized we hadn't seen a kid that runs around identifying as a superhero/vigilante type. I instantly remembered a photo my mom took of me jumping round the house in Superman underwear or tying a towel around my neck as a cape. That's what made me instantly relate to Green Poncho. I too was that young kid (still am in my head), pretending to be a hero or vigilante.

I went so hard for this show that I had to attempt to do it justice by writing it up in an article for Black Nerd Problems' website. The head writer of *Craig of the Creek*, Jeff Trammell, hit me up to say that he was talking about the write-up with his producer on the show and how they loved it. Man, that meant the world, because I believe in giving folks their flowers while they here, plus this is one of those rare shows where you fucking know the people behind it care, actually get it, and are really pushing for progressive and inclusive content in each episode. The show was created by Matt Burnett and Ben Levin, who are white; however, you don't get these episodes and characters without Black writers and Black artists of different genders working together and influencing each other. Which is to say this show can't happen without the likes of Jeff Trammell, Kellye Perdue, Ashleigh Hairston, Tiffany Ford, Najja Porter, Dashawn Mahone, Lamar Abrams, Richie Pope, Pearl Low, Nick Winn, Taneka Stotts, and Shakira Pressley. As well as POC storyboard artists and writers like Michelle Xin, Amish Kumar . . . the list keeps going.

The writing staff on *Craig of the Creek* looking like a UN Summit, and that's what the fuck I am talking about. *Craig of the Creek* is what happens when writers and artists with range from different walks of life come together to create real, earnest stories and characters for all audiences. When I say all audiences, I mean adults, kids, queer, nonbinary, Black, POC, the list goes on and on and keeps going on and on and these creatives keep covering it. Every so often I'll hit Jeff up to tell him that the whole *Craig of the Creek* staff are legit doing the Lawd's work, and one time he said back to me, "Lol, Omar. Mark my words . . . We over here planning things you gonna be telling your grandkids about," accompanied by a GIF of the wrestler Roman Reigns doing a mic drop.

I thought, "They are already going the distance with this show and wanting to go even further?" That's the type of content creators I fuck with. They know what they're doing matters in the long run. Matter fact, there's an episode on the show where Craig's mom, Nicole, is getting her hair done and her hairdresser, the owner of the salon, is a Black woman with bright red hair. I sent a tweet with a picture of this scene talking about how detailed the creators are with the hairstyles of their Black girls and Black women on the show. This woman on Twitter, Kryssie, responded to the tweet, saying, "Omg that hairdresser has hair like me [smiling face with heart-shaped eyes emoji] I'm 34 . . . Never seen it." *slams palm on table with enthusiasm* That's what this show fucking does, man. To be Black, watching this show *Craig of the Creek*—we're so used to "how they see us" in the media. The way Black characters and people are depicted by writers and creators that are not Black or don't have Black people in the room. There are so many cartoon shows and live-action shows where tropes of colorism or tokenism are blatant or a running gag due to this white gaze commenting on its idea of Black culture.

However, whenever I hear *Craig of the Creek*'s theme song, I know that this is a time *when we see us*. When we get to see ourselves earnestly in this adult show disguised as a children's show. *Craig of the Creek* lets kids growing up now see themselves on television in these characters, while being kind enough for those of us that are older to see ourselves in these creek kids and adults as well. All this time seeing Green Poncho in these episodes, I thought I saw myself, but when his character development came, I was not ready at all. It was June 2020 when the "Into the Overpast" episode aired. I knew it was going to be fire because the title card had Green Poncho posed in the air shooting an arrow with lightning striking behind him as an homage to *The Dark Knight Returns* comic book. In the episode Craig and Green Poncho are retrieving his boomerang arrow that Craig shot earlier. They run into Maya, one of Green Poncho's enemies. Maya avoids Poncho's arrows, disarms him, then tosses Craig into some bushes when he steps in. Green Poncho crawls toward his bow, but Maya then steps on, squats down, and says, "Come on, Omar. It doesn't have to be like this. You can still come back." It's the first time we hear Green Poncho's actual name.

My wife, Tasha, sat up from the couch, we both looked at each other in a "what the hell?" moment, and she said, "Did they name this kid after you?" I thought, "Man, no way." It's so weird to see that your favorite character that you've been following for a year shares your name. This was the episode we find out Omar's story as he and Craig escape Maya and dodge the King's forces looking for them. We then enter a flashback sequence where Omar explains how back in the day, he and Maya were friends and met a boy named Xavier. They found out that Xavier is the King's little brother. When Xavier inherited the title of king from his older sister, Omar and Maya were told by Xavier to fight each other to see who'll serve as his best friend. Omar didn't want to fight but Maya did. This led to Omar falling out with her, his exile from the kingdom, and him being saved from the King's forces by an archer girl wearing a green poncho at the overpass.

Dude, we learned Poncho's name, which freaked me the hell out, then we learned that he's not the first Green Poncho, that it was a girl that he got the mantle from. What?! The writers legit gave him a whole hero origin story that's still not over yet! In the flashback we saw that Omar's personality is nothing like it used to be before he became the Green Poncho. Fam, this kid was joking around, reading comic books, making puns, and being lighthearted. I tell you that was my entire childhood. Scratch that, that's my entire adulthood now. I never felt more seen than when we saw Omar fighting Maya in the flashback and she told him, "You never take anything seriously," because I've heard that my entire life growing up. I had to clutch the pearls on that one. The best part of the episode was finding out that he likes pineapple on pizza too. That solidified it, this kid is my fucking guy 'cause I love that shit too. It's savory and sweet, dammit.

Yo, I never identified with a character more than this lil vigilante. First thing I did after seeing that episode was watch it again screaming, "Let's fucking goooo." Then I asked Jeff if Green Poncho's name was coincidentally Omar from the start. He hit me back, saying, "Nah, bro, that's all you. I did that for you. Thanks for the love and support." He then sent a screenshot of what he told me a year ago on March 4, 2019: "Omar. Mark my words . . . We over here planning things you gonna be telling your grandkids about." Man, I don't even have the words. Which makes this hard 'cause I gotta put it in words. I've fucked with shows before, I've loved stories on shows, but *Craig of the Creek* is *the* show for me that I relate to. Episode after episode, they do not miss, they don't beat you over the head with a message. They show different types of kids being able to be children while subtly showing how easy it is and can be to normalize queer relationships, such as Craig's older cousin Jasmine casually telling Bernard (Craig's older brother), "I'm texting my girl-friend, mind your business," proving that Lauryn Hill wasn't lying, this could all be so simple.

Craig of the Creek does the work to make that so. That work begins, ends, and is dependent on the audience and those that may become a part of the audience from different cultures and walks of life seeing themselves and relating with the characters and stories. I was thirty-five years old when I finally saw myself in a character after watching this show. I'm going to be watching *Craig of the Creek* with my children (as well as having my nephew put it on for my children to watch when he's babysitting them as I did him) so they don't have to wait as long as I did to see themselves.

The Disney Two-Step

WILLIAM EVANS,
aka Tiana's Security Detail

THERE'S A SCENE early on in *The Departed* when Dignam (Mark Wahlberg) is interrogating Billy (Leonardo DiCaprio) in the hopes of convincing him to be an undercover agent. The scene intensifies when Dignam begins to press Billy's background and the duality of his personality: "You were kind of a double kid, I bet, right?" "You have different accents?" He was exposing the vulnerability of Billy's accommodating identity. Trapped in two worlds, Billy assimilated, sometimes on a weekly basis, to the crowd he serviced in hopes of fitting in or not facing ridicule.

I think about this a lot when it comes to how diversity works in the media and political space. Because the demands and desires of diversity have grown louder at about every level of human interaction, many institutions feel they are caught between wanting to be more progressive in their representation and opportunity while not pissing off their core base and support too much. And by core base and support, I mean white people. There is forever an attempt to appease one group and not piss off the other, whether we're talking left-leaning politics or network programming.

There is perhaps no bigger entity that has mastered this half-in, half-out two-step than Disney. Well, rewind, perhaps there is no bigger entity than Disney. Full stop. And maybe resources, practice, and some mystical charm strung around the statue of Mr. Disney himself have contributed to how it is more versed at it than anyone else. Perhaps it was the easiest target first. While Disney now is all things to all people, the most common association that populates someone's mind when Disney is mentioned is either the mouse or the princesses. And for a while, the princesses weren't great. Outside of the very real and valid feminist critique of what the princesses used to be, which were bystanders in their own stories, they were mostly white. And if they weren't, well, I mean, Pocahontas shouldn't exist as a Disney entity and there's not much more to argue on that.

Now, Disney has produced more diverse characters than just about anyone. The landscape is full of women of color doing amazing and active things. Ruling kingdoms, solving crimes, opening a restaurant with the best gumbo in New Orleans. It has been an amazing thing to watch, from my youthful years where Snow White looked like Black people might startle her to seeing Moana dodge arrows and swing to her escape from a pirate ship. But I guess my question is, what exactly is Moana?

Well, she's Polynesian, I think that's one of our few exacts. Though that itself is not a definite, as *Polynesian* is such a catchall for the many different cultures, dialects, and traditions of many people. The film is set in Samoa, but is kind of portrayed as Hawaii for American audiences? Maui in the film is a demigod who is huge and bullish and a buffoon in many ways. But he's based on or at least named for the actual Maui from Polynesian culture, a thin teenager on his journey to adulthood. Not to mention the erasure of Hina, the companion goddess of Maui, who never appears in the film. I mean, we already have one heroine here so . . . see you on the other side of the ocean, I guess?

The mixing and ambiguity of marginalized characters and cultures in Disney films is not a bug. It's a feature. It's a calculated risk of building bridges into cultures but never venturing too deep to ensure (white) American audiences will walk the length of it. If I can show you a sanitized culture with some hallmarks that seem cool and exotic without committing you, the viewer, to investing in it, I can check the box on diversity and not turn disinterested white folks away. Maybe the starkest example of this is the *Aladdin* live-action movie, where we revisit a fictional Muslim city where our hero goes from street rat to sultan. The animated *Aladdin*, a thrill ride, was released in 1992 in a much less connected world where ridicule and concerns rarely interrupted big business in real time. Specifics to Islamic culture were nonexistent in '92, but their erasure was more stark in 2019, when there was much more pressure to get cross-cultural experiences right. But I can't imagine the anxiety of trying to replicate one of the most known Disney properties that occurs in the Middle East in an increasingly hostile Islamophobic climate. Well, you just erase any association with Islam or Muslim identities from the film. You get close-enough casting. You call turbans "hats." You work in some spitting camels and monkeys hopping through the streets and hope people forget the significance of where the story takes place. And I guess, if you're willing to do that, then maybe you didn't have much anxiety about it to begin with. So, never mind.

As Disney is much bigger than just multimillion-dollar movies, this philosophy is existent in much of its outreach—i.e., cross-cultural projects. Princess Elena is definitely Latina but most definitely not any specific culture. The Indian detective Mira's city aesthetics and holidays borrow from many specific Indian cultures that don't intersect. And yes, Disney spends what I'm sure is some minor king's ransom for consultation on these projects where they are close enough to appeasement and haven't ventured far enough away from the status quo. But it raises the question of how long will we continue to have consultants informing white filmmakers and showrunners instead of employing creators who are versed at making movies and TV shows and also have a strong familiarity with the source? Which, ya know, maybe that's the next generation of Disney, in another twenty years or so. But the intent is rarely a fully realized effort, and it's hard to divorce the model of using marginalized experts with proximity to the story that white creators want to tell from that.

As much as some would scapegoat marginalized people wanting the media they consume to be more representative and forcing Disney's hand in submitting to that, it's about the choices that Disney has decided to make. I think about how *Frozen 2* was the big animated tent-pole movie for Disney in its release year, and I was curious if it would do anything to answer the fact that people of color didn't exist in the first movie. Well, *Frozen 2* rectified that in ways that I'd generously label as nefarious. Outside of the fact that Arendelle apparently relaxed its immigration laws because Brown folks could now be seen walking the streets, the way the othered people are seen is used as a bigger issue. In the movie, the Northuldra tribe is basically its stand-in for a fictional Indigenous tribe. It is revealed that the conflict between Arendelle and the Northuldra had been a false narrative given to Elsa and Anna—an opportunity to be a commentary on how we struggle with past tragedies toward a group of people. When we realize that Anna and Elsa's grandfather was the villain, the agitator who tried to conquer the Northuldra, there is a very clear moment where the princesses could've tried to reckon with their family history. One where they were not responsible for the fallout, but also had been given—and believed—false tales of its origins.

At this point, we've been given a movie and a half to know that Anna and Elsa are good people. We know they are flawed but kind-hearted women. They pursue what is right and just with generosity and empathy. This is a classic "sins of the father with a chance at redeeming the family by doing the right thing" scenario. But *Frozen 2* doesn't do that. Instead, it builds in a way to make the princesses blood related to the tribe through their mother. Which has two immediate effects: First, it allows for a quick reconciliation of the aggrieved Northuldra to instantly forgive and now trust the rulers of a kingdom responsible for its oppression. In the movie it happens in seconds, so fast I had whiplash while seated in the theater as my eight-year-old appropriately asked me what just happened. I had few answers. It was the true wish fulfillment of those that say shit like, "I don't know why you're still mad about slavery," or even those "the only race I believe in is the human race" bastards.

The second issue is the investment factor. *Frozen 2* doesn't make (let's just call a non-spade a non-spade) white people reckon with their family lineage and what trauma their ancestors caused upon another people. It makes the investment partial to the personal stakes of the white folks involved. By making the princesses some de facto descendants of the Northuldra tribe, now the tribe's struggle is the princesses' struggle as well. The action to right those wrongs comes from there and not because it would've been the human thing to do in the first place. This tactic is tried and true and problematic as all hell. It is the politician that doesn't support gay rights until their son comes out. It's the white executive that speaks with authority of their role in society by positing their adopted, marginalized children. *Frozen 2* is the animated version of what fighting the good fight for big business looks like now. We can reckon with systemic and colonizing actions against the oppressed. But only as long as we make it the struggle of the beneficiaries too. And oh yeah, Anna and Elsa are biracial, I guess. I think about this all the time now.

And if Anna and Elsa are biracial now, what is Tiana from *The Princess and the Frog*? Single race, multispecies? For all my love of

Tiana's characterization and my lightweight unhealthy adoration of Anika Noni Rose, it's impossible to not see that *The Princess and the Frog* started a thing where Black voice actors are cast for Black-human-identified characters in movies where the character is only a Black human for part of the time. The math is simple here. You've got the big Disney princesses that preceded Tiana like Cinderella, Snow White, Pocahontas, Princess Aurora, Hua Mulan, Ariel . . . Tiana was the first Black Disney princess and the first one to get turned into some shit that wasn't a person. Hell, Ariel became MORE human. Where can a sista sign up to become MORE human as her plot point? Now, if you give me a story of a woman in New Orleans wanting to open up her own soul food spot, who also happens to get transformed into a frog, yes, I'd rather her be Black.

The fact that Tiana is turned into a frog isn't necessarily the problem. This is my [*Game of Thrones* spoiler warning incoming . . . .] Missandei dying theory. Folks were mad when Missandei got merked and tossed off of a castle wall. And yes, it was upsetting because Missandei was a great character. But yo, you missed me with the actual problem. The situation wasn't that a Black woman got killed on *Game of Thrones*. The whole brutal point of the show was that no one was particularly precious and that fairy-tale narratives were subverted and often dismantled. The problem was that Missandei was the only Black woman of note on the show. And so when she dies, you now have zero.

With Disney, Tiana being a frog most of the movie is made more significant because there are now zero Black princesses who get to be Black women for the majority of the movie. The solution isn't necessarily for *The Princess and the Frog* to not exist but for there to be more Disney movies with Black princesses. Now because of Disney's influence, this has become *a thing*. Take a movie like *Spies in Disguise*, where Will Smith is an ultra-cool Black 007-type with way more charisma, but the catch of the film is that he's a damn bird for most of it. And then, you have a movie like *Soul*. I don't really know where to begin with *Soul*, but for the uninitiated, here's the pitch: Joe (Jamie Foxx), a Black high school music teacher whose dream it is to play his own gigs as opposed to teaching uninspired kids how to hold a trombone, gets his big break. In the process of celebrating his first big gig, he falls into a manhole, uncovered as they frequently are. And then poof, Joe is dead (or as we learn later, he's in a coma). But his soul is moving toward the "Great Beyond" nonetheless. Joe freaks out because it isn't his time yet and finds himself mentoring a very reluctant soul in the "Great Before" named "22" (Tina Fey). Eventually hijinks ensue that land both Joe and 22 on Earth. Except 22's soul is in Joe's body and Joe's soul is in . . . a cat. Through this misadventure they both come to understand living life for the moment, what their true spark is, and how to repair relationships with themselves and others.

Listen, Pixar has a formula. They know how to circle the human heart and often in the last act devour it like sharks. We are almost helpless to their very well-structured emotional manipulation. They aren't making bad movies. And *Soul* isn't a bad movie. But the weight that *Soul* tries to carry seems too heavy for the folks that created it, specifically when dealing with the pronounced Black elements of the movie. It's important to know at least one very big preproduction note about the film: Joe, when the film was conceived, wasn't originally Black. Who knows how much of this story was constructed with a white protagonist in mind before this change, but here's the exercise you can do to articulate how much that matters. Was White Joe (sorry, that's the best code name I got) a musician too? Was he even a teacher? What was in place of the barbershop scene? (I don't think any of us can see White Joe going into a Sport Clips during this movie.) What was White Joe's conflict with his mother? Was his father still alive? Yes, these are loaded-ass questions, but it makes it easy to see the "Black checklist" in *Soul*. Depending on how generous you are, they either make the Black aesthetics in *Soul* feel authentic or well within the realm of stereotypes. There are scenes where the possible copy and pasting feels prevalent in the film. Take Paul, a very brief antagonist of Joe, who makes fun of Joe and tries to crush his dreams at every interval. The comeuppance for Paul happens later in the film. Terry, the record keeper from the Great Beyond, who is obsessed with finding and retrieving Joe (pardon the slave-catcher vibes, but I didn't write the movie, yo), finds Paul and briefly pulls Paul's soul out of his body because she believes that Paul is Joe. Yes, somehow, the record keeper for millions and millions of souls who have passed on mistook one Black man for another. In a movie where Paul is white and this is just "the bully getting scared straight" this probably goes off as a typical gag. But when you have so many examples of unprovoked violence placed on Black people, which includes, way too often, mistaken identity, this joke isn't hitting the same.

Perhaps the most damning thing about *Soul* though? Probably the gentrification of Joe's life by 22. We've seen movies before where people switch roles, or in this case switch bodies, and through experiencing a differing perspective help solve each other's problems. The problem is, the culture divide between Joe and the aesthetic we attach to 22 (a middled-aged white woman) isn't simply different perspectives. It implies that a simple tell-it-like-it-is approach would solve Joe's problems. Whether it's his relationship with his mom. His bully. His career choice. It flattens the complexities that occur in these Black relationships and treats them like they operate in a bubble. When 22 stands up to Joe's Bully (Paul) in the barbershop it assumes the anxiety from Joe is just a product of a typical antagonist relationship. It erases the factors of Black masculinity and the tightrope that Black men walk in their efforts to be accepted within their community and not seem threatening outside of it. When 22 helps facilitate Joe repairing his relationship with his mom, it is spawned by 22 being abrupt and speaking out of turn to his mom. It plays like a very typical parents-not-supporting-my-dreams conversation. But there is an erasure here of the weightiness of Joe's mom being a Black widow and a business owner in the city. Of wanting her Black son to have easy-to-see hallmarks of success because his father did not. This shouldn't be as generic a moment as it is, but the revelation is flat. Both of these examples carry the pathology that Joe has just made these situations too complicated to untangle. And that it really just takes this witty and naive middle-aged white woman to solve his problems. Problems that we assume came from years of friction during Joe's life, she solves in about five minutes of total screen time. And ya know, that's cute. I'm sure there are plenty of people that responded well to that. "Joe was just in his own way, he just never stood up for himself and thank god 22 showed him the way." But there's a lot of historical context missing in those moments. For example, we don't get to see why Joe's mother would be apprehensive about Joe pursuing a music career. It assumes she's just like every other parent who has a pragmatic approach for their children. But there's a story that feels particularly unique to this Black woman who has owned her own business for decades, now seeing her departed husband's face when she looks at her son. Her son, she believes, is underachieving. And if we don't have the screen time to tell that story, we should at least feel the weight of it. Maybe not have the mouthy never-been-a-real-person-before character break down her concerns so easily. That feels reductive, to say the least. And at one point, 22 steals Joe's body. And when the smoke clears, Joe ends up apologizing for his behavior. Which is after he saves 22's soul. I mean, we got Black abduction. Magical Negro stuff in the last act . . . It's a lot, fam. It's a whole, Black, lot.

Movies like *Spies in Disguise* and *Soul* can be enjoyable films. But it's a weird way to go with the pressing want and need of diversity to promote these marginalized characters in the name of representation just for them to transform into a thing not representative of the community you're wanting to appeal to.

Maybe it's generous, but I still think these blunders or oversights are more neglect based than malicious. The *Mulan* movie debacle feels different though. I think about all the press of *Mulan* being this big tent-pole achievement. About how they weren't going to disrespect China and its folklore this time. How the location and the actors involved proved that they were taking this seriously. And yes, the actors were sort of representative of what *Mulan* should look like. But behind the camera it was the complete opposite. The tone changes from that tone of "we're doing the right thing this time" when you see it for what it was: white people telling someone else's story in a location exotic to them. This was far from the only problem with *Mulan* from a cultural perspective, including things Disney couldn't really control like the lead actress being a fierce defender of the Chinese state and its violence against protestors in Hong Kong. But then there's the Xinjiang thing. And to be more acute, the filming in Georgia thing.

I couldn't give a damn about what outrages Republican senators have these days . . . or the length of my personal existence . . . but Disney made a big show about the possibility of no longer filming in Georgia over an abortion heartbeat bill. And ya know what, this ain't *that* essay, but big business taking a stand on "something" that people feel is a worthy social fight? I'm not mad at that, not even a little bit. Butttttt when that same big-ass company decides to film in Xinjiang, which has been a specific region where China has been committing human rights abuses to Uighur Muslims for years, it does make a brotha tilt his head and say, "How, Sway?" What is this supposed to mean? Was it merely an oversight? Was the Georgia thing virtue signaling for progressives in the U.S., thinking no one would notice or care about these issues outside of our borders? Is this some Muslim-hating, self-described liberal Bill Maher shit?! It's pretty confusing, if you're not cynical. I am cynical. It just feels like some bullshit to me.

When I say that there are people at Disney that care about diversifying its media, that's not to be flippant and assuming. I've had the privilege to meet a great deal of people working with the Mouse who take these things seriously and do all they can to make a more equitable entertainment complex for the widest range of people. But there's a limit to the power folks have if they aren't making the biggest decisions as far as movie scripts and casting calls. And at the end of the day, Disney didn't become Disney because it didn't want to maximize profit. TV shows and movies with marginalized figures as the focal point may be an untapped resource, but that still isn't bigger than predominantly white audiences that may or may not care about reconfiguring the social climate for the movies they already love.

It's hard to imagine that Disney doesn't know what it is doing. Disney is huge and fucks up sometimes. And just like every big company, cares enough about power dynamics and how representation affects the consumers it is selling its product to. But to say that Disney has made some misfires with how it treats diversity is to assume that they are mistakes made from lack of knowledge or misaligned execution. With Disney, it's often neither of those things. It's just that few have the surgical precision to split the baby so cleanly.

Y'all Mind if I Wyl Out over Black Love and POC Love Real Quick?

OMAR HOLMON,
aka Erotic Ebony Fanfic Artisan

MAN, I BEEN a Marvel kid from jump. Matter fact, Storm, aka Ororo Munroe, aka Hadari-Yao, aka Beautiful Windrider, aka Blue, aka Ms. Sun's Out 'Cause I'm Out, was the very first superhero doll action figure I ever got. Mom bought her as a gift for my sixth birthday. We went to the store to get cake mix and I saw Storm hanging out in the aisle in her X-Men fit in that toy box. I knew upon sight that she would become the GOAT based off the vintage fit alone. Y'all don't hear me. I said THE VINTAGE STORM X-MEN FIT, muhfuckas: silver fox hair, all-black outfit with the gold lightning bolt on the chest that lit up so you knew it was real. You know what the fuck I'm talkin' 'bout—that classic Ororo Munroe; that "I am every woman" Ororo Munroe; that throwback "you see we never ever do nothing nice and easy, we always do it nice . . . and rough" Tina Turner–"Proud Mary" Ororo Munroe. NERD! Oh, it was a wrap ever since then. Storm was, and still is, the Beyoncé of comic books. I been in the stands stanning for this Ororo Munroe ever since. So when Marvel had Storm and T'Challa, the Black Panther, get married in *Black Panther*, vol. 4, #18 (2006)?! Jagged Edge's "Let's Get Married" (the remix version tho) was on full blast while I read that shit.

Are you kidding me? You wanna talk about power couples? You wanna talk about Black on Black on all-Black everything excellence? You wanna talk about a goddamn Marvel moment?! They got married in the middle of Civil War, when superheroes were being told to sign with the government by Iron Man, and Captain America was saying, "Yeah, fuck that noise." Those two were still in attendance at Storm and T'Challa's wedding! T'Challa told them they better act fucking right while they were there too. It was Black superhero Hollywood in attendance for their wedding, man. BET covered their wedding! Prince played the reception. Charles Xavier told Storm that she's about to become more than a goddess or hero. She's now become the ambassador of human–mutant relations. Proof that they can coexist. A role she was born to play. Charles Xavier told Storm that she got the juice now, man.

Even Uatu the Watcher, a cosmic being that records the major historical events of our solar system, showed up for this wedding. Storm and T'Challa had Uatu the Watcher, a being that's millions of years old, eating hors d'oeuvres at their wedding ceremony. There is no greater fucking flex. None greater. They even allowed a number of white folks in as well. They had to sit in the back tho. Yo, even Dr. Doom sent a gift letting it be known he was mad he ain't get an invite. Dr. Doom was out here mad he ain't get to dance to Prince live. Dr. Doom fucks with Prince.

T'Challa even brought Storm to the spirit world for her soul to be judged by Bast, the Panther God, to bless their union. Bast stared Ororo right in the windows of her soul, growled, then licked her face saying, "All right, y'all go on ahead now." This union was everything. We got some adventures with Storm and T'Challa. They went on a world tour and had some adventures. Then six years later, the Avengers vs. X-Men crossover was happening. The Avengers and X-Men were beefing due to the cosmic entity known as the Phoenix Force coming back to Earth for a host. The Avengers showed up on the X-Men's door to take custody of Hope Summers, who would be the host of the Phoenix Force. This caused a rift in the X-Men and led to the Phoenix Force being split among five mutants. Namor the Sub-Mariner was aligned with the X-Men and was one of those five mutants. Shit got wild when Namor chose to flood Wakanda for hiding the Avengers. T'Challa then annulled his marriage with Storm when she arrived during the aftermath, seeing her as siding with the X-Men. For the record, Storm and the X-Men had no idea what Namor was up to. Fam, this was the biggest "what the fuck?" moment. T'Challa can be stoic but bruh is mos def not heartless. We throwing away six (real-time) years of marriage as a wack-ass "major" consequence of this "major" summer crossover event? Get the fuck outta here with that mess, man.

I was beyond livid. Marvel, what the hell, we coulda had it all! Six years may seem like a long time in real time, but in comic book time (since these characters really don't age), that's maybe what, a good two and a half years? At best? We never got to see all the mechanics of their marriage that could be. You don't give these two Black characters this amount of power up on a platform then just toss it away for a 2012 Avengers vs. X-Men "war" that won't mean anything in a few months, man. Reginald Hudlin and Scot Eaton didn't redefine T'Challa's beginnings in this series for this shit right here. You gotta give the fandom way more than a couple story arcs of marriage. Does T'Challa do dishes? Who is the better cook between the two? Who claims the right side of the bed? Who is the better driver? Naaah, you gotta come with more character development and growth as a union than that, baby.

This shit fucking hurt for a good while. Storm running round with Wolverine, and T'Challa appearing ever so often singing, "*I can love you better . . . but not at the moment tho, 'cause Marvel ain't lettin' us be great or have it all,*" outside her window, specifically in Hickman's *New Avengers: Time Runs Out* storyline. But then a hero comes along with not only the strength to carry on but the strength to write them wrongs five years later in 2017. Those heroes are Ta-Nehisi Coates and Brian Stelfreeze bringing the power couple back together one mo 'gain in *Black Panther*, vol. 6, #13. T'Challa is dealing with the gods/orisha that have protected Wakanda abandoning them in their time of need. This leaves T'Challa with many questions about how gods operate. So, who better to talk to about godly shit than the woman worshipped as a gawd her damn self, Ororo Munroe? Yeah. Hell yeah, man. T'Challa, the pragmatic scientist, asking Ororo about her experiences as a goddess in an expensive-ass room somewhere outta our tax bracket? Drinking the finest Wakandan champagne? T'Challa trying to get a better understanding of where the Wakandan gods stand with his people? Storm helping enlighten this man dealing with religion, history, and context so much bigger than him.

Grrmmmm-hmmm! *rapper hearing a sick beat growl* That's the jam I want on my French toast. Ta-Nehisi Coates and Brian Stelfreeze gave our ship wind to its sails again. This was evident when T'Challa asks Storm, "And what of you? What became of all your worshippers?" "Silly king. I need no religion," Storm replies. She then says, "And I only require the worship of one man," while holding T'Challa's face in her palms and kissing his forehead. Let's fucking go. Let's fucking go, Black-ass love. Come on. In later stories in the series Storm is there to bail T'Challa out, bail Wakanda out, and once Coates starts the Intergalactic Empire of Wakanda storyline Storm is on the front lines showcasing why she is Top Five Heroes and Bad Bishes Dead or Alive.

Lemme be clear, this isn't to say these two characters aren't interesting in their own rights or need the social construct of marriage in order to be prominent. I'm just big on follow-up, especially since we never had a chance to see this couple develop. I mean, come on, man, they were given a backstory of knowing each other as kids from way back in *Marvel Team-Up* (1980) with Storm saving T'Challa's life. That mythos was expanded upon in a retcon to set up for their marriage. Also, I'll shut up when you can tell me a prominent Black married couple on par with T'Challa and Storm. I'll wait. I'll wait even longer. Mister Fantastic and the Invisible Woman been married for how long again? Peter Parker got married to M.J. back in 1987 (then had that taken away in the *One More Day* storyline in 2007). Luke Cage and Jessica Jones got married in 2006, they're still married. The X-Man Northstar (Jean-Paul Beaubier) married his Black boyfriend, Kyle Jinadu, in 2012. No prominent all-Black or -Brown married couples tho.

So, forgive me if I am happy to see T'Challa and Storm still being something of an item all these years later, and I'm still wondering, what do they do for date night? What could Storm get as a gift for the man who has everything? Is T'Challa used to folks wanting to take one pic with him in it and a selfie with just them and Storm? Do they have Thanksgiving in Wakanda or the X-Mansion? What are the Black American cultural faux pas, culture gaps, idioms, and slang that come up in conversation that Storm has to explain to T'Challa? These are questions we need answered. Though their marriage is over (for now, dammit), with their romance hinted at continuing, hopefully we can see more of that.

You may be saying, "Dude, get over it." To that I say, "I hope your firstborn child loses their first championship high school game or academic decathlon." You knew what this was, fuck was you still reading for, then? But hear me out tho. I grew up on Marvel, man. As I'm older now, married now, hindsight be one hell of a drug when you're a consumer. I'm going to have bars for that ass. I'm just sayin' I enjoy seeing Black and Brown characters flourishing and exploring aspects of a relationship (as well as enjoying being alone). If I'm being reflective about it, perhaps that's because my parents were divorced, so the way relationships are and could be are pretty different growing up under that point of view as a kid. Again, you start to look for other Black and Brown couples in Marvel and they're not too common.

Looking back, the ones I can recall offhand are Storm and Black Panther as a pair again, Monica Rambeau and Brother Voodoo (a funny whatever-ship from the *Marvel Divas* comics), Misty Knight and Sam Wilson, Monica Rambeau and Adam Brashear, Surge and Prodigy from X-Men (very short-lived but counts). I'm sure I may have missed some, but I'm talking post-Blaxploitation era and into the 2000s. Take the time to think about it tho, it's really only a handful. Ya might've noticed I listed Black-Brown interracial couples on that as well. I noticed a pattern at Marvel where a majority of their white characters that star in their own solo titles are in relationships with people of color, which is dope when done correctly. Do y'all remember when Cindy Moon, aka Silk, debuted in *Spider-Man*? Silk was bit by the same spider that bit Peter Parker but was kept away for years in a bunker to protect her from an enemy tracking her. When Peter and Silk meet, they have this animal attraction to each other and can't help but make out.

Man, we ain't seen Peter do that with any other woman or person with Spider powers . . . but okay. It comes across rather fetishy, as Cindy Moon is Asian. Thankfully she becomes a character outside of Peter, but that initial presentation feels like a ball drop and reinforcing for an exotic stereotype/trope. But there are examples of it being done well as well: there's an issue of *Secret Wars: Secret Love* (#1, 2015) where Iron Fist is doing Misty Knight's hair in bantu knots. I mean, it don't get much more "awww" and cute as fuck as that, does it? It's a good example of showing a person learning an element of someone else's culture and participating in it. A similar scene occurred in *Creed* where Adonis Creed (Michael B. Jordan) is doing his girlfriend's (Tessa Thompson) hair. Beautiful real-world representation in two different ways. Yet, we often see more occurrences of a white person taking part in an aspect of a culture that's outside their own.

Marvel has a big majority of comic book titles that have a white character shipped/paired with a person of color as the main love interest. Which can serve as a reflection for those in those relationships in real life, 'cause representation. However, one, usually those POC love interests are new characters and only exist as a love for the lead character with no agency of their own. Two, there are certain POC characters that will have or appear in their own title, and they are dating a white partner as well. Three, we don't see many people of color in interracial relationships with other people of color. The first interracial couple I saw in media was in an X-Men comic: Storm and Forge. Storm kissing Forge, the genius mutant inventor of the X-Men, was my first time seeing in comic books two Brown people kissing. At that age, I knew Storm was Black and Forge was Indigenous American, but the impact didn't really hit me then.

I looked at the page thinking, "Hey, look at these Brown folks kissing. Nice. I'm currently too young to understand the significance of this, but somewhere in me I do know it is significant. It will probably affect me subconsciously throughout my life in some way that will hit me later . . . perhaps while I'm writing an essay. All right, let's see where the action scenes are in this issue." This was my first comprehension of an interracial couple, not realizing at the time that my sister and brother were products of an interracial marriage. My mother is Black, and her first husband was a dark-skinned Brown Tamil South Indian man. I realized just how close to home this was when I was reading an issue of *Ms. Marvel*. Ms.

Marvel is the hero identity of Kamala Khan, a Pakistani American Muslim girl from Jersey City. In one issue we see Kamala's brother, Aamir, marrying Tyesha, a dark-skinned Black West African Muslim woman.

Aamir and Tyesha are supporting characters in Kamala's book, but this wedding was incredible; we see two people of color with different cultures meeting each other in the middle in solidarity. Aamir and Tyesha end up surprising each other at their wedding by wearing traditional wedding garbs from each other's culture. Aamir shows up wearing a boubou (a traditional West African formal attire for men) because, as he tells his sister, Kamala, "I wanted her to feel safe. Not like she has to give up the things that are important to her just to fit in with us. So I wore this instead of a kurta." Tyesha shows up wearing a shalwar kameez (a traditional combination dress worn by Pakistani women usually accompanied with a long scarf or shawl called a "dupatta" around the head or neck). My moms had similar experiences going into a different culture, and her meeting in the middle was learning Indian dishes from her sister-in-law that married into the family too. Years later, after my mom got married again and had me, she was still making Indian dishes. Funny part is, I didn't know that some of the dishes she made for me to eat were Indian. I didn't even know she knew how to make Indian food. I just ate whatever she made without question. It wasn't until I was in an Indian restaurant with my father in 2016, where in passing he said, "Your mother made this better," while eating his order. Seeing the confusion on my face, my father then informed me of all this information I just told y'all.

There's a picture of my mother with her first husband's family where the women are all in saris and she's in this fly-ass '70s-era fit Black as fuck. Being her son, I too am Black as fuck and my wife happens to be Punjabi Indian (from Australia). When I was visiting her extended family in India with her, I saw a crispy bread dish my mom used to make that they were serving. My wife told me it was called "puri." I told her I'd called it "pocket bread" since I was a kid. I ate that dish for years not knowing it had a proper name. At our wedding I dressed in Punjabi attire and did a dance number with my wife because I'm pretty sure I had to prove I could dance to get into the family as the final test. Black folk dance at a wedding for fun; Indian folk dance as a trial by fire. I passed. You don't know trill till you see a whole family flood the dance floor for a number. My god. It just goes to show that interracial doesn't mean white + POC as the default as we're seeing in media. People with dark skin, Brown skin, or Black skin can be in an interracial relationship or biracial as well.

Also, let's be clear, I'm not trying to stan for marriage as the be-all and end-all of relationship evolutions, I understand the dynamics of relationships are way different, as we have folks that are polyamorous, asexual, nonmonogamous, or open with their relationships, as well as other expressions of partnership. I'm also not saying that because I am in an interracial marriage I JUST wanna see more POC + POC interracial relationships. No. My reader, what I'm saying is I want to see Black couples, Indigenous couples, Asian couples, Aboriginal couples, Arabic couples, Pacific Islander couples, front and center. Black/POC with other people of color as a norm for interracial up in this muhfucka. Not solely white + POC as the main definition of interracial with Black/POC characters created just for a white lead who will disappear to the wayside once a new writer takes over, a storyline finishes, or the series concludes before a new series starts over. Oh, and I want that across all genders, all nonbinary gender–conforming folks, and all sexual orientations. We gon' mention that off the strength, fam.

We may be far off from Marvel exploring all those routes simultaneously across the board with their characters but have TV shows and other comics doing the work in that regard. But listen, y'all ain't got to mind me tho. I'm just talking my shit and unpacking all these feels from the icebox where my heart used to be (I know, I thought long and hard about making that reference). I'm just so happy to see that there's still something between Ororo and T'Challa that doesn't literally involve the end of the world for them to get together for old times' sake. I'm just happy to see Black people out here expressing love to each other in a healthy way for all of us to see all up in these panels, nah mean? I'm just here to shout out Aamir and Tyesha Khan being respectful and adhering to both their cultures as they join in union, ya feel me? Power to the power couples!

Whenever I Watch *Underworld,*
I Feel Like Kate Beckinsale
Wants to Break Up with Me

WILLIAM EVANS,
aka The Black Lycan Student Council President

THERE ARE A great number of things that I should and still kind of love about the *Underworld* series while fully realizing that it's not exactly the *Dark Knight* trilogy for vampire flicks. I mean, making werewolf transformations happen in live action ain't never been easy, and this latest movie had rumbles of a lawsuit because its story strayed a little too close to the game *Vampire: The Masquerade,* but still. Despite its can't-really-walk-in-the-daylight weaknesses, I can still watch undead or emo beasts of the night merge supernatural powers and gifts with modern-day weaponry and feel like I didn't waste a couple of hours. Give me gadgets and full auto pistols with UV light bullets. Give me a man that transforms into a beast in mid-run on the walls. I'm here, fam. For all of it. Especially a really attractive protagonist letting them thangs go in a sleek black zero suit. Well, about that.

Maaaaan, listen. I want you to flash back to 2003 with me, when a young William was in his early twenties, brimming with the confidence of a mediocre white dude. I was smart, in prime athlete shape, I knew all the house dances, I could get in free to the fall ice-breaker depending on what frat was hosting it; it was lit more than a decade before anything would be called lit. *Underworld* had me hype, because vampires. Kate Beckinsale was basically coming off of being the extremely pretty "it" girl with previous flicks like *Serendipity* and *Pearl Harbor*. So, when I saw the trailer of Beckinsale breaking out of romantic-interest plot-point role and moving into undead-but-very-much-badass heroine out to restore balance and fend off the coming vampire-lycan war, I was all in. I mean, fam. Selene is not here to play with you heauxs.

Still-frame game turned up to eleven. So yes, muthafuckin' yes, I was up in the theater ready to see all this glory. I'd tell you who I took to the movie, but I don't remember and that's not important anyway. That night was about me, Selene, and some pale-on-beast violence.

And then, about an hour into the movie, I felt like Selene got up from our dinner, went to the bathroom, and then had the waiter send me a note like, "Sorry, I had to leave. I know that's rude to stick you with the bill. But the chicken was dry anyway, so don't pay full price." At first I thought the movie depressed me because it only has two color schemes in the whole film. But nah, I was depressed because Kate invited me back to the spot, asked me to come in, then told me to sit on the couch and watch TV by myself while she went to bed. I sat in the theater like . . . do I just sit here in my seat till she gets back . . . or go home?

Watching any of the *Underworld* films makes me feel like Kate Beckinsale is completely bored with my existence, fam. I feel like she invited me over to the crib to chill and listen to music, but just speaks in deep sighs all night because she actually hates her own vinyl collection. And because she's talented and gorgeous, I'm over here like, "Kate, what can I do to make it better? What can I do to engage you and make you happy?" And she, while still rocking the black leather and badass cape, just looks at me and says, "Baby, I don't really know. Nothing is probably going to help. Get taller maybe?"

If Selene ain't banging them hammers or using the vampire/Dark Knight gadgets, she looks like she at the DMV on a Monday. Like nobody wants to stand in this line, but what you gonna do, not drive? All I want Kate to do is get her license and have good hair in the pic, man. All I wish for Kate to do is discover online registration, yo. She for real out here on that Diddy, "if you don't *blank expression*, you don't eat." Maybe I'm projecting. I dated a woman once who was always down to go out with me, but turned into posing for the *Mona Lisa* when we would link up. She hit me up three years later saying we just got together at a bad time for her, because a family member had a long-term illness and was in their last stages. Bad breaks, ya know. I'm not a lycan, I have a heart and understand.

So I thought maybe that's what's going on with Kate Beckinsale. We don't know all there is to know about celebrities' lives. Maybe someone in her fam was going through some rough shit when *Underworld* dropped. By *Underworld: Evolution* I was like, "Oh, same shit, okay this shit must be terminal." When I saw *Underworld: Awakening*, I said, "Aiight, somebody been dying of the same shit for about a decade now." Ain't no more excuses, yo, Kate just rather be getting a root canal than playing Selene. Kate rather be washing her hair than playing Selene. Kate probably screen-test Selene while still wearing the breathing mask she slept in, fam. We can't try to call it something else anymore.

I still learned how to enjoy the films though, you just gotta temper your expectations. Selene the type of person you make pay up front when you splitting the meal. Don't ever let a Selene type go second in the "I'll do you, you do me" scenario. Ain't nobody trying to be intimate with someone carrying the enthusiasm of a bus stop when it's their turn to put in work. You can't let a Selene be your agent if you ever want to get booked for any gigs. You gotta meet people where they at, and Selene ain't never gonna be in the cheerleading section. Or anyone's hype woman onstage. You call Selene when you think you did something stupid and you need validation and she gonna be like, "Ehh." You don't call Selene when you accomplished something big to share the news cuz she gonna be like, "Ehh." As long as you know this going in, the films are still watchable. Well . . . mostly.

It looks like *Underworld: Blood Wars* was the end of the line. For *Underworld*. For bored badass Kate. I hope so, fam. Not because I need the *Underworld* films to stop, but because I know what it's like when you have to do some shit you don't want to do so that you can do what you want to do. I don't know what Kate wants to do, but it obviously ain't this shit. Be warned, Evangeline Lilly, this could happen to you. Just because you're a gorgeous and athletic white woman who can do action doesn't mean you gotta cash in for bad movies. Choose projects you want moving forward. Remember, Beckinsale and Biel did that so hopefully you won't have to go through that.

As for *Blood Wars*, did I see it? Yeah. Selene's apathy just made me want to be there to comfort her more. I didn't try to hold her hand though. She'd probably forget I was there ten minutes later anyway.

An Open Letter to Gohan:
You Gonna Stop Being Trash
Anytime Soon or Nah?

OMAR HOLMON,
aka Senzu Bean Beyond Burger

I–I DON'T EVEN know how to begin this, because thirteen-year-old me can't come to terms with the situation. Lemme start this off by saying *Dragon Ball* and *Dragon Ball Z* are staples of anime fighting shows. The lead protagonist Goku and his friends basically beat people's ass who try to take over Earth or destroy the universe. Damn near every fight has him power up to a new form capable of beating his tough opponents. That is the *Dragon Ball* franchise in a nutshell, as best as I can even hope to describe it (use Google for the CliffsNotes). So, I was eating cereal watching the new *Dragon Ball Super*, seeing Goku and enemy turned rival and friend Vegeta transform beyond Super Saiyan God mode, fight mofos from a different universe, meet the king of all twelve universes, and get the fucking Super Dragon Balls. I'm like, gotdamn they're doing the most, then I noticed two things: one, there weren't enough raisins in my Raisin Nut Bran cereal (y'all slacking), and two, where the hell was Gohan?

Gohan wasn't around at all? Then I heard it mentioned in passing that dude had a business meeting he couldn't get out of . . . *wipes hands down face* Yo, this has been a long time coming and I hate to be the one to bring it up, but it's time someone said aloud that Gohan straight up let the *DBZ* fandom down. Well, maybe it's the fandom's fault. Way back, Gohan's dad, Goku, sacrificed himself against a strong enemy named Cell during the Cell Games Saga. Gohan beat Cell and that was supposed to be the baton pass for Gohan to replace his dad as Earth's top fighter and protector. The fandom wanted Goku back tho, so when the Majin Buu Saga came, Goku took center stage again and Gohan kinda fell by the wayside. I'm just saying, dude was supposed to be the truth, supposed to take over the rock from his pops, Goku, but it's like homie straight up peaked in the Cell Games. Gohan's win on Cell is basically his one platinum hit (with features). My mans was a fucking baby-face animal that's not a killa, but don't push him!

Gohan was voted most likely to succeed in *DBZ* and been chilling, making beats for five summers in his mom's basement. I'm talking, "Damn, homie, (LITERALLY) in high school/*Dragon Ball Z* you was the man, homie . . . The fuck happened to you?" Now if you gonna try and say, "Oh, he got a wife and kid now. He's a family man," that ain't no excuse. He couldn't dust off the NordicTrack? My man couldn't hop on Groupon to get a discount at a Bikram yoga class? Okay, the fandom didn't let you succeed your dad, but you mean to tell me you couldn't hop on the antigravity Bowflex at all (is anyone even getting these references) just to keep in shape? I don't wanna hear y'all blaming his mom, Chi-Chi, for trying to make him a scholar either. Chi-Chi wanted him to get a good job, which he did, but she ain't want 'em to be a fucking punk. Chi-Chi knew it was downhill once he started that Saiyaman phase and began to train Goten *immediately.* The fandom's also so quick to be like, "Well, Goku wasn't around," "Goku was training all the time. Died. Stayed dead. Came back—" Lemme cut you the fuck off right there.

How many times did Goku save Earth's ass? How many times did homie *die* for Earth? Then he went and tried to train his son to take over and fucking *died* again when Gohan got cocky with Cell. Bruh, we ain't blaming that man's pops for this specific shit right here. If my daddy had to train all the time 'cause Earth was always in danger from 'roided up rando aliens trying to run the natural resources, I'm not crying about his ass not being there for me, 'cause he'd say, "Oh, you wanna pull the 'my daddy wasn't there to toss a football with me' card? That's 'cause I was making sure you had a damn atmosphere over your head to even toss the damn thing."

No, sir. I'm doing push-ups 'cause I'm gonna be damn sure able to windmill the rock when he gets knocked and passes it to me. Not Gohan though . . . this guy legit went from child prodigy to State Farm customer service agent. Look at ya mans now . . . LOOK AT YOUR MANS AND DEM! You may also say, "Well, he's a pacifist." That still ain't no excuse 'cause I know a couple pacifists that ain't letting certain shit pass their fists . . . Man, y'all know why we here. Let's put this horse out to pasture.

sets timer

DEEP INHALE

"Let Nas Down" should be playing anytime Gohan appears on-screen.

Gohan stay dressed in business casual clothes lookin' like he in a fuckin' Allstate commercial.

Goahn lookin' like a walking J.Crew mannequin.

Gohan lookin' like he 'bout to fap to his calculus book.

Gohan lookin' like that geek chic phase NBA players were struggling through.

Gohan the dude at work by the watercooler talking 'bout how much he benched in high school.

Gohan the dude at work by the copy printer going through a midlife crisis.

Gohan the dude at work washing ayebody else's dishes.

Gohan the dude at work that gets his stapler ran daily.

Gohan the dude at work saying, "Did you try holding Ctrl + Alt + Delete?"

And I know just what the fuck you are thinking: "Oooh, but he still has the mystic power level and—"

Mystic Gohan ain't do a GOTdamn thing.

Mystic Gohan is the softest soft drink on Earth as far as I am concerned.

Mystic Gohan is an alternate costume L for Gohan to rock.

Mystic Gohan is the fucking Frank Ocean of *DBZ* and we still waiting on that new power level to show up.

Mystic Gohan is straight up Michael Jordan's Secret Stuff for the Tune Squad in *Space Jam*.

Gohan is like blueberries, he's trash in everything except waffles (the Namek Saga) and muffins (Cell Saga).

Gohan'll have one good round at Taboo and then chokes each turn afterward.

Gohan'll be the only dude coming in to work on Saturdays.

Gohan'll have Tobey Maguire playing him in the live-action film.

THEN. THEY. HAD. YOUR. BOY. OUT. HERE. IN. A. TRACKSUIT. MY. G!

Bruh, that shit ain't even Under Armour!

Gohan out here in the Generic Windbreakers #4 from WWF WrestleMania 2000!

Gohan out here in the Juiceman infomercial dude's early bird special tracksuit!

They legit got Gohan in the Magic Mike *breakaway sweats?*

They legit got Gohan in the fucking knockoff Nike sweat suit?

Why Gohan's tracksuit the same color of Oscar the Grouch's living room?

Why Gohan's tracksuit look like an outtake from *You Got Served*?

His power level may be over 9,000, but I guarantee that outfit was under $9.

Gohan rocking the exact same outfit as the gym teacher (Hayato) from *Rival Schools*.

IF SOMEBODY DON'T GET GOHAN OUT OF *HOME MOVIES*' COACH MCGUIRK ALTERNATE COSTUME RIGHT THE FUCK NOW.

feels self running out of breath

hears announcer shouting, "DOWN GOES GOHAN! DOWN GOES GOHAN!"

sees Gohan hit the floor

starts fading from lack of air

. . . but the audience raises their arms in the air to give their energy for me to keep going

Gohan need to go to Scared Straight for Super Saiyans.

Gohan need to go back to appropriating Namekian culture.

Gohan need to put the Saiyaman durag back on 'cause nothing was ever the same since.

Gohan need to get a Cobra Kai gym membership.

Gohan need to stop listening to Fleetwood Mac and put DMX back in the playlist.

Gohan need to get his business-in-the-front, party-in-the-back mullet back and remember who the fuck he is.

Gohan need to watch some of his old AMVs to remember who the fuck he is, because he's one episode away from his final form being a Yamcha cry meme.

TIME

The Want to Protect Taraji's
Proud Mary, Critiquing the Choir,
and How We Judge Black Art

WILLIAM EVANS,
aka The Bourne with an Afro Supremacy

"I'M ROOTING FOR everybody Black."

It's hard to articulate all the ways in which Issa Rae's now infamous quote both summarized and galvanized the sentiments of Black folks when she calmly delivered those words during the 2017 Emmy Awards. Black people do this, often to our dying breath. Whether it be with TV awards or Black quarterbacks in the playoffs, seeing a Black person compete in a realm that is not necessarily populated by Black people can often be the tiebreaker when there's no previous vested interest. It is the very American adage (ironically) of *everyone loves an underdog*. But with Black people, because of how often *we* are the underdog.

I get it, Issa, I do. I think the context is important here. In intent, I'm sure Issa's *everybody* means truly everybody, not just everybody recognized enough to make it to an awards show. That's an important distinction, because rooting for everybody Black and rooting for everybody Black that got nominated for an Emmy are worlds apart, even when they are conflated with each other. Black art doesn't have to equate to Black art excellence. But so often, Black art gets scrutinized in the same way. So then the question is: What do we do with Black art that doesn't meet our expectations? How do we manage it and acknowledge it? And ultimately, what is our commitment to it?

This dilemma has existed forever, but I found myself more interested in its exploration with the release of *Proud Mary*, the Taraji P. Henson special ops–type action movie that was released in January of 2018. When the trailer and art for the movie dropped the previous year, there was a great deal of excitement for an abundance of reasons. *Proud Mary* looked like *The Bourne Identity* with a Black woman. Assassin-level training. Master of disguises. Hand-to-hand combat, one-woman-army type of shit.

First and foremost, Henson is very easy to root for. Often unfiltered, authentic, and rooted, Taraji feels like one of us that had the talent and limited opportunity but busted her ass and made it. She's a legit premier talent on TV and an Academy Award nominee. So if she's doing something, we're going to show up and support, because if Taraji is winning, we feel like we're all winning.

Second, there's not a whole lot of predominantly Black action films out there that get major releases. And definitely not with a woman as the protagonist who looks like a complete badass. After getting about seven different Black Widow knockoff movies with a white woman killing everyone in sight, then yes, Black people are excited for the possibility of seeing a Black woman in that type of role.

And last, the promotion was unapologetically Black. The trailer, art, and design were all gorgeous, and while there wasn't much ongoing marketing to pull from, the initial images were easy to feast upon.

All of that explains why we wanted it to be good. But does that make it good? In this case, no. Sadly, no. With the naked eye, you could say that reviews on *Proud Mary* were split. The critics were tearing it down, but there were plenty of fans championing the movie, qualified as that praise may be. Of course, one's love or disdain for any kind of media is often a subjective venture. If you don't have a vested interest in providing a balanced critique *cough, like being a reporting pop culture site, cough* then you are going to most likely bring your preferences and, yes, prejudices into it. You might honestly believe that *Proud Mary* is a good film. Or you might feel that *Proud Mary* is a film you wish desperately to be good. By the objective critique of the movie, all indications would be that it's not very good. So, I would guess the question is, why does that matter?

Proud Mary brings into focus the question we tepidly approach: What exactly do we do with art that may or may not rise to excellence when Black people are behind it? It is a loaded scenario for sure. If a movie filled with predominantly Black people comes out with too much hype and is terrible, a simple dismissal of the film isn't the resolution. If Black art fails, we don't have the luxury to question the production alone. Was it sabotaged? Was it unfairly marketed? Did it tank because it wasn't catered enough to the white gaze? Is there a penalty to Black authenticity? All of this may sound like conspiracy when rattled off in this way, but there are concrete reasons for the skepticism. We've seen these things happen before, so we are reluctant to trust a system of fair review for things we either do enjoy or really want to enjoy.

But if we consider the fact that it may not be good—whether it be *Proud Mary* or Gabrielle Union's *Breaking In* or Paula Patton's *Traffik* (with the hard *K*, no less) that released later that year—when it disappoints, well, what is our responsibility then? What is omnipresent is what we collectively fear as a worst-case scenario. There is the possibility that if *Proud Mary*, the action film debut that was produced by and stars our beloved Taraji, is bad, that the possibility may never come up for her (or others like her) again. We drown in a sea of white mediocrity every day (how many *NCIS* shows are there now?) but are all too aware how easily Black stars and their ventures get benched if they don't succeed.

It is a tangible fear. If Gerard Butler stars in a terrible movie, he will have another starring role the following summer. If Taraji gets a taste of being a leading woman in a movie (two in the last two years), none of us want to see her go backward from that.

This ties into half a hundred other questions about how we treat Black artists compared to white artists and what the standard of quality should be. As I watched the conversations about *Proud Mary* rage on, the most frequent defense of the film's shortcomings typically came in the form of comparing it to similarly mediocre-to-bad white films. Do I think a bad Taraji-led film means she shouldn't get another opportunity at the character or a similar role? Of course not. But that's because I think Taraji is a good performer in a poorly written movie, not because other films as bad as *Proud Mary* already exist. For instance, I thought the *Red Sparrow* movie with Jennifer Lawrence was bad and pretty unoriginal. And yet, I saw a lot of people saying, "Well, if they can keep remaking that movie premise, then we can have *Proud Mary*." I mean, sure. But that doesn't make *Proud Mary* good . . . that just makes two bad films.

This is, of course, part of a bigger phenomenon. Black people are fiercely protective of their art and artists because we know how easily they can be degraded and nullified. I think about how *A Wrinkle in Time* was supposed to be an exploration of the source and a visually extravagant film . . . for a younger audience. But it happened directly after *Black Panther*. And because predominantly Black films are still treated as monolithic (even among Black people), there was discussion and push that we needed to support *A Wrinkle in Time* like we supported *Black Panther*, ignoring the fact that those films had completely different visions and audiences. So when *A Wrinkle in Time* did not do MCU numbers, it was seen as a disappointment. But like, your twelve-year-old thought *A Wrinkle in Time* was pretty cool. And that was the original aim. It's an example of how the impulse to push for the success of Black art is born from the necessity of protecting it preemptively. This is an experience we know well: we've watched what white media consumption can do to a Black star that has either served their purpose, didn't kneel to "good Negro" ideals, or ruffled sensibilities outright. The early and brief careers of Eriq La Salle and Isaiah Washington demonstrate this. Possible Terrence Howard more recently. Fading Black stars aren't just forgotten. They are often buried. And because we've seen that play out so often, we have made it more difficult to critique some media in a social space. Some of the best examples of this have happened on Netflix, with the releases of *The Get Down* and *Luke Cage*.

Count me as one of the early adopters of really digging *The Get Down*. I was thirsty for a POC-led period piece that wasn't centered around slavery. And so, I was on board for all of it, which means that I was willing to give it all the rope I could manage. And while I still think a couple of episodes from the first season (and by God, just the first season) are still pretty good, the show is almost hard to watch at times. Once I had a brief reprieve from being starved for that specific kind of content, I was a lot more objective in admitting the many flaws the show had. Still, I saw myself defending it, often against people that didn't embrace it. "This is a show about the birth of hip-hop that's filled with Black and Brown people, what the hell is wrong with you?!" We joke about not wanting to get dragged for saying something bad about a thing that Black people love, but it's a real thing. There is a sense of betrayal, that we are cracking some foundational defense if we aren't all in agreement that this very Black thing is the very best thing.

We saw this with *Luke Cage* too, where there are still plenty of people that claim it's the best of the Marvel Netflix shows. Which seems laughable to me, as some of the acting and the derailed third act of the first season alone take it out of any "great" qualification for me. But I did *enjoy Luke Cage* about as much as any of its rivals. And I wanted it to win. I needed it to win. And it did win enough when it was all said and done. Even if it wasn't the big prize.

In a similar vein, I wonder how history will treat *Lovecraft Country*. Here we have Black, pulpy horror, the likes we haven't experienced on TV. It captivated so many Black TV fans that yearned for more each week. But after the first few episodes, the cracks begin to show in the narrative. Some decisions the showrunners made didn't do them any favors. There was the trope that to show passion in lovemaking, someone had to come close to being physically hurt. You had the producers patting themselves on the back for including a transgender character that neither spoke during the show or had any significant involvement. And just a lot of "if Black people had the power, they'd terrorize white people" vengeance fantasy at work. In a dark and almost affirming way, maybe it shows that Black writers and creators are mainstream enough where they can be held accountable for the same social miscues that their white counterparts are. But honestly, nobody wants to enjoy their art with that lens.

Essentially, it comes down to what do we, as Black consumers that want to support Black artists, owe those artists if the work doesn't hit the level we want? I don't believe in any way, shape, or form that Black art has to be exceptional to warrant support. I think work that doesn't rise to some profound level should be supported, regardless (provided it isn't straight up damaging or harmful). I really wish that *Proud Mary* crushed at the box office, even if I don't think it is a good film (it didn't, by the way). But the why is worth investigating.

The film was shown in the second-lowest number of theaters of any that grossed in the top ten during the week of its debut. Much was made about the disparate marketing for the film before its release. It seemed that Sony/Screen Gems had given up on the film before it was ever birthed. What began as a modest but respectable marketing push dwindled to the point that screenings weren't even held previous to the release. When questioned on the curious move, Screen Gems would state that because *Proud Mary* wasn't a critic-friendly film, that it would let filmgoers decide for themselves. Well, that worked out great. Because the people that make movies may be a lot of things, but idiots probably isn't one. I'd say there's a more realistic answer. I would venture to say that it may have never had a shot at being a great film. With an estimated production budget of $14M (and making a little over $20M domestically), it's hard to imagine putting it in the same ballpark as other big-name action films. *The Commuter*, which opened on the same weekend, had a budget of at least $40M, and that looks like a younger sibling to your average Liam Neeson not-as-smart-as-it-pretends-to-be action film. Neeson hasn't made a financial blockbuster film as the lead since the last *Taken* movie in 2014, but my dude's dance card is full for the foreseeable future. How many more action films does he have in his future, you ask? More than Taraji.

At the same time that Black art doesn't need to be monolithic in its content, neither does it need to be in its quality and output. I'm not an advocate for more bad or uninspiring art in the world, but I also believe that not all art has to be all things to all people. And this is mostly true. But the stakes for Black art that doesn't hit a particular greatness threshold always feels at risk of being reduced to scarcity, or being critiqued for not doing more. Not every Black movie needs to justify its existence by being *Moonlight*. But not every Black moviegoer should feel they have to go to every Black movie just to keep Black movies being made either.

For Dark Girls Who Never
Get Asked to Play Storm

WILLIAM EVANS,
aka Preacher of the Mutant Gospel

THE NERD COMMUNITY is a really tough bastard to please. The Black nerd community, maybe even more so. Still, because we, the Black nerd coalition, rarely get what we want, throwing us a bone is often a good way to buy yourself some goodwill and keep our adamantium claws from coming out. Storm of the X-Men is probably the biggest get-out-of-jail-free card that may never get played. In 2014, Bryan Singer, who gathers accusations like Google inquiries, announced that he had found Cyclops, Jean Grey, and Storm for the next X-Men films. You may now know these films as *X-Men: Apocalypse* and *X-Men: Dark Phoenix*. Or more accurately, the movies that basically killed the X-Men franchise.

Now, the first thing that pops up is how young the actors were when they were cast. Like, could be Famke Janssen's (the original X-Men movies' Jean Grey) kids young. But that's not very surprising. *X-Men: First Class* was a prequel to the original X-Men films, and *X-Men: Days of Future Past* was a sequel to *First Class* (which was still a prequel to the original films), but then *Days of Future Past* does some time travel shit and kind of erases the timeline of the original and . . . you know what, everyone is younger now. Just take my word on this. It's trash but it's canon. Like Jar Jar Binks.

So, we can talk Sansa Stark playing Jean Grey (we saw how that turned out) or Tye "You Might Remember Me from *Mud*, Actually Naw, You Probably Don't" Sheridan playing Cyclops, but come on, fam. This is a Black Nerd Problems production . . . you know we're gonna talk about Ororo da Literal Gawd.

I do not come to bury Alexandra Shipp, however easy she makes it. We could talk forever about Shipp equating the conversations about colorism in her being cast as Storm as racism toward her. Or about her stating most racism she experiences is from Black people (starting to get the idea Alexandra might need a primer on the definition of *racism*). We could talk about how we should've seen her uninspiring performance coming based on her performance in the Lifetime *Aaliyah* biopic, which to be clear was a train derailing while passing through a forest fire. Even bad movies like that can be a vehicle for the brilliance of its lead, like Chadwick Boseman in *Get on Up*. Or most small films that Tom Hardy stars in. Or Viola Davis on planet Earth. None of that came from Shipp's performance in *Aaliyah*, and I sincerely hope folks younger than me don't associate that with the singer's legacy. But that's kind of the point: none of this is about Shipp as much as what it represents in Hollywood. Which would really suck for her in that position if she weren't so terrible at handling the complexity of it.

What this is about is the way that Hollywood continues to pretend that no impact or history lies in the darkness of someone's skin. Well, when I say "Hollywood," I mean directors like Bryan Singer. And when I say "someone's skin," I really mean Black women. Brothas can fall victim to skin shade discrimination as well, but outside of skin color, they don't have to deal with the impossible beauty standards of women, let alone a dark-complected woman.

Plenty of people will say (with or without venom): "What's the real issue, it's not like they cast a white woman as Storm, does it really need to be this complicated?" Yeah, you bet your all-shades-of-Black ass it does.

Even as a fictional character, Storm is a feminist symbol for Black women the way that most assume Wonder Woman has been for women all these years (the box office response of the first Wonder Woman film bears that out). Storm has always been powerful, goddess-like, and African. And no, not Charlize Theron South African. Her dark complexion has been depicted throughout her comic book history (there are exceptions with some artistic liberties over the years, but few and far between). Storm has become a beacon and symbol for women with darker skin for decades now. The unwillingness to recognize that is just another thunderbolt in the side of a demographic of women who frankly are plenty used to it by now.

The stigma of Black women that are darker being deemed ugly, less desirable, or just plain less than goes back a lot further than the X-Men. Unfortunately, time has done little to eradicate that notion. It's why Lupita's rise to fame was constantly met with "I don't get it, I don't see why people think she's beautiful." Or the *New York Times* calling Viola Davis "less classically beautiful than [Kerry] Washington." Or why there were about seventeen things wrong with Zoe Saldana playing Nina Simone, but one of the most talked about is how much lighter she was than Nina was. Black does not equate all Black. For Nina, to disregard her struggle in the world because she was dark-complected is to disregard her true story. Now, Storm is a fictional character, she does not have a daily grind, struggle, and catalog of insults, dismissals, and microaggressions that have to be accounted for. But living and breathing Black women that embrace the idea of Storm do. I think about Tiffany Onyejiaka's essay on colorism where she states, "And this is what Hollywood needs to realize: That casting agents, producers, and directors tend to gravitate toward a very distinct type of black girl who fits the 'Halle Berry' aesthetic: slim, light-skinned, and classically attractive in a Eurocentric sense." She wrote that in 2017 and little has changed.

You would assume that comic book movies and shows are where you would see the quickest change to this, because of the blank-slate nature of new castings. It's easy to create excitement or at least headlines with comic book portrayals. There has been a slight uptick in casting dark-skinned Black women in these TV shows and movies, though the lion's share seemed to happen in *Black Panther*. Lupita Nyong'o, Danai Gurira, and Letitia Wright are incredibly uplifting to see on-screen, breaking the norms. But again, they're all in the same movie more or less. Outside of Wakanda, you have a few actresses like Lashana Lynch in *Captain Marvel*, Viola Davis in *Suicide Squad*, and Anna Diop on *Titans*. After that the well runs pretty dry for significant roles. This isn't an easy measurement. Is progress a film like *Black Panther* with a large grouping of darker-skinned actresses? It certainly can't be the promised diversity of *Wonder Woman*, where a quartet of Black women show up on Themyscira with little to do and even less to remember about them. I think progress may look like a lead protagonist role or, dare I say, a love interest. You've got Lupita in Wakanda then like Zendaya and Zoe Saldana. That's your list. (Never sure how to count Zoe considering she's green in *Guardians of the Galaxy*, but her skin tone absolutely counts in, say, the *Star Trek* movies.)

I do empathize with actors and actresses in these cases to some extent. This is a passion and an art for them, but it's also a job. And regardless of the state of the economy, turning down a gig ain't really something you're trained to do. I have no idea if Shipp was a Storm fan previous to accepting the role. Maybe the symbol that is Storm was a source of power and pride for her just like many other Black women. But that empathy doesn't really do much to alleviate the consistent knocking in the back of skulls of Black women that have been passed over because they were too dark. To simply dismiss this as a nonstarter of an issue is really just another level of "I don't see color," but instead it's "I don't see the difference between one Black person to another."

Because (somehow) I'm still an X-Men fan and because I'm an Ororo Munroe stan, I was hoping Alexandra Shipp would kill it. Lord knows that we were in need of a good Storm performance after all these years (for the record, I think bad writing did hurt Halle in the first *X-Men*; everything went downhill after that though). Are the number of darker Black women in roles growing? Ever so slightly. Can women like Lupita and Danai be game changers? I certainly hope so. We don't know how we would be getting Teyonah Parris as Monica Rambeau without the prior representation of those women. I'm happy to watch all these women kill these roles, but let's be honest. None of these roles is Storm. That's just math. Or weather. Whatever. But with more attention paid to colorism in casting than before and actresses like Dominique Jackson, Janelle Monáe, and Yetide Badaki openly petitioning to play the goddess, it feels like there's at least a chance. Black women of all shades, especially those that are often passed over for glamorous roles, deserve a chance to see themselves throwing lightning from the sky.

How My Black Ass Would
Survive Every Horror Movie

OMAR HOLMON,
aka The Guy Keeping Freddy from Getting Shut-Eye

THERE COMES THAT point when I am watching a scary movie (having been forced to) where the suspension of disbelief just straight up shuts down. I hate how Black folk get axed in horror movies by doing out-of-culture shit. Neither I nor any of my peers—dare I say, any Black person—ever gone to investigate a strange noise heard in the distance while outside. Yet, Black folk still die first in the horror movies. Or they die as fodder for the white characters to get away. What the fuck?! How, yo? If Black people got more accurate portrayals in horror movies, those movies would be over in minutes. The monster or killer wouldn't even happen to cross paths with the Black folk in horror movies. I'm not saying we're better survivors, I'm just . . . Actually, yeah, that's exactly what I'm saying. Maybe it's just me, but I see plotlines going way differently when facing off against some of the horror icons. I'll take the forefront with how I would handle these certain horror villains and thriller situations.

Let's start with one of the biggest horror icons in the game, Freddy Krueger from *A Nightmare on Elm Street*. Freddy got the claw hand thing going and he mostly merks folks in their dreams. Cats would usually try to stay awake in order to avoid Freddy, but when that fails, they're stuck in a nightmare where he is in control. That does seem scary, but there's a reason Freddy's ass kept that shit in the burbs. He wouldn't be trying to get in Omar Little from *The Wire*'s dreams.

Freddy should know better than that—all I'm saying is, he tries going in a Black dude's head? He getting jumped. Early. Timberland boots contouring his face on sight, and immediately after that me and my whole squad are gon' roast him for what he's wearing. "Look at your fit, boy! Look at his watered-down Fruit Roll Up–looking-ass *Where's Waldo* sweater, doe! This dude out here with beef jerky skin thinking he gon' scare somebody?" Freddy wouldn't even be able to handle the fucking jokes being snapped on 'em at damn near light speed. There's nothing to protect Freddy once a brother gets in his Toph earthbending roast stance with the hand at an acute forty-five-degree angle.

Also, what Freddy gonna do in a Black woman's dreams? Not a damn thing! He'll get crushed by the tempered glass ceiling they face. Oh, it ain't a problem for them since they gotta punch through that shit daily, but Freddy can't. Freddy Krueger ain't winning a fight against any sister in her dreams, period. The man's already bald but would get snatched bald again somehow. Freddy never been in a dream where the white privilege is working against him. I would have loved seeing Freddy try to come up in my mom's dreams. He'd be doing the dishes, taking out trash, filing her taxes, and using his knife gloves to do mani-pedis QUICK! I'm not hearing it with you, Fred.

Let's talk about the other horror movie MVP, Jason Voor-

WILLIAM EVANS AND OMAR HOLMON

hees from *Friday the 13th*. First and foremost, I'm nowhere in any part of America where walking round with a machete and a hockey mask is a regular thing where no one bats an eye. I see a dude in a hockey mask and there isn't a goal, a referee, or ice in the vicinity? I know it's time to go. Also, I'm pretty sure everyone hears that *ch-huh-ch-huh-ch-huh-ha-ha-ha-ha* sound when Jason is around, more than likely because he is making it himself. As far as tactics, I'm running. Now I know everyone is like, "Ooooh, Jason is slow but he catches you." FUCK. OUTTA. HERE. WITH. THAT. SHIT. They always trip over something in the woods (I'm convinced everyone has been tripping at the same spot in the same woods in movies for years). I ran track in high school for this occasion fucking specifically, man. You're not just running for your life; you're running for the team. I'm making it to my fam to be like, "Man, you ain't gonna believe the shit I just saw . . . I was out soon as I saw dude. I fuckin' ran, man. Y'all woulda been proud of me." Worst-case scenario, I know Jason is weak against water, so in that case I'm gettin' Sharkeisha or Solange to take Jason down 'cause their fighting style might as well be waterbending from the *Avatar: The Last Airbender* series.

Man, this is easy survival shit. Who else y'all got? Aliens and Predators? What, you thought you were gon' trip me up with that one? NOPE. Not a problem. Dealing with Aliens is simple. I'm not going into space. If I was one of those folks that applied to go on that one-way trip to Mars mission (remember that shit?), then I'd have a more strategic answer, but since I have common "nah, I'm good" sense, Aliens wouldn't be a threat. However, Predators are a bit different. Predators go to planets looking to start shit, so there's no avoiding that shit—the hunt is their rite of passage. Predators are similar to the Black experience with police, as they lie in the cut and then decide to come at you because they got the power to do so, because (as we've been reminded) we're the most dangerous game. The main difference is there's a code with the Predators. You fight back to take 'em down and they'll dap you with respect, as Michael Harrigan (Danny Glover) showed us. Or you can help them out in the field against an enemy like Alexa Woods (Sanaa Lathan) did. Alexa teamed up with a Predator to take out some Aliens and she was rewarded by getting a Predator insignia recognizing her as a warrior by the clan (#NotAllPredators?). So, at best, I'm helping out Predators somehow. I'm straight up telling them, "Look, man, I'm showing my allegiance with you, so who we goin' after? Drug lords again or Aliens, 'cause I don't like either of those motherfuckers no way no how anyway."

I'm tryina tell y'all this shit is way easier than they make it out to be in the movies, man. All right, who next? Y'all gon' say I forgot about Michael Myers from *Halloween*? That I did not. I'm straight up going toe-to-toe and pound for pound with Michael Myers. You wanna ask why? 'Cause fucking Busta Rhymes gave him the fucking jumping front kick (in Timbs!) out of a window. Since that is technically a WWF move, and I hold true to the theory that whoever gets hit with a WWF move in a fight automatically loses (even if they win), I'm nailing Myers with that HBK Sweet Chin Music and letting the chips fall where they may.

Who the fuck is next, man? How about Sadako Yamamura/ Samara Morgan from *Ring*, you say? Pshhh, please. Whole premise of her movie was you watch this tape, then you die in seven days 'cause she comes after you from the television . . . Dude, it's 2020, there ain't shit worth dying for on a VHS tape, even if it's labeled NSFW. I'd only give her this scenario if there was a torrent for this shit, man. That's the only way anybody I know going to peep her wack-ass tape. This was a simple fix 'cause as soon as I see her coming out the TV I either change the channel, break it, or chuck it out the window. If she comes out my laptop . . . arghhhhhh . . . I think 80 percent of me says I'd give it the Falcon Punch. Next!

Esther from *Orphan*? Esther was posing as a nine-year-old girl, but she was actually in her late thirties and mad disturbed. She might not be in the same league as Freddy and them, but my mother loved this movie and my brother had the perfect retort for the entire film: "Nope. Noooooooooooooooooooooo way. I'm not going out like that. I'm scoop-slamming her like Matt Hughes and doing some UFC knees if need be. Taking her right back to the orphanage and not even stopping the car when I kick her out. Shortest movie ever. If you went to get popcorn, too bad, you missed the entire film." Next!

The serial killer from *Scream*? Ain't nobody round here scared of that Saturday-morning *Scooby-Doo* villain mask, yo. Again, man, this is a serial killer that can only flourish in the suburbs on some big fish, little pond shit. His whole fit and MO is out the ordinary in the burbs but not in the big city. How you gon' flourish in New York when your fit don't scare anybody 'cause we done seen it all on the subway. If it's me and I see dude jump out, I'm automatically assuming he's a street performer. I'd give him some change and keep it the fuck moving like, "Okay, buddy, yeah, you're a serial killer, yada, yada. Look, I already gave you a dollar . . . we're done here."

Is that all y'all got for me? That all there is? Man, I'll throw in *Jurassic Park* as a bonus 'cause it ain't horror really but that shit ain't fun neither. So check it, there's no way on any part of the universe would I be caught at Jurassic Park or Jurassic World.

Like, what's a better survival plan than utterly refusing to go because there's a muhfucking park . . . with muhfucking actual dinosaurs. No. Just hell no. But for argument's sake, let's say I'm a ten-year-old that wants to go on a field trip there or whatever. Son, MY. MOM. WOULD. NOT. BE. HAVING. IT. First off, I'm going to assume she isn't sending me to the Flintstones' trap house because A) she loves me, and B) she would tell me if I wanna see dinosaurs I better take my ass to the museum and pet one of the dead ones on display. I could hear her now sayin', "Must be out your mind talkin' 'bout some Jurassic World. Why don't you go clean your room and see if you find any fossils in there, 'cause you ain't cleaned it since they cloned the first damn dinosaur anyhow." News would break about the dinosaurs getting out days later. Mom saying, "Oh, you still wanna go to some Jurassic World now? I didn't think so."

Is there no one else? Huh? Some of y'all might be reading this saying, "Oh, you forgot Norman Bates." I'll beat the mama's boy outta Bates. What else you got? Alfred Hitchcock's *The Birds*? That ain't nothing but a Popeyes/Church's Chicken/Crown Chicken/Chick-fil-A commercial to me. *The Hills Have Eyes*? I know they ain't looking at me. *Jaws*? I'm good right here ten toes down on the beach. Pennywise? I don't entertain clowns or muhfuckas in clown shoes, go on with that mess. Chucky? Y'all talking *Child's Play* is straight up child's play, there's nothing I can do worse to Chucky that his sequels ain't already do to him. Still, Chucky ain't nothing a punt kick can't take care of. Get that Garbage Pail Kid the fuck outta here. Go. Go. Go. Go. Go. Go. Go. Who's next?! Huh? Ain't a scary movie alive, character or scenario, that got me shook. I'm prepared for anything and every damn thing. Ain't nothing gon' get me or catch me slipping. What's that? Hold up, did I hear someone say, "What about *The Exorcist*?"

. . . All right, so . . . I mean . . . I— No comment. End the chapter, yo. End the damn chapter, they out here bringing *The Exorcist* up and I do not fuck with that level of supernatural. Mmm-fucking-mmmmm. No, sir. Better do like Bob Seger and turn the page, 'cause we done here.

Jordan Peele Should Get His Flowers while He's Here

OMAR HOLMON,
aka Get Out . . . of My Dreams and into
My Dark Twisted Fantasy

THERE'S NOTHING I love more than character development in real time from performers. Seeing them excel when they don't stay in their lane, refusing to be pigeonholed. I love seeing it occur when actors go from comedic roles to serious roles and vice versa. I'm all about celebrating. I'm also about praising that range when it occurs in order to give people their flowers while they are still here. Too often we see an artist's body of work go under the radar and only appreciate it fully once they're gone. I'm just trying to get ahead of that and in doing so give that man Jordan Peele his flowers while he's here. Jordan Peele did a whole cultural genre reset when he went from comedy to horror. *Get Out* really changed the game and he did not slow down from there. Lemme give this man his credit from the beginning to his current progress save point at this moment.

takes a deep breath When J. Cole said, *The real is back, the ville is back / Flow bananas here, peel[e] this back*, he meant Jordan Peele was going to not only go bananas but the entirety of the fruit basket on Hollywood cinema. Jordan Peele got drafted to the 2003 cast of *Mad TV*, and then like every hacker in every movie scene where there is a hacker breaking into a system, he said, "I'm in." Peele said, "Y'all want jokes, huh? I got your fucking jokes right here. I got your comedy sketches right here." All the while plotting for the lane change. First Jordan Peele had to bide his time tho. He warmed his way into America's hearts with jokes and shit. Got households used to his face on TV making audiences laugh out loud. That was the first step, the second step? Operation *Key & Peele*.

Comedy Central was desperate after they fucked up the *Chappelle's Show* ride. It needed someone to fill the void. It should be understood I don't give a fuck if that wasn't the actual case 'cause this is the narrative in my eyes. Comedy Central asked Keegan-Michael Key and Jordan Peele for a show. If they could hold their ship together. "Can y'all make muthafuckas laugh? The TV streets need a sketch show from us. We need this hit. We need a banger show. Can y'all do it? Can y'all get this shit done?!" I like to imagine Keegan-Michael Key and Jordan Peele hearing this, then looking at each other and giving the Matthew McConaughey–level "all right, all right, all-fucking-right" to signify the comedy game was 'bout to change. This was it, baby. This was what those years spent grinding on *Mad TV* was about. This was comedy WrestleMania.

Key & Peele hit them TV screens with the same energy as a buddy-cop/team-up movie and nothing was the same. Muthafuckas weren't ready for this Harlem Heat all-Black everything tag team in the comedy game. I said *looks over shoulder* biiiiiiiiiiiiiitch, no one was ready for the skits. Ya boys were nice. Lemme rephrase that, Keegan Key and Jordan Peele were fucking nooooice. Muthafuckas knew the show's skits by heart. They got funny and addressed race shit, stereotype shit, and that surreal shit. They took the trope of magical Negroes that show up in movies to help white folks and upped the ridiculousness of it in a sketch where two old, wise, magical Black men rivals, Mr. Stanley (Jordan) and Carl (Keegan-Michael), battle each other to be the one to offer advice to the "troubled white boy." The sketch was like the magical Negro version of the movie *Highlander*. There's another one where Keegan-Michael plays Mr. Garvey, an inner-city teacher having trouble as a substitute teacher at a school for white middle-class kids. You know how some teachers or most white people can butcher the pronunciation of Black or ethnic names? Mr. Garvey does the same thing when trying to pronounce these kids' "common"-ass English names like Ay-Ay-Ron (Aaron), Dee-Nice (Denise), Jay-Quellin (Jacqueline), Je-Seeka (Jessica), and Balakay (Blake). Not only is this my favorite sketch, it's a brilliant play off this misconception of English names being the norm or easier to pronounce than Black/ethnic names. Every Black/POC person has a story 'bout their name being butchered in pronunciation into something outrageous. These were the top-tier sketches that the comedy streets needed. *Key & Peele* gave the world five seasons of jokes. They made themselves household names for five years. On top of the world and then they decided to end the show. Best thing about them is that they did it like Outkast, they were still a duo, but they were both going to do their Outkast *Speakerboxxx/The Love Below* solo routes at the same time. The stage was set right there for the swerve.

Everyone heard that Jordan Peele was getting into horror and said, "What? The dude that did that comedy action movie about getting his cat back? That Jordan Peele? The funny guy?" Everyone had their opinions. Folks had their doubts. Maaaan, Jordan Peele dropped the trailer for *Get Out* and Loooooooord. Everybody shut the fuck up. *Get Out* changed the horror game on some FUBU shit (For Us, By Us, for those born after 1992). A horror movie where the micro- and macroaggressions were the large portions of the scares. I remember being in the theater in New York watching *Get Out* and that shit was a whole-ass experience. It felt like the *Black Panther* feel but for horror movies. Jordan Peele did that shit, man. I like to imagine that Jordan Peele was standing somewhere overlooking a city with his hands behind his back like Thanos, while his film gained notoriety, traction, and praise. The success of *Get Out* made everyone look at Jordan Peele and wonder, "How long were you planning this? What else do you have in the pockets?" Jordan Peele peeled off from comedy, swerved into horror, and said, "Oh, we not done yet. I got more for that ass." Jordan Peele did the DJ Khaled voice and said, "Another one," not only dropping his second horror movie, *Us*, but then producing and writing the *Candyman* 2021 remake with Nia DaCosta directing it. Do y'all know how hard Black folk go for *Candyman*? Candyman was, to me, at least, the first Black slasher horror figure. His film became a cult classic with Black folk and cemented him, to me, at least, as a Jason or Freddy Krueger type icon in his own right. Yes. Jordan Peele got on and is putting people on. We love to see it.

You'd think it would stop there. You'd think Jordan Peele would be happy having proved that you can't pigeonhole an artist. You'd think folks recognizing that he got the comedy and horror game on lock would be enough. No. Nope. It ain't. Jordan Peele showed up in a teaser trailer rocking a black suit and stepping through a door. Not just any door. The motherfucking *Twilight Zone* door. What. The. Fuck? Jordan Peele went on to become not only the executive producer for a *Twilight Zone* remake but the narrator as well. That's comedy, horror, and now a sci-fi element of horror? How many championship belts is this man Jordan Peele going to take? How much flex can one man possibly flex on us? Y'all don't hear me tho, this is what stunting looks like. Everybody thought it was all jokes with Jordan Peele. Everybody thought he was just going to keep it comedy for his career. No, no, no, folks. Jordan Peele dipping his hand in all the dishes in the kitchen. The man is cooking a bunch of recipes right now.

I wanna know what the fuck is next so I don't get surprised. Is he going to go into rom-coms next? The man was already in *Toy Story 4* with his mans and dem Keegan-Michael Key. We gotta add children's movies to the list now too! Jordan Peele is legit putting together an Infinity Gauntlet of a résumé, with all the gems being his movies, plus the big moves he made and is continuing to make. *slams fist on table* See that's what the fuck I am talking about. That's the come up we love to see. Jordan Peele's career is looking like a heist movie at this point. This feels like a long-game heist to steal the stat quo from Hollywood one piece at a time and I am enjoying it. Does that make him Danny Ocean? Jordan Peele has really changed what a horror movie can look like and I'm hoping he will continue to do so. All the while swinging back and forth between comedy and horror to show that he can do both with ease. This is the shit I am talking about, not many people can get away with or do what Jordan Peele has done across genres. So those that have should get their flowers now as well. I love when performers fly under the radar, but it's good to let them get the recognition and praise they deserve while they're still around to take it in.

Top Five Dead or Alive:
Red Hood in the DC Animated Universe

WILLIAM EVANS,
aka The Fifty-Eleventh Robin So Far

LOOK, FAM, EVERYONE got their rituals, nah mean? Some folks like to eat a particular meal every first of the month. Some folks rearrange their furniture. Me? I watch *Batman: Under the Red Hood.* Every. Month. I be scoping all these DCU animated films and for the most part, I can dig something out of all of them, but they all be fighting for second place, yo.

Red Hood is the muthafuckin' John Boyega over the couch reaction to *Star Wars,* but for all Batman animated films. Please believe, this shit go prison-yard hard through every phase. And I know folks love *Mask of the Phantasm* and *Return of the Joker* for good reasons, but you know what those movies ain't got? Jason. Muthafuckin'. I Boosted the Wheels. On the Batmobile. When I Was Barely Double Digits. Todd. Which, no matter what flick you prefer, ain't no debate. Red Hood as a character, through any DCU animated film, is Top Five Dead or Alive.

Fuck the whole industry!
You tried to get rid of me?
Y'all must be kiddin' me!!
    —Keith Murray, "Special Delivery"

Man, you can call this shit tradition at this point. If you run with Batman and rock the red. Stop. Yellow. Stop. Green. Stop. Then you know you gonna have to get dead and get brought back at some point. But Jason Todd was the original, fam. And the way that shit starts? With Jason getting blown da fuck up after getting the cape beat off him with a crowbar? Sheeeeeeiiit. Not everybody get an honorable death like that. Well, all the Robins kind of do, but still.

Also, the movie improved upon the source, cuz the comic book version was ehhhh. Some ol' Choose Your Own Adventure type shit where some bitter muthafucka that must have hated their younger brother voted to have Jason killed off. Well, guess what, bastards? Your boy came back with a vengeance for ayebody.

What's worse is that he made sure to let folks know that just cuz he came back, don't mean that something happened to him. He hit Batman with that "oh, you think Ra's' little dip in the pool turned me rabid?" Naaaaaaah, fam. Jason been on that *Murda Muzik*. Batman kept that impulse in check, but your boy out here "No Church in the Wild" for his brand of justice. Always has been.

Scared to death, running like I got bears on me
(Run!) My Timbs start feeling like they Nike Airs on me
    —Ghostface Killah, "Run"

Yo, but why Jason Todd about to win *American Ninja Warrior* off the strength of his rooftop game? First time Batman chased him through these Gotham streets was mostly by vehicle, but when Bats and Nightwing tried to bounty hunt your boy? Fuck that. Your dude bailed on a helicopter and then went *Bourne Supremacy* through the skyline. Even Nightwing can't shut the fuck up about it (played brilliantly by Neil Patrick Harris).

Jason out here turning in his forty time at the combine, jumping out of windows, turning 180 degrees, and shooting fire extinguishers to delay his pursuers. Dude did the triple jump onto a blimp (a fuckin' blimp, fam!) and set up in position. Then he readied the pistols like it was a turn-based strategy game, just waiting on Batman to hit the corner. Not to mention him cutting the cable off his ankle midair. Not to mention the long game he had set up with the bomb posted in the train station for his getaway. Nah, man. Y'all ain't gonna have me believing the Red Hood ain't play all the *Ninja Gaiden* games.

> *Yeah we got A-M-M-O, but you'll get beat like MMA*
> *I got Dracos, Ninos, Automatics; that's my DNA*
> —Lil Wayne, "Fly Away"

Can we talk about how Jason took that Batman training and went next level with the spec-ops weapons training? Can we talk about how your boy combined gadgets, hand to hand, and an NRA membership? Yeah, obviously, this is what separates him from Batman, but yo, Jason ain't develop that same fear of firearms that Bruce did. Times two, cuz your boy always carry a pair. And a blade.

Did I mention he got Batman's arsenal too? When the Black Mask's mercenaries showed up your boy went dual-wield God mode. He out here moving like Aang if Aang carried a couple extra clips and had Quantico-level marksmanship. You see the way this dude side-to-side drills while never leaving his target?!?!

He out here on skates, man. He out here going Kyrie Irving on these dudes. Chow Yun-fat could never. Max Payne ain't got enough agility perks, and Jason ain't even got Bullet Time, yo. If your MCM can't strafe with the left thumbstick and aim with the right like Jason, then your MCM is trash.

I ain't even got to his fight with Batman near the end. Well, not the very end. That's a bad example cuz I do love how they always make sure that Batman can go next level on his former apprentices when he needs to. But under the gargoyles, Jason was giving Batman all he could handle. He done disarmed your boy. Mask off like he was Miles Morales or some shit. That knife in the cape, trap? Next level. The bomb in the mask trick? He just showing off.

> *With so much personality, what do you want from me?*
> *I could be by myself and enjoy the company*
> —Kanye West, "Whole City Behind Us"

Let's also be real, after watching so much of our beloved Batman be the stoic stalwart, having a lead character in a Batman film with this much personality is my shit. He ain't as chatty as Nightwing (it's part of his charm), but every time dude speaks, that shit kills. From the introduction of the Red Hood, he was out here dropping bars and one-liners wasn't nobody else fuckin' with. When he threatened the drug trade for 40 percent, his mouth was as lethal as the AK he was pointing. Your boy tossed the heads of each lieutenant on the table talking about, "That took me two hours. Want to see what I can get done in a whole evening?"

He was also the monosyllable gawd in this movie too. He watched one of his project spots get bodied: "Hmm. Cute." He got hit half a hundred times and thrown into a building: "Ow." And you can't do that without the gawdbody voice acting of Jensen Ackles, who you probably know as Dean from *Supernatural*. Or you don't cuz I don't know too many Black people that watch that *Supernatural*.

But whatever. Point is, he murder death kills that role. Whether he's insulting Batman, talking to himself, or using some callback humor on the Joker, he's out here doing the Cowl's work.

We can't close this part without acknowledging one of the best-delivered lines in the movie after he done set up Nightwing and Batman for the Wu. Over the train, your boy yelled, "*You haven't lost your touch, Bruce.*" Flipped the game all the way upside down and left our hero shook parts one and two.

> *Thought you'd be different 'bout it*
> *Now I know you not it . . .*
> *So let's get on with it*
> —Kanye West, "Blood on the Leaves"

One of the most gangsta things about *Red Hood* is that the story flips back and forth until its climax, when you see what Jason really wanted. It ain't about him taking over the drug trade and just being a criminal. It ain't just about being a better Batman with more permanent solutions. Ain't even about getting revenge on the Joker for himself. Nah, man, your boy Jason was on that Sinestro Corps shit. He was trying to show Batman that absolute force might be the answer. And then . . . after all the turns, that shit got mad sentimental.

He was mad at Batman for not doing away with the Joker and was legit hurt that he, Jason, wasn't the last straw. "After he took me away from you . . ." Maaaaaan, I wasn't ready. I wasn't ready for that turn, yo. Jason been trying to act detached and business as usual about this shit, but your boy was mad hurt that he wasn't avenged enough. And I ain't even mad at him, yo.

We been asking the why on Joker's life for a minute now, but this shit was the most personal. And when he couldn't turn Batman, he was like, "Fuck it, we can all die, then," as he had the place wired to explode (which led to that incredible Joker shit with "I'm the only one that's going to get what he wants tonight!").

> *Everyone who doubted me is askin' for forgiveness*
> *If you ain't been a part of it, at least you got to witness*
> —Drake, "Forever"

Once a month, fam. I be all up in animated Gotham, memorizing lines, sculpting my mobility workouts around Jason's flow, perfecting my one-line dialogue in case anybody ever try to move in my corners. Bring your best heroes, villains, it don't matter. Jason is what the truth looks like. Red Hoodie Up.

If My Black Ass Was Enrolled in the X-Men's School, Charles Xavier Would Have Been Fed Up

OMAR HOLMON,

aka #1 Mutant Draft Pick on the FBI's Most Wanted List

Mutatis mutandis ("Changing [only] those things which need to be changed").
—Xavier's School for Gifted Youngsters school motto

I GREW UP in an X-Men home, man. My sister's favorite character was Beast. Pretty sure my brother was a big Cable fan. Mom rolled with Storm. Cyclops was my guy coming up. I always loved what the X-Men stood for. The X-Men debuted in comics back in 1963 and served as an allegory for the civil rights era. At its heart the series is about humans that happen to be born with mutations that give them powers or cause them to look a certain way. The people with these mutations got discriminated against because of them and became known as mutants (*Homo superior* if you nasty). [Quick sidenote: The original five X-Men used for this allegory for victims of racism and discrimination were all white. We don't see more mutants of color till the 1975 X-Men roster. Funny how when it's white characters as mutants who have powers that are

161

discriminated against and hated, America can understand. I'm just saying, it would have been interesting to see how things would have gone down if some of the original X-Men were Black mutants to really drive home the point with art imitating life.] Anyway, y'all know the rest. Charles Xavier opened up his School for Gifted Youngsters to teach mutants to control their abilities and to adapt to the world by fighting for a better tomorrow.

Yeaaaaah, I was thinking 'bout that shit, and the older I get the more I agree with Magneto's advanced course in Muthafuckas (*Homo sapiens*) Never Loved Us and X-Men squad leader Storm's Intro to Everybody Gettin' Stabbed 101 class that she been teaching since the early '80s. I already told y'all how my dad was with me growing up when it came to knowing history. I realize two things now: Dad was militant as fuck about African and African American history as well as the treatment of Indigenous folks, and I've gotten the baton passed from him (Mom was a different type of hands throwing). Plus, more and more as I grew older, I started to realize for myself that yeah, Magneto's fireside chat mixtapes really resonated. If I'd attended the School for Gifted Youngsters, then my parents would have enrolled me during the late '90s/early 2000s, so let's say I hit puberty, discovered my powers, got transferred, and I spent my high school to college years at the school. Let's imagine . . .

> **CHARLES XAVIER:** Class, let's welcome a new student, Omar Holmon. Omar, would you mind telling us what your mutant ability is?
>
> **ME:** No problem . . . Jesus Christ himself has pleased me with many gifts. One of many is knocking people the fffffuck out.

Yo, I would have had Charles Xavier fed the fuck up for real, for real. I know that shit from fucking jump. Maaaaaaan, listen,

I woulda had questions as soon as I heard Xavier talking 'bout some . . .

CHARLES XAVIER: The X-Men are sworn to protect a world
   that fears and hates them.

raising my hand

XAVIER: Yes, Omar?
ME: So, we gotta protect oppressive-as-fuck nonmutants like
   them? *points out the window to a crowd gathered at
   the school's front gate*
XAVIER: *hard sigh* Yes.
ME: Does that count toward our final grade, 'cause real talk,
   if not . . . I'm good.

Let's say the original X-Men were my older classmates or teach-ing assistants, but obviously they're always going on field missions. I'd be complaining my ass off if Jean was my TA. I'd be at her office hours like, "This BRB note been here for like a week. Jean Grey ain't ever here, fam. She done died like fourteen times already and came back. The fuck, man? How she not teaching religion is beyond me. She and Jesus probably fucking got a web series together in heaven."

I'd be all up in the cafeteria wylin' out with discussions, man. It wouldn't be all serious 'cause I'ma be joking round with roasting my friends like, "Jubilee, I know you ain't ripping on me, girl. How long you been here again? When the fuck you gon' graduate, my mutant? How many credits you missing, Bilee?!"

We'd be talking about X-Men's past adventures from the com-ics, movies, and TV show 'cause I'd bring up the shit I gotta get off my chest like, "Aye, why can no one tell me how Darwin got knocked by Sebastian Shaw [*X-Men: First Class*]? His mutant ability was to be able to adapt to anything and he still got killed? How does that even work? I saw Darwin grow gills in swim class. I was trying to spar against him in the Danger Room and he beat my ass just by roasting me, man. He said, 'What X-Man rocks glasses in the field? You *Dexter's Laboratory* lookin' ass, boi.' He literally adapted to every situation and threat, but he got merked? And he doesn't come back to life, but Jean Grey done died twelve times since last Thursday and—" *sees Jean Grey* "Shit! MS. GREY!" *runs toward her* "I NEED TO TALK TO YOU ABOUT THE GROUP PROJECT!"

It'd be all love with everyone, but every so often I know I'd be overhearing mutant conversations saying people that look like me are getting shot down in the streets and just have to retort with a high-pitched "Ehhhhhhh. You're a telekinetic white dude . . . Don't nobody know that shit unless you're too lazy to get up and get the remote, homie." Now, if it's a mutant that looks like Beast or Nightcrawler saying that shit, that's different. I could legit see having to explain how Black Lives Matter. "Y'all shouldn't be rocking All Mutant Lives Matter shirts because the conversation happening now is to bring awareness to the Black lives being taken by police. Also, if we keeping it real, Black mutants are five times more likely to get killed than white mutants, so the shirts you made should say Black Mutant Lives Matter. What? It's true. Fuck you mean 'Why I always gotta bring race into it?' Really, I'ma Black mutant, homie. That's like two strikes. Look at Bling!, she's a queer Black woman who's a mutant, that's straight up four strikes. We serious right now?"

Listen, they could put me in as many classes with Iceman that they want, I wouldn't have any chill whatsoever. I'd have mad presentations on why Magneto was right in my social studies class. I'd be raw enough to rock a "Magneto Was Right" shirt while doing it too. Catch me up in Hank McCoy's class and he'd be talking about the proper procedure for time travel.

HANK MCCOY: Time is fluid. I know everyone wants to go
back and kill Hitler but—
ME: *high-pitched* Ehhhhhhh. I could name some people that
would go back and stop the transatlantic slave trade instead.
MCCOY: As tempting as that would be, the fragility of ti—
ME: You can keep talking, Mr. McCoy, and I'ma listen to
you keep talking, but I'm letting you know now if we
ever go back in time and you don't see me . . . you'll
know why. Also Rust Cohle the gawd told us "time is a
flat circle" so you wouldn't have to.

There'd come a time where I'd be called into the field for my first mission to see if I'd want to become an X-Man upon graduation. We'd be up against Mystique, Cyclops would be talking about our attack plan, and Xavier would be telling us the situation via telepathy as we land on-site.

CYCLOPS: X-Men, move ou—
ME: Hold up, Sunglass Hut Sensei. Xavier, what exactly did
Mystique do again?
XAVIER: She's attacking anti-mutant protestors and holding
them hostage.
ME: . . . Yeah. So, what's the problem? 'Cause I'm not . . .
Seeing. One.

Now, the way I see the days before my graduation plays out like this. Cyclops calling me into his office and hitting me with the real talk about my future and shit. If I wanna just go into society or stay on as an X-Man.

CYCLOPS: Let's talk about what do you wanna do after gradu—

ME: Hypothetically speaking, X-Force was the black-ops squad of the X-Men that merked threats before they happened, right?

CYCLOPS: . . . . Hypothetically speaking *gets up out of seat and closes the blinds* that would be the ideal goal for a black-ops division consisting of mutants. However, said division would be unassociated with the X-Men, operating without their knowledge or protection.

ME: Hypothetically, when can I start?

CYCLOPS: . . . You should take the Blackbird out for a ride at about 1300.

ME: 'Nuff said. *leaves office*

CYCLOPS: *does Birdman hand rub* My mutant.

Yo, put me up in X-Force and lemme run through these anti-mutant oppressors with my woes. I'm sorry but sometimes muthafuckas gots to go. I'd be with that shit, man. Tired of Xavier talking 'bout "protecting a world that fears and hates us." Fer real? Do you not see those big-ass Sentinels they send after our asses? These cats hate us so much they went out of their way and made a literal large-ass system of oppression in giant robot form. Fuck that noise, man. Why don't these anti-mutant humans get these Sentinels to help them out when they in a jam, then? Fuck, I gotta get jet lag for and help people in a different time zone when they got the Iron Giant walking around? Also, I got so many questions about Sentinels too. Who funded these shits? How are these shits allowed to just roam around, they not dropping property value? Who gave them this red-and-purple-candy paint job? I mean the X-Men's school is based in New York, so at least paint them in Yankees or Mets colors. The city officials really spent millions of taxpayers' money for these Sentinels? They really said, "Fuck the education fund, fuck the housing fund, and fuck all that. What we really need to do is fund these giant robots to harass mutants minding their own business. That's where it's at"?

I can't have that on me, man. I'm not having it. Fox Studios out here making horrible-ass movies about us and we let that shit stand? Naaaaah, man. No. They. Gots. To. Go. If my file from my time on X-Force ever became public record, I'd have Xavier calling me up and putting Magneto on the phone so he could tell me, "Yo, chiiiiill. You wylin'," but I'd tell them both, "All I'm saying is, the *Homo sapiens* ain't got no love for Magneto and Professor X? The *Homo sapiens* ain't got no love for Magneto and Professor X and the X-Men? We saved y'all asses how many times and y'all don't love us? Y'all don't love us? Well, let it be known, then!"

Go On: An Evergreen Comedic Series That Helped Me Navigate Loss

OMAR HOLMON,
aka I'm Mr. Cry on the Inside

HUMOR IS A beautiful lock-pick set, the perfect tool for any situation. Humor can open people up, it can get you out of trouble, it can even be a defense mechanism to protect you. However, these things usually stop short when death is involved. When dealing with the loss of someone, humor often becomes a tool without a "right time" to be used. To me though, humor is a way of making death, this infinite unavoidable circumstance . . . somehow a bit smaller.

> *Death is a joke you don't make*
> *once it's in the room*
>
> —Thuli Zuma

My first best friend in this world was my mother—she was my tag-team partner, my first audience, my first roommate. She died on September 9, 2011. Since that day it has not stopped being September 9, 2011. On the best days, I'm at her bedside still trying to make her laugh. On the worst days, it's the voicemail saying that she is gone, or my first step into the loud silence of her hospital room. She once told me, "It was always you and me against the world," and when my teammate needed me, I wasn't there. The last word I heard her say to me was "Go," assuring me I could go to a job interview and come back. But for the first time in my life, I was too late. My way of dealing with not being there when she died was not talking about it. The weight of it would pop up sometimes in strange places . . .

"Yeah, lemme get the strawberry ice cream with Reese's Pieces . . .
[*Oh god, she's really gone.*]
tears running down face but still wanting ice cream
. . . Lemme get some sprinkles on that too . . ."

. . . but I'd push it down and keep it moving. I didn't consciously deal with it until I was watching NBC's show *Go On* about a radio talk show host named Ryan King (played by Matthew Perry).

After losing his wife, Ryan goes right back to work as if nothing has happened. Worried about him, his boss and best friend, Steven, forces him to attend a support group. Under threat of losing his job, Ryan agrees, but doesn't take it seriously. While Lauren, the group counselor, is running late one day, Ryan invents a game for the group to determine once and for all who has the most tragic story. It's a tournament dubbed "March Sadness" by Owen, a kid that has been coming to counseling for months and remained quiet up to that point. It was the hilarity of this scene that got me hooked on the show's handling of loss and humor.

Lauren warns Ryan that if he doesn't deal with what's happened, he's going to explode. After learning the hard way that she is right, Ryan reveals to the group (and us) that his wife died texting him while driving. "She needed to tell me to buy a bag of coffee, so at least it was important . . . I don't know how to do this."

It's weird how my real-life loss connected me with this group of fictional characters: Anne, who lost her wife; Owen, whose brother was in a coma; Fausta, whose children and husband were deported, as well as others dealing with their different issues.

In one episode, Ryan thinks he's going crazy as he begins to see his dead wife, Janie, around the house. I'd had a similar experience. I was sleeping, but I could swear someone was sitting beside me petting my hair. It felt like my mother beside me, and we were back in our old house. I knew it couldn't be real, but that familiarity of home resonated so strongly that I needed it to be. I was in that state where you aren't sleeping anymore but can't immediately open your eyes. I finally forced myself to wake up, sat upright, and called out, "Mom?" This was the first time I had said her name aloud in an empty room in a year. When Ryan brings this up, fellow griever Anne assures him that it's normal. I began to feel relief as well.

Go On was never preachy in its approach to navigating through loss, it was always sincere and honest, which is what draws me back to rewatching it every so often. I related most to Owen. He only opened up to Ryan about his brother being in a coma organically through their mutual love of video games. Owen hadn't been able to bring himself to visit his brother, so Ryan volunteers to go into the room for him, to talk to Owen's brother and sing to him, as Owen said it was something they always did for each other . . .

It turns out to be a prank—Owen sends Ryan to a stranger's room—the way he and his brother used to mess with each other. In doing that with Ryan, he gets the push he needs to finally go and see his actual brother. Ryan gets him back beautifully with a prank that makes Owen believe he broke the vase holding Janie's ashes. It's this playfulness within the group as everyone grows closer that kept drawing me in.

I felt like I had found a shortcut to talking about everything I needed to unpack by watching these characters do it for me. This show was my group where I didn't have to speak but still processed everything internally. And right when I thought this defense I had been developing through this loss was helping me out, the show goes and calls me out on relying on it too heavily. For me, my mother dying was the worst thing that could happen. Now that it's happened, there's nothing left to be afraid of. This mentality changed my personality. I became way more blunt in how I gave advice/opinions, indifferent to good or bad things that happened to me (how do I phrase this without sounding like a sociopath?), and far more comfortable talking with people about grief and loss. It's hard to put this into specific words, but the defense I'm talking about is a shift in how I've come to engage with emotions and people. Even when using humor.

Here's an example of what I mean. When I was eating with friends not too long ago, one friend got a phone call from his mother. When he rejoined the conversation, I asked if everything was all right. He replied, "Yeah," in a tone like "my mom's being a bit much" manner.

ME: Oh, trouble with your very-much-alive mom, hmmm?
    You know how hard it is to hug a field on Mother's Day?
HIM: Well, she just made a suicide threat again, so . . .

The table got quiet and the "oh shit" look instantly appeared on the faces of our friends sitting across from us. I stared at him for a moment before saying my initial thought aloud, which was . . .

ME: DAMMIT!
HIM: *nodding and smiling* Yeah! Yeeeeeeeeah!
ME: Arghhhhhhh, dead mom doesn't beat that, does it?!
HIM: Nope! Dead mom doesn't trump suicidal mom, Omar.
    What now?!

We were laughing about this while our friends were looking at us like, "The fuck is wrong with y'all?" He then talked about this issue with his mom (which none of us had previously been aware of). In turn, I told him about the mental illness my mother dealt with (which none of them knew about either) and how it was growing up around that. We weren't playing pain Olympics but instead showing that, although we weren't able to fully relate to each other's experiences, we had a parallel of understanding. That understanding comes from a bond through our black humor. Not everyone can have or hold the conversation in that way because not everyone has gone through or dealt with what we were talking about. Casually talking about that while making jokes looks wild from the outside in, I know, but my friend and I both have that same shift with how we engage, so this was a comforting conversation. However, *Go On* literally talked about this, with the grief counselor Lauren telling the group and Ryan specifically that you shouldn't rely on that newfound defense or personality shift to navigate through life at all times, because it can hurt or make others uncomfortable unintentionally. I knew she was right 'cause a friend told me that they hated crying in front of me 'cause I would just look at them like a science experiment. Sooooo, that's something I continuously work on.

Go On thought of everything, dammit. I loved the show so much, and the fact that it was canceled after only a season wasn't fair but was fitting, as that's just how life is, isn't it? You take the great things for granted and get so hurt when they're taken away. My mom used to tell me constantly, "I'm not always going to be around to do this for you," to which I'd reply, "But you're too stubborn to die," every single time. The day she was on her deathbed she told me, "When I go, don't bring me back." In that moment the only thing I could say was "Given the weight of the current situation, that's the most gangsta shit you ever said to me." The thing is, no parent should ever have to bury their own child, so a child burying their parent becomes this privilege, a privilege none want but still have to acknowledge.

I'm still workin' on it, but this show helped me realize that it's all right if it's September 9, 2011, today or even tomorrow as well, but when it stops being that day, I don't have to feel guilty about it because moving on doesn't mean forgetting. It just means you remember in your own way, even if it happens to be recalling all the funny moments. How we choose to go on isn't important, just that when the time comes, we do.

The Sobering Reality of
Actual Black Nerd Problems

WILLIAM EVANS,
aka The Reluctant Sword

OCTOBER 31 WAS a Friday, and despite the fact there was already plenty of reason to celebrate because it was Halloween and the end of my workweek, it was also the opening day of Ohio's comic con as a part of the Wizard World circuit. I clocked out of work, threw on some jeans and my *Attack on Titan* Survey Corps shirt, and headed straight for the convention, since there were precious hours left in the day. Once I made it down there, grabbed my press pass (we outchea), and made it to the floor, it was as I expected: steeped in glorious geekery. As Leslie Light, a Black Nerd Problems editor and writer, had written about so eloquently before, not everyone can make it to New York or San Diego for the mother and father of all cons in North America, and the smaller ones definitely have value.

As this was my first year attending, I was just trying to make the rounds and soak in as much as I could without committing to anything or really planning on writing about it (you'll see how that worked out). At some point, between my buying an original sketch of Master Chief and taking a picture of a homie in an awesome Deathstroke cosplay (*Arkham Origins* edition), a guy came up to me pointing emphatically: "Awesome shirt, man!" I thanked him. It is in fact an awesome shirt, so I get that a lot.

"Check this out." He put a long box on the table in front of us and pulled out a replica Survey Corps blade. While not sharpened steel, it was solid metal and polished, a nice collectible whether you intended to hang it on the wall or wander into the woods beyond Columbus and hunt Titans. I nerded out with my newfound friend and enthusiast for a moment before making my way to the very display he had made the purchase from.

The display was glorious: just about every bladed weapon from nerd lore was on the tables, all handled with care, all available for a price. There was Jon Snow's Longclaw, Cloud Strife's Buster sword, Nariko's Heavenly Sword, and many, many more. I picked up Buster and marveled at its weight. This thing was awesome. I had no idea where I would put it, but that doesn't mean I didn't contemplate dropping some credits on it. I mean, come on: *FINAL FANTASY VII* MEMORABILIA!

And then I got really, really sober and put it down. I smiled at the vendor, told him how great all the stuff looked, then walked away. Maybe it was because the autopsy of twenty-two-year-old Darrien Hunt, the cosplayer in Utah, was just released and confirmed that he was shot at least six times by police, at least four of them in his back. Darrien was killed in September 2014 for carrying a plastic sword as part of his *Samurai Champloo* Mugen cosplay, about a month before I stood in front of a vendor and walked away from his awesome collection of replicas. Darrien never drew the fake sword, but when the guns were pointed at him, he ran. Away from them. And they shot him to death anyway. Suddenly, the idea of carrying around a giant sword wasn't as appealing.

I want to be clear and realistic about something: I am aware of two things simultaneously. I am über-aware of the violence against Black men and boys based solely upon the fact that someone was scared of them by default. I talk about that a lot, constantly really, because Trayvon Martin and Jordan Davis and Michael Brown and Darrien and . . . and . . . and . . . happen a lot. Constantly really. But I am also aware of my personal disposition. When the debates raged on after Michael Brown's death at the hands of Darren Wilson in Ferguson, Missouri, one of the people arguing in favor of the killing was Ben Stein. He answered the pleas of people stating that Michael was unarmed by saying, "He was armed with his incredibly strong, scary self." From a physical stature, I would be counted among the strong, scary men Stein refers to. But I'm also older than most of those men I named. Maybe my life has been saved multiple times without my knowing because some cop or Second Amendment lifer thought that older translated to "not as much of a threat." Who knows what magical combination of Black and wide shoulders and graying beard unlocks the secret of being Black and safe to exist. But Walter Scott was fifty when he was shot in the back. Philando Castile was thirty-two. Maybe the lesson is that nothing truly saves you.

I don't know the answer, but my age has brought me at least one thing: recognizing what I hold precious. When I was younger, I was much more reckless. My interactions with police officers were seldom cordial, but I had been conditioned to think, "This is a thing that happens." One friend got pulled over and got a ticket. One friend got pulled over three months later and never made it home. As a teenager, I thought the outcomes of interacting with the police were random. "Nothing to be done." And because of that, I took less care. I wasn't antagonistic with cops, but I seldom entered a situation thinking, "I must do whatever it takes to get home alive." Because I didn't think it was up to me. And maybe even scarier to think about in retrospect, I'm not sure I even thought it was up to them.

But you get older and you accumulate things. Like a sense of purpose, a direction. For me, mostly it's been a family. I don't think I have a particularly healthy approach to my own mortality, but I am very concerned about the effect my premature death would have on my wife and daughter. Now, I'm at least aware of unnecessary risks. No matter how mind-boggling fucked that is. And that's the point really. How the fuck is it that my Friday-night comic con experience was hijacked by me doing the math on if I could get to my car safely with a giant, cartoonish sword strapped across my back? Why was this something that concerned me at all? It sure as hell didn't concern the cool white dude who had shown me his Levi blade earlier. If I'd run into him again and if he'd asked me if I picked one up myself, I wouldn't know how to tell him about my reluctance to open myself up to possible harm. I wouldn't know how to engage him on a level that says, "I'm glad we met and share an affinity for this same piece of art, but because I'm Black and aware of the world around me, I don't feel comfortable indulging myself at the same level you do." It's a tough conversation to have. It's a tougher situation to articulate. It's toughest though just trying to live with that doubt in your head.

We were probably naive for a while. Even people such as myself that talk about the violence toward Black bodies in all manners of aggression thought that nerd shit was off-limits or at least not viewed as a threat. "It's a costume!" we would all yell in our glass cases, now fogged and yet unbroken with our exasperation. Darrien Hunt changed that.

And we didn't need him to be shot in the back while running for his life AWAY FROM COPS that had their guns drawn on him, but it's a lesson we learned nonetheless. The name Black Nerd Problems originated from funny vignettes that Omar and I used to trade back and forth that really had to do with relating our nerddom to other people. Like, "If she legit thinks *Gotham* is the new *The Wire* . . . #BlackNerdProblems" (from Omar). It was fun and comical and facetious. But a real Black Nerd Problem is not knowing if your cosplay will get you killed. Or if phaser = wallet = forty-one empty shell casings later. Or feeling compelled to write this chapter in the first place.

Bury the Stringer Bell
but Let Idris Live

WILLIAM EVANS,
aka The Dude That Knows Where the Fuck Wallace Is

ALL PRAISE DUE to Idris, fine as he wanna be, every man—and I do mean every gotdamn man—cursing his own genetic makeup cuz of Idris. Got more jobs than that Black woman you still ain't paid for the emotional labor. Got more talent than a bored-ass Jamie Foxx after his show got canceled. Dude canceled the apocalypse in *Pacific Rim*, then got COVID-19 and canceled that shit for himself too. Idris, never change, never stop having your Madonna moment, your marrying beauties half your age even though you look three-fifths of your age your damn self.

But it's time to admit that Stringer Bell—yes, that String; yes, that Bell—might have been the most beloved punk ass in TV history. String the Destroyer. String the original Roc Nation brunch president. String the Sunday Truce–Breaker. Was a terrible fucking person. And no, not the "well, he was a drug dealer, of course he was terrible" moral high ground terrible. I mean even on *The Wire*, where there were no angels, he was still a lower demon terrible.

String studied the game, watched the film, knew all his history, and still blew a 3–1 lead. String came up in the drug murder game and only bodied his own people. Sexy-ass Judas. Chicken hawk Black sheep in wolf clothing. *Tropic Chocolate Thunder*. He's the dude pretending to be the dude pretending to be another dude. He never won shit. Stringer Bell ain't won shit except a *Drug GQ* magazine cover and summa cum laude of a Baltimore community college. Show me a Stringer Bell accomplishment and I'll show you a nigga doing half a life sentence for his decisions. String's face too pretty for tatted tears.

String will date your partner though. Let you take that bid and pipe your beloved. There's some hoes in this house and String is *Home Alone* with no intruders. Stringer Bell is Mr. Steal Your Girl. Or correction, Stringer Bell is Mr. "Let You Rot in a Jail Cell, Kill Your Underlings, and Then Pay Someone to Murder You in the Prison Library" Steal Your Girl. You ain't feedin' D'Angelo's kid, String. You ain't taking that little nigga to the Druid Hill Park. At least take him in as a ward, String. You ain't got no Ned Stark in you, bruh. West Baltimore lookin' like Iron Islands under your watch, String.

How you gonna set up two of the most dangerous men in the game against each other? How you gonna work Robert's Rules into the drug game? Does the chair know we gonna look like some punk-ass bitches, String? How you gonna kill a kid cuz he no longer likes killin' other kids, String? How you obsessed with no paper trails but you run a copy machine business? How you let a downtown dude steal your money like that? How you gonna try and send your lead enforcer on a suicide mission cuz your feelings hurt? How you ain't hard enough for this game, String? How you not smart enough for this game, String?

You know why we loved Avon, String? Cuz that man stood for something. Like, the entirely wrong shit, but he stood for something. Avon didn't want nothin' from nobody except his corners and maybe to drop some bodies on the block here and there. But the bodies were to remind people that those were his corners. What you ever stand for, String? Besides to take an oath in court. Besides to leave a prison visit when D'Angelo punked you about Wallace.

You know why we loved Omar, String? Cuz that man had a code. Don't never put your gun on nobody who wasn't in the game. What code did you have, String? Besides speaking in codes to make sure you weren't caught on tape talkin' that drug talk? Besides giving customers the code to use the copy machines in your store?

I'm sorry if Stringer Bell was your favorite. I'm sorry you find Baltimore Benedict Arnold sexy. I wish he had a floating eye. I wish he had a hook for a hand. Like a Captain Hook–type metal appendage covered in smallpox. We didn't ask for a perfect presentation of a man just to get an articulate Demogorgon. I'm just glad we didn't get a Stringer prequel story with Idris. I would've watched every second of it.

An Open Letter to the Starks: Y'all Should've Taken Better Care of Your Direwolves

OMAR HOLMON,
aka Middle Earth's Direwolf Dog Walker

HEY, STARK CHILDRENS,

Gather round and lemme holler at y'all with a story for a minute 'bout some loyalty shit. I like dogs, but I'm not a die-hard dog person. I'm not the "you can lick me on the mouth" type, know what I mean? Now, my brother, Travis, *loves* dogs though. In 2003, he brought this little black pit bull puppy with a white arrow on his nose over to Mom's house. Travis named him Exodus. I was playing with the puppy then watched as he wandered by the kitchen table. Mom, knowing what was coming, shouted, "OhoOo—OoOoO—OooO—TRAVIS! He 'bout to pee!" I took my sock off and tossed it at the puppy, he understood the gesture and peed on it. He even looked back at me midstream as if to say, "Aye, man, thank you. You're all right." I lost a sock that day but gained a friend in Exodus. Whenever we met, he always remembered me for the assist.

It needs to be said that Exodus was the coolest dog I've ever met in my life. When he walked into a room everyone would go

WILLIAM EVANS AND OMAR HOLMON

"Ayyyyyyye! Exodus!" like he was Norm from *Cheers*. Exodus never barked and felt more like the chillest person than just a dog. When not engaging with anyone he'd just stare out the window picking out which squirrel he was gon' to fade once he made it outside. One time when visiting him at Travis's place, Exodus was on top of the balcony while I was in the driveway, a good forty feet away. I saw a huge snake Harlem-shaking his way toward me. Before I even reached the "shit" portion in my "Ohhhhh shit" yell, this dude Exodus was already by my side, muscled up like, "What's the problem? Who got a fucking problem?" For years we'd run through the woods together, and even in his old age he'd be limping but still goin', which just reminded me that the homie was getting on in his years. Exodus was getting worse as he got older. One day he sneezed so hard that it shook his head violently and left him bleeding from the nose profusely. My brother had to make a hard call on letting Ex live after that, as he could literally die from blood loss should it happen again (which it easily could), or putting him down. The doctors weren't telling Travis which way to go with his decision, so Travis did what he thought was best not for himself or the family, but for Exodus. In September 2015, Exodus, the most chill dog I ever came to know and love, his watch ended.

Now I said all that to say this: if I was living in y'all's world as a Stark and Exodus was my pit bull–breed direwolf, on my fucking life if shit went down and he dies fighting beside or for me and mine, I'm not coming back alive either. I'm going Fall Out Boy (*goin' down swinging*) back-to-back with Ex like the cover of *Lethal Weapon* on some "I'm not gon' bury my direwolf! My direwolf gon' bury me!" But you fucking Stark kids, man. You fucking Stark kids out here losing y'all's partnas? I said partnas! Not pets. Not companions. Muhfuckin' partnas, ride or dies, your fucking sigil bannermen out to the wild, man. Couldn't be me. Y'all got the game all the way fucked up. Fuck the North remembering right now, the hood still remembers how Sansa's wolf, Lady, went out. Lady was the first Stark direwolf to take the fucking L, an L that wasn't even hers to take too. Ned had to fuckin' ice Lady because Cersei was pettier than all fuck, man. Shit, you mean to tell me the glass ceiling comes for your gender no matter the species too, doe? For really real? Ned walked over to her somber as hell and Lady was like, "Oh hey, man . . . you gon' take this collar off? Kinda tight around the neck, nah mean? Oh, you're petting me? Never spent much time doing that before but okay . . . ummm, what's with the knife? Whoa! WHOA! AYE, I AIN'T E'UN DO NUT-TIN'!" and she really didn't, remember? Lady got *Gone Girl*'d because earlier, Joffrey was being a fuckboy then turned that fuckboyedness toward Arya, holding her at sword point. Arya's dog, Nymeria, saw that shit and kept it a fucking buck running up on Joffrey with the chompers to his hand. Arya tossed Joffrey's piece into the river and they bounced from the scene of the crime. Arya had Nymeria dip 'cause she knew they'd try to earth her for what she did. What they didn't know was that Cersei would take the punishment out on Lady. Fucking foul, man. Lady, you deserved better, you pretty thing!

Then they came for Robb Stark's dog. The big homie Grey Wind, man. Grey Wind was the fucking Arn Anderson enforcer of Rob's army. Grey Wind grew the fuck up and was fighting by Robb Stark's side copping more bodies on the battlefield than your local morgue. Grey Wind was the definition of an animal, man. My man was taking no shit. NO SHIT. When you got a direwolf going into war with you? Going off and collecting fades all on his lonesome, then coming back to you as if clocking off of a nine-to-five? You better do everything in your power to keep that muhfucka alive. That canine Grey Wind was real as hell, but what Robb do? Had him locked up 'cause the boy would get antsy around folk. Grey Wind got that taste for blood and was lookin' at folks like they weren't even fit to manicure his paws. Then what the hell happened? Robb Stark got fucking GOT at the Red Wedding while his homie Grey Wind, aka the Bad Weatherman, was locked up.

Them cats came out after betraying Robb and went straight for Grey Wind to kill him. Grey Wind had to be like, "Oh, this is that bullshit I was talking about. *10 stabs* Y'all wanna stab me? Y'all wanna kill the realest soldier in the platoon? *34 stabs* You ungrateful-ass bastards. *56 stabs* YOU WANNA EUTHANIZE ME? WELL, COME ON, THEN! *67 stabs . . . 87 stabs . . . 109 stabs . . . 118 stabs . . .* Shoulda ran up north with Nymeria when I had the chance . . ." Man, remember back to what Robb said when the Starks first found their pups and Theon was bein' a buzzkill saying, "The pups may die anyway, despite all you do," and Robb chimed in with, "They won't die. We won't let them die." Okay, Robb. Sure. Fucking sure. Y'all two for fucking two right now and the count only increasing.

big sigh What the fuck, Starks? The direwolves are like your own personal version of '90s Death Row Suge Knight. Robb, the fuck you locking him up for? "Ooooh, he gets really bloodthirsty and antsy." . . . And? Muhfuckas out here choppin' ya daddy's head off on the block, kid! Trust NO-damn-body. The North remembered that shit till the (Michael) Boltons came up in the spot with the fuck shit. Fuck shit has killed more people and especially direwolves in this series than . . . I can't even finish the joke because I figuratively can't think of anything else. Fuck shit is the leading cause of animal companion death in Westeros. Fuck shit almost got Jon Snow's dog, Ghost, clipped on that dumb shit too when Jon locked him away. Jon locked his boy up and got the acupuncture treatment to the abs in a mutiny after he became head of Castle Black. Jon Snow came back to life and Ghost was lookin' at him like, "And that's what ya dumb ass gets for putting me away. The fuck wrong with you, man? You think an oath gon' stop fuckboys from doing fuck shit? Hell no! You know what stops them? Me, these fangs, and that Valyrian steel piece on your hip with me on the hilt. Lockin' me up . . . must be out your fucking mind, man. I should howl at Nymeria to get me 'cause y'all on that dumb shit up here."

Ghost made it out alive there and thank *GOT*, but then . . . then they got my boy, man. They got Shaggydog, man. Shaggydog was my fucking favorite direwolf. He had only like, what, four appearances on-screen? Shags had the best fucking entrance. Stepping from out the shadows down in the underground crypts of the Stark family, growlin' at Summer and Bran till Rickon called for him while stepping out the pitch blackness of the underground tunnel. "Heeeeeeere, Shaggy-dooooooooog." THAT WAS MY SHIT. You gon' tell me the only all-Black everything dog, the wildest, most fuck-all-y'all wolf in this piece got fucking GOT when Rickon and Osha got caught and taken to the Boltons? THEY KILLED SHAGGYDOG OFF-FUCKING-SCREEN? THEY KILLED MY MANS OFF-SCREEN, DOE? COME ON, MAN! NOT SHAGS! NOT FUCKIN' SHAGS. On everything, if that was me? Rickon, if I was you, I wouldn't be around to see how that shit played out with the Boltons, because once you kill my dog, I'm killing everybody. There's no taking me in alive or unconscious, you gonna have to merk me because I'm only here to settle the fucking score with no mercy rule in place.

Now we come to Summer. Everybody is like, "Oh, Summer sacrificed himself for Bran when them White Walkers were attacking him during his meeting with the three-eyed raven." The fuck he did. Bran, Summer been there for your ass since you got knocked out the tower. Guarding your ass day in and night out. Letting you warg into his mind free of rent and shit, escaping with your ass passed up north, encountering fuckboys human and magical, and then when y'all finally got some peace in the caves with the three-eyed raven, you had to go and be THAT guy. You using your wargin' skills like it's the internet to go back into the past and shit. Summer lookin' at you like:

"Aye, man, maybe you should listen to the old raisin-lookin' dude in the tree and not stay in the past all long . . . Oh, you just . . . you just gon' warg back there anyway. Okay . . . You know I see what you see, right? Oh, you just . . . see an army of frozen popsicles and you going to walk through them . . . oooookay? Oh, you see the fucking original Mr. Freeze ice king but you not gon' run? He sees you . . . he sees you! ANNNNNNNND HE GRABBED YOU! ANNNNNNNND HE KNOWS WHERE THE FUCK WE AT! GREAT! FUCKING GREAT! Oh . . . oh, y'all goin' back into the past . . . OH, GREAT, YOU SEE HODOR BACK WHEN HE WAS IN HIS PRIME AND YOU STARIN' INTO HIS SOUL AND YOU JUST CREATED A FUCKING TIME PARADOX AND ALL HE IS HEARING IS HOLD THE FUCKING DOOR! GREEEEEEEAT! THIS IS ALL FUCKING PERFECT! THE FUCK, DUDE! BUTTERFLY EFFECT, MAN! I'M A WOLF AND EVEN I KNOW ABOUT THE FUCKING BUTTERFLY EFFECT, OH MY GAAAAWD!

"You just went back in fucking time and gave Hodor a K-22 paper jam! Wait . . . HOW THE FUCK DID THE SNOW MEN GET HERE SO FAST? They're killing the leafy Cabbage Patch Kids now? OH, SHIT, THEY CLAPPED THE RAISIN DUDE IN THE TREE TOO? OOOOOOH MY FUCKING GAAAWD, YOU GOT TO BE SHITTING ME. *sees Meera calling to him as Hodor drags Bran to escape* MMMMM—yeaaaaaah *looks at invading horde* uhmmmm *looks back at the squad* . . . You know what? . . . Fuck it. The afterlife gotta be better than this shit. West Side Westeros wigits! Was bumpin'? Folk gang! Gang! Gang! Gang! Gang!!"

Please, Summer ain't sacrifice shit. Summer just saw his boy fuck up the damn timeline . . . or maybe it was supposed to happen all along, or maybe because Bran did that . . . You know what? Nope. Summer didn't even wanna figure that shit out or deal with the comments section in the next scroll that got sent out by raven. This shit is wyld out here, man. Y'all Starks had the red and black nWo wolf pack, man. Y'all had a literal six-pack, man. Y'all Stark kids were soul connected to the views from the six (literally) and now y'all down to fucking two.

Sansa, you exempt from this 'cause the L found you and Lady. Y'all ain't seek that shit out . . . I mean you coulda told the truth instead of pleading the "I dunno" when the king asked what happened, but whatever. Robb and Rickon . . . SMDH. Bran, I don't even wanna fucking make eye contact with your ass for another five episodes, dude. Arya, good shit. You knew what was up before all of us. Jon, I wish I could say good job for not doing that dumb shit again, but as soon as you got a dragon you forgot about ya boy. You left Ghost up north after he went to war for you in the Battle of the Bastards without so much as an "All right, well, see you the fuck later, then." Ghost straight up missing an ear, tail can't even wag, bloodstains all in the white fur, and you really just left dude with a fucking look like, "Aiight, man." Ain't even pet that good boy, you fucking loser. Then what happened? That drama went down with Dany, forcing you to join the Free Folk beyond the wall. You ran back into Ghost, smiling like "hey, boy," and Ghost looked at you with the Thanos "You could not live with your own failure. Where did that bring you? Back to me" stare into the windows of your damn soul. Ghost still as disgusted with you as we all are. Sheeeeeeeeit, Ghost and Nymeria . . . you all we got, baby. Good job making it out alive, y'all. Y'all ain't get the *All Dogs Go to Heaven* route like the rest of your family so wrongly got and we all applaud your jerseys going up in the PetSmart rafters. Job well done, y'all. Job well fucking done.

EPILOGUE

After a few months Travis got another pit bull, a gray one this time around. A rescue he named Raja. Raja was used as a bait dog for fighting, so he got them Jon Snow scars on him, but he is very happy with his new life now.

Haikyuu!! Roughly Translated Means "Ball Is Life"

OMAR HOLMON,
aka You Got Swerved

LEMME TELL YOU something you should already know. There's an anime for just about everything. You want pirates and ninjas? Anime has you covered. Cooking competition? There's an anime for that. Magical girls saving the day? Anime put that shit on the map, pay homage. See, *pours ginger ale into a highball glass as if it's scotch* the beautiful thing about a good or well-written anime is that it'll make you care about something that's not in your area of expertise or realm of experience *sips ginger ale slow because it burns like scotch*. Now, there's anime you watch and then there's anime you get immersed in. When Will and a few other friends were talking about this anime on Netflix called *Haikyuu!!*, I decided to check out a few episodes at 8:00 p.m. one random night not knowing what it was about. I stayed up till 4:00 a.m., watching that show entirely enthralled. What's it about, you ask? It's an anime show about high school boys' volleyball teams going hard in the muthafucking paint.

Soon as *Haikyuu!!* had its protagonist, Shōyō Hinata (aka "Jump-

189

man, Jumpman Jumpman, that boy spiking something"), stepping on the court saying, "Y'all smell all that IcyHot in the air? Woooo, we gon' be ~~hoopin~~ nettin' on the courts here today, boi," I was hooked. If you haven't seen this series, I guess you don't know ball is life. Here's the quick rundown: Hinata is Kevin Hart in height but got these tall dreams of spiking volleyballs in faces after seeing Karasuno High School's #10 volleyball player, dubbed the Tiny Giant, in action at nationals on television as a kid. The Tiny Giant is Katt Williams in height but Vince Carter in hops. This is what gets Hinata into volleyball. However, his middle school has no boys' volleyball club, so he practices with the girls' team trying to get a setter for spikes. His friends who are all involved in other sports join his janky-ass pickup volleyball club so he can at least play in one actual volleyball game. They play and get murdered by Kageyama Tobio's team. Kageyama is the setter for his squad and can play every position, and they bust Hinata's shit in. I mean ESPN-highlight-reel type embarrassing ass-busting. We see that Hinata has no technique or experience, but his talent, reflexes, and hops are disgusting. I'm talking dunk-from-the-foul-line disgusting. Hinata's raw athleticism is so nasty it puts Kageyama on notice. Hinata swears that he'll bust Kageyama's ass one day. A year later they end up at the same high school as freshmen on the Karasuno Crows high school boys' volleyball team. A team now known as fallen champions, or the "flightless crows," since the Tiny Giant's departure.

The great thing about this anime is that it doesn't solely focus on just Hinata and Kageyama. This is a sports anime that focuses on the entirety of the team. The starting lineup for the Karasuno Crows is as follows: team captain Daichi Sawamura, ace Asahi Azumane, left-wing spiker Ryūnosuke Tanaka, libero Yū Nishinoya, middle blocker Shōyō Hinata, setter Tobio Kageyama, and blocker Kei Tsukishima, with vice-captain and substitute setter Kōshi Sugawara and pinch server Tadashi Yamaguchi. There are more folks on the bench too that come to shine as well, so it's important to know all the names of the players as well as the team managers Kiyoko Shimizu and her apprentice, Hitoka Yachi, 'cause these muthafuckas out here doing work! Everybody plays a part in making this team wild card challengers. As far as I'm concerned this squad is the '92 Olympics Dream Team. The series creator, Furudate Haruichi, captures the essence of teamwork and that's what won me over. Mind you, I'm no expert in volleyball.

Back in my teen years at Hackensack High School (go Comets!) I ran track, but volleyball was my favorite spring activity in gym class. Every day before track practice, my best friends, Phil and Elvis, along with our other teammates and I, would go to the main gym and play volleyball. We played so often that the girls' volleyball team would play against us before their practice. It always started out fun and cordial until the girls got warmed up and started spiking on us. Looking back, I now realize that this was where we all learned about intersectional feminism, 'cause those girls came together to Stone Cold Steve Austin mudhole stomp the shit out of us once the score got a little too close for their liking. Mind you, there wasn't a damn thing we could do about it either. One time, I saw my boy take a jump serve to the chest, North Face still on, and he got laid out. I stood there lookin' at his chalk outline, then at the server, and she had her blowout blowing in the wind (there wasn't even a draft in there) while pointing at us to pick out who was gon' get that pain next.

That ain't stop us though. We'd still be fighting on that underdog shit. I'll never forget seeing Phil, a 220-pound shot-putter in track, dive to dig up the ball and slap it to me with his left hand as his chest hit the floor. I bumped it up on instinct just as Elvis Allen Iverson'd himself into the air and knocked it over the net. We're all cheering as the ball looks like a prayer to God floating in the air. Yeah, well, that prayer got stamped "return to sender" as Tamika jumped up to hit the ball full force for a spike. She Onyx slammed (the rap group, not the Pokémon) the rock right in front of us while shouting, "Get that weak shit outta here." I'd hear her saying that in my head for the rest of the year, because she sat behind me in social studies and whispered it to me repeatedly.

I relive that shit every time I watch *Haikyuu!!* I love it. I then realized exactly how deep in the *Haikyuu!!* fandom I was when I found myself buying a Karasuno Crows cosplay uniform. It is the only cosplay uniform I own and will ever need. These kids built different, man. These other school volleyball teams kept talking about how the Karasuno Crows use to be great but been trash for dumb long now. The way they talk about the "flightless crows" would make you think it's been like ten or twenty years since this volleyball team has seen greatness. The team only been bad for like four years, yo! Like damn, the old coach had to retire, and things fell apart, it happens. The third-years Daichi, Sugawara, and Asahi had to hold it down for three years till they got this all-star roster, matched with an enthusiastic faculty advisor, Ittetsu Takeda, who got the old coach Ukai's grandson, Keishin Ukai, to be the new coach. They were tired of being called flightless crows, yo. Teams calling these dudes' skills butt to their face. Maaaaaaan, they don't say that shit no mo when the Karasuno Crows step on the court! The powerhouse schools kept thinking they'd dog walk them Crows and wound up eating crow. These boys busted they asses for three anime seasons to make it to nationals in season four.

Look at the résumé! They took on Date Tech and its Iron Wall. Date Tech specialized in blocking spikes. They blocked Asahi so much prior to the start of the series that that grown-ass-lookin' man had PTSD from not being able to get a spike off. Had that man looking at his hands thinkin', "Am I even an ace?" Karasuno took their Iron Wall down piece by piece—piece by fucking piece—for Asahi to get his confidence back as the goddamn ace of the team. Asahi sent them a spike that had the same stank on it as Mercury during retrograde. Then they beat Aoba Johsai and its powerhouse setter and server Tōru Oikawa. Oikawa's serves packed the same strength as a fucking howitzer and was blowing the team apart. Them serves never saw a Burger King commercial in their life because they weren't letting anybody have it their way. That boy's serves were a thing of beauty, man. Karasuno had no choice but to just brace for impact. But still, Karasuno pushed the Aoba Johsai team so hard that they had that boy Oikawa crashing into the announcer table just to make a set from out of bounds to keep the ball in play. That pretty boy crashed into a table and stumbled back up into the game hustlin' hard. Still got bodied. Who next?! Who else wanted it with the Brandon Lee–blessed Crows of Karasuno High?! Even Shiratorizawa Academy, one of the top eight teams in all of Japan, had to kiss the fucking ring. Its captain and super-ace Wakatoshi Ushijima was talking all that shit about Karasuno being nothing. All that shit about crushing the young jumpman Hinata, and what happened? Dem Crows mobb deeped Shiratorizawa Academy on the court with their teamwork. Ain't nobody fucking with Karasuno High of the concrete parking lot. Well . . . actually a lot of teams fucking with them now that they in nationals.

Listen, as it stands, Karasuno is facing Inarizaki High. Its boys' volleyball slogan is "We don't need the memories." It became my second-favorite team on the strength of that slogan alone. That slogan sounds hard in any context. You know a team strong as fuck when its slogan is better than a presidential campaign slogan. Yo, watching Karasuno in tournaments and now nationals is stressful as fuck for me, man. This is my NBA Finals. Y'all talking 'bout ball is life in terms of basketball?! Nah, man, please know when you hear me screaming "ball is life" I'm talking about these anime high-stakes high school volleyball matches. My wife had never seen the show, so I rewatched it with her and saw her crying when Tsukishima, the most lax and analytical member of Karasuno, screamed in excitement after getting a winning block against Ushijima from Shiratorizawa. She wiped her tears away saying, "What the fuck?! It's high school volleyball, why am I crying?! Why is the show so good?!" I looked at her and said, "It's okay. Ball is life, yo." She looked back at me and yelled, "BALL IS LIFE."

I ain't ever seen a team want the W as hard as these Karasuno Crow boys. Daichi the team captain got knocked out crashing into Tanaka when they both dove for a ball. My man lost a tooth and was bleeding from the mouth. He told Tanaka, "My fault, you called it but I couldn't stop my body. That's on me. But hey, look, you put us up in points." That's how you lead muthafuckas on a court while you get taken off the court. Daichi was out there putting his parents' dental insurance to use for the love of the game, baby. That's the heart I'm talking about. That's the captain of a team I wanna serve under. Matter of fact, *Haikyuu!!* is the anime universe I wanna live in. *Haikyuu!!* is where I wanna own a mortgage. This whole atmosphere is where I'd thrive.

I don't even have to be on the volleyball team. Lemme be the water boy. Lemme get these kids hydrated with Alaskan glacier water. Fuck, I'll even be the ball boy just so I could say I was there to witness the greatness. I would love to be on the team, but the way my passion works, they'd have to censor my trash talk. Soon as the shit talking started from another team, I'd make it a point to receive every ball in play. I'm talking running outta bounds, jumping off walls, diving into the audiences for this shit. That's me. That ball ain't touching the ground on my watch. Not while I'm breathing. Not with these teams out here saying we flightless crows. Saying we can't and ain't fly when that's literally our volleyball club slogan? Lemme put the Denzel Washington voice on as I say this cause no. Nooooo. I don't accept that. Ever. I reject that. Karasuno ain't come all this way just to say we came this far. I would still be civil and shake hands with the other team after we win. I just noticed each team that loses always says "We'll beat you next time" respectfully, and Karasuno members are always polite in telling them "We won't lose!" in response. Listen, if any team steps to me after a game saying that it'll beat me next time, I'm letting it know, it gon' get its shit rocked . . . again. Fuck they think this is? Our team captain lost a tooth for a dive. Y'all ain't got that kinda heart. Y'all soft. Your spikes felt like sprinkles being placed on cupcakes. Weak. Your serves were nothing but soft serve ice cream. Lacking. Fuck outta here with that shit. Listen, I'm all for friendly competition, but they are not ready for the real-cash shit level of trash talk I'd bring to the court when provoked.

Haikyuu!! got me wanting a #13 Karasuno Crows jersey, man. I'm dedicated to the team, yo. There was an episode when the third-years were thinking of retiring and the ace Asahi told Sugawara and Daichi that he was staying on to try and get the team to nationals. He said, "I'm not even going to college anyway." That's what the fuck I'm talking about right there. He knows ball is muthafucking life. Fuck a college degree. It's about getting the team to nationals, graduating, opening up a convenience store like Coach Ukai, and then getting that #1 draft pick for the Neighborhood Association volleyball team. Don't you dare say ball is life if you ain't 'bout that life like Asahi. My #10 Shōyō Hinata Karasuno jersey cosplay uniform that came in the mail says I am 'bout this fucking life right here, baby. *Haikyuu!!* got me in my local YMCA on the v-ball court nettin'. Working on my serves to make it out the hood. Got me thinking I gotta turn my life around at thirty-six years old 'cause I went to college like a loser when I shoulda been ballin'. Argh, it may be too late for me to go pro, but when I'm in my Karasuno jersey cosplay with the short shorts to match, I know I can still go Crow.

I Read Mark Millar's *Jupiter's Legacy* and I Saw the Father I Am and the Father I Hope I Never Have to Be

WILLIAM EVANS,
aka Papa Power Trip

HOLIDAY WEEKENDS, IN the imagined psychic lie I construct for myself, are supposed to be super-productive days. I spend the waking hours of the workweek doing a job that does not feed my creative necessities, so being off for three days or more should be my "get shit done" days. But recently, at the praising and properly hyped recommendation from Black Nerd Problems contributor Ja-Quan, I found myself instead venturing into my comics to-do list. I had only meant to read the first couple of issues of *Jupiter's Legacy*. I had only meant to read the first volume of *Jupiter's Legacy*. I had only meant to see how *Jupiter's Circle* started. Within a few hours, I had read the entire series, including the *Legacy* vol. 2 conclusion, the single issue that released this week. Yes, Mark Millar is a brilliant and innovative writer. This is a known and verifiable thing. I wasn't surprised at the efficient and beautiful locomotion of the story. I was most drawn in by the proposal and questioning of legacy itself, as it's something I feel the grip of each and every day.

Jupiter's Legacy essentially begins with a Caesarian story: the plot to murder a king. After being granted powers on a remote island during the 1930s, the Utopian, the world's greatest hero, leads America back to prominence. For a time. Along with his fellow heroes (once dubbed the Union), time has moved on even if the Utopian and his puritan ideals have not. He's a father of two children, both inheriting superior powers, both initially unable to live up to their father's incorruptibility. Eventually, the Utopian has alienated enough people over a long enough timeline that they have imagined a world that continues to spin without him in it, with his own son, Brandon, providing the final wound on the senate floor.

Reading through this series, I realized that I am no one and everyone in these panels. While this story is of course wrapped in flight, heat vision, telekinesis, and the stakes of the entire world hung above the head of its characters, it is at its core about parenting and parentage. To know me for a day is to know that I think that my father is a brilliant man. And while either an endorsement or a detriment to that statement, I am also aware that I am very much my father's son.

I graduated with my undergrad from The Ohio State University at the age of thirty-four. My father graduated with his master's degree in chemistry before he turned twenty-four. By the time he was thirty, he and my mother were sacrificing a lot on the way to lifting us (and my yet to be born sister) from the previous lower economic state that both of their families existed in. He ascended highly within his job at a Fortune 100 company and worked tirelessly there and at home, all of which was a precursor to my sister and I having little excuse to not succeed in some fashion once we left the nest. My father, who is a good man, was, but is, far from the pillar of humanity that is depicted by the Utopian in the *Jupiter* series. I am not the colossal fuckup filled with jealousy and murderous intent that was the Utopian's son, Brandon. And maybe like the comic, we do exist somewhere in the space between the gods and the Earth they dare not land upon. My father seized on his potential early, while I floated in the undisciplined current downstream from the waterfall he conducted. And yes, I'm aware that is not a condemnation of me, that I was not a failure because I didn't become my father, at least not at the speed he did. But once, I was a boy with a father. And once, I was a boy with my father's gifts cloaked in the tower of what he had achieved thus far. No amount of self-esteem makes those constructs disappear overnight.

Legacy is often an abstraction, a word that feels big the way that Titans are. Or the way a parent did in the first memory you can pull in which you needed to be lifted to reach something above your reach. In *Jupiter's Legacy*, Millar is the architect of a story doing double the work. On the surface, the story is an informing of what these heroes will leave in their wake, being the first of their kind to shape the world in this way. But while in this fantastical story the heroes are trying to shape the world into something befitting their kids, they also have the responsibility of shaping a nurturing childhood for their kids, befitting the type of individuals that will contribute to that very world they want to protect. No matter how we slice it, the Utopian fails on some level at this. I mean, he is murdered. The social capital he built in life is used as a Trojan horse by his son and fellow heroes to make power grabs in his wake. What the Utopian was willing to bet on was the powers he and Lady Liberty passed down and the unlimited opportunity they provided to their children would be enough. It would carry them to worthy and ambitious futures.

As I get older, I feel the reach of legacy more and more, hoping to turn out my pockets. Begging to see what I have accumulated, what I have gained that's worth passing down. Every accomplishment, every missed opportunity, every close call, feels like something being etched into my stone tablet. Some of this, of course, is pure ego, but there's an equal part of this that is a true question of: What exactly have I done or am I doing that will outlive me? My parents' legacy, thus far, is elevating their children above structures that limited opportunities for themselves. If I hold the line, send my daughter to a good school, enable an environment that is conducive to her succeeding, the same thing my parents rose into, is that success? Is there credit for not going backward? I have confidence that I have made *some* impact in the worlds I move through, but is a legacy still a legacy if it doesn't tangibly benefit my child?

There's a further analogy from *Jupiter's Legacy* that relates to my own story. I've always assumed my sister held the larger potential between the two of us. Better artist, wider thinker. But outside of our wildly different personalities, I was the oldest. I felt compelled to maximize the gifts I had early because they looked so much like my father's gifts. And because of this, adulthood was a lot more of a straight line for me. I had an idea of what I should be doing because our head of family seemed to lay it out for me. My sister was told to take her gifts and just figure it out. Because she is so wildly different than our mother as well, there was no real blueprint for who she was in our household. In *Jupiter's Legacy*, Brandon, the man that would slay his father, has a sister, Chloe. I rooted for Chloe, the daughter of the perfect parents, the way I root for my own hardworking sister, optimistic that she is also forging a legacy that she can be proud of. Chloe doesn't have a part in her father's demise, but she may not have had access to his guidance as much as Brandon either.

But that's not my story to tell. The one I can tell is the story of what attempting to build a legacy may cost you. Or cost my father. I remember when my father began to withdraw further into himself during my teenage years. I don't think my adolescent sensibilities had an opinion of it at the time. When I was angry at him, post-divorce, I pointed at that as some evidence of something. Of him withholding something owed to me, despite the mounting gifts before me with his handwriting on them. Today, I get it. I totally get it. Not because isolation is a thing that one does, but because it is a thing that *I* do. Sometimes it is for the sake of creativity. But sometimes it's because it is my best way to see the world I'm trying to impact. It is a single-view stargazing that pulls me away from those I want to affect most. Before reaching the part of the series where the Utopian finally breaks down, finally submits under the weight of trying to be everything to everyone, I wondered, "How does this character deal with all of this?" Isolated, depended upon. The pressure of having such a heavy hand on so many people's futures.

In the end, what Millar so expertly crafts in *Jupiter's Legacy* (and *Jupiter's Circle*) is how family is defined. What lasts. What's usable. And probably most important, what on earth is supposed to come next. What makes for an excellent and thoughtful superhero story is rooted in a much more relatable theme of what we are owed by those that raised us. What our responsibility is in accepting those gifts. And ultimately, what we choose to pass on.

Hajime no Ippo Is Just a Manga about Boxing but I'm Over Here Crying My Guts Out

OMAR HOLMON,
aka Volg Zangief's Cutman

"YOU SHOULD CHECK out this boxing manga," he said. "You'll love the action and story," he said. Seven years later, chapter 1202 of *Hajime no Ippo* has me staring up into the rain like Vegeta. Remember when P. Diddy shouted, "What I'ma do now? Huh? What I'ma do now? It's all fucked up now." That's how much of a wreck this chapter and series has left me. And I hate that I love that. This is all my friend Ayinde Russell's fault. In 2010, he told me to check out *Hajime no Ippo*, created by Morikawa Jouji in 1989. I've been hooked ever since. I started the series when it was about eight hundred chapters deep. I read it every day and everywhere I went for months. It's safe to say major shares of my emotion are invested in *Hajime no Ippo*.

I'm nervous even writing this because I'm so passionate about the series and I want to do it justice. *Hajime no Ippo* is an incredibly beautiful story about a kid that falls in love with boxing, but it's also the most devastating literature I've ever kept up with. If you know the series, you know what I mean. If you don't, then in order to understand the heartbreak you need to get familiar with where it all started for Makunouchi Ippo.

The story takes place in the real-world setting of Japan in the late 1980s, where we meet Makunouchi Ippo, the most polite, modest, and good-natured kid. Period. It's impossible for you not to love this kid. He doesn't have time to make friends as he helps out with his mother's fishing business. His father died at sea saving a crew member's life. Ippo gets picked on often due to his polite demeanor. By chance, pro boxer Takamura Mamoru happens to be jogging by one day and sees bullies attacking Ippo. Takamura embarrasses the bullies with ease. Ippo is amazed seeing this before passing out. He wakes up in the Kamogawa Boxing Gym (thanks to Takamura), and this is where it all comes together.

That same day, Ippo learns the first steps to throwing a proper punch from Takamura. Ippo hits the heavy bag so hard that skin from his knuckles flies off. Takamura realizes he has power and that his work on the fishing boat has given him the muscular build to be a serious threat as a boxer. Takamura gives Ippo a tape of Mike Tyson, explaining that Tyson's demeanor was the same as Ippo's in his youth until he became reborn. After viewing the tape and seeing Tyson's transformation, Ippo asks the question that'll haunt him and us for years to come: "What does it mean to be strong? How does it feel to be strong?"

Right there, that's the moment our boy Ippo gets with the shits. We then witness the trials Ippo endures to prove how serious he is about becoming a pro boxer. Now, there are so many key moments that I can't cram into this paragraph from early on in the series. All you need to know is that Ippo earns not only the right to get trained at the gym under Takamura's coach, Kamogawa Genji. He also earns respect and a rival in Miyata Ichirō. Creator Morikawa Jouji is a master storyteller. I'm focusing on Ippo, but there are so many other characters' stories that get told as they step into the limelight. The cast is so well rounded that you at times forget who's the main character, as Ippo's friends and opponents shine. There are few over-the-top opponents that are "evil" as opposed to being straight arrogant asses. Everyone fights for their own reasons and we see them all, getting glimpses into the path that's brought them in front of the protagonist at the time. Morikawa is able to humanize each character and describes their fighting styles so they stand out. [Fun fact: Morikawa used to be a second (a cornerman in boxing), which explains the in-depth research and visuals he puts into the manga. Every punch and style on display by these characters is explained and a point is made to pay homage to the real-life boxers that made them famous.]

I pointed this out to my father, who grew up on boxing. I told him about a character named Mashiba Ryō that utilizes the Hitman fighting stance and flicker jab made famous by "Thomas 'the Hitman' Hearns!" Dad interjected excitedly. "We used to watch the Friday-night *Fight of the Week* on television and listen to it on the radio. It wasn't closed-circuit back then," he says.

Morikawa is paying respect to eras even before my father's time. He goes all the way back to the 1920s, when Ippo's signature move, the Dempsey Roll, was created by Jack Dempsey. The technique consists of Ippo weaving his head in a figure eight motion to avoid punches while simultaneously using that momentum to punch from left and right angles.

I love hand-to-hand combat in manga, comics, animation, and live action. What I love even more is a character that isn't saved by anything but their own strength. Morikawa emphasizes training in this series like no other I've ever seen. We spend months with Ippo during his training regimen, which always varies. Coach Kamogawa is old, experienced, and super-innovative to put Ippo in the best condition for his fights. One fight may require leg strength, the next building a stronger, thicker neck to withstand punches from an opponent coming down from a higher weight class. Lemme tell you like Coach Kamogawa told Ippo: "Not everyone who works hard is rewarded. However! All those who succeed have worked hard!!" Not a damn thing comes easy in life. It's all about that training on training on training, boi. Much like in life, in a fight there are no guarantees things will go your way. However, the more prepared you are for what's to come, the better your odds.

Morikawa literally shows us this in each fighter's training regimen. He stresses the particular muscles that develop on each page, along with the effect of their developing. It's all cause and effect with intricate visual detail. There's no Senzu Bean, Hidden Trap card, or forbidden *jutsu* that'll make it a short or easy fight. Just a Gold's Gym membership being put to use and that's what the fuck I'm here for. Ippo follows Coach Kamogawa's instructions as if they were commandments. That shit is law to him. Kamogawa made Ippo's in-fighting approach and Peek-a-Boo style his best weapon. The trust that buds between Kamogawa and Ippo is one of the relationships in *Hajime no Ippo* that separates the series from its contemporaries. The bond between the trainer and his pupil. Ippo will always do everything in his power in the ring to show his appreciation for the time and belief Kamogawa (and others) entrusts to him.

What Ippo lacks is a killer's instinct. He is the nicest, kindest kid. He just wants to see how far he can go. How strong he can become. That mentality will only get you so far. After a devastating loss challenging the #2 world ranked boxer Alfredo Gonzales (I was sad for weeks), Ippo is at a crossroads. Takamura tells him how it is point-blank. He draws a line in the ground (ironically where Takamura first tested Ippo's decision to become a boxer) and tells Ippo not to cross it unless he's ready to become a whole 'nother monster. That's the only way he'll survive going for the world title.

Takamura is telling Ippo not to get Coach Kamogawa's hopes up on him if he's not willing to take that next step.

Ippo now wonders if he has what it takes to cross that line and become a monster. It's not in his demeanor, he fights and moves forward on courage and because that's all he knows how to do. What does it mean to become inhuman? Whenever Ippo comes back to that line in the ground Takamura made, he goes around it every time. He sees that inhuman quality in his boxing rivals and friends and wonders about himself. This internalization and constant questioning of himself make Ippo so human and relatable. That questioning is really the heart of the matter. I love when we see characters in a story at an impasse like this. It's reflective of real life in sports shit. How far are you willing to go to be the best? Did you come all this way just to say you came this far? And can you live with the toll that becoming the best or inhuman will take on your body?

At the time Ippo was living with those consequences, having suffered from being punch drunk. *Punch drunk* is a boxing term for a cerebral concussion from blows to the head. It causes confusion, hand tremors, memory lapses (it can even lead to dementia). It's hard to tell if the condition is short term or permanent at times when symptoms are displayed. It seemed temporary for Ippo. However, in his comeback match, Ippo gets knocked down and doesn't remember it. From there the writing is on the wall. Ippo gives his coach a meaningful look before heading back out to fight. Once I saw the look, I said, "No. Not like dis. Not like dis!" as Ippo delivers a crushing soliloquy about this being as far as he can go.

"After this, I don't think I'll be able to continue. I don't think I can go with you anymore, Coach. I'm so sorry. At the very least I want you to see the new Dempsey Roll we created together. All that time that you spent on me. I want to show you that it wasn't all for nothing. Please watch me!"

We only see a glimpse of the new Dempsey Roll, as Ippo gets knocked out before it's in full gear. His final goal is showing the new Dempsey Roll they toiled over as a parting gift to his coach. Arghhhhhhhh, Ippo's apology to the coach broke me, man. Especially since the creator, Morikawa Jouji, has been having health issues regularly. These health issues have caused delays in the series. It is evident the creator is apologizing to his fans through Ippo's words.

During my junior year of high school, in track and field I had an accident in the pole vault field event. It was during a windy day at a track meet. After two good practice jumps, I went for a third because I wanted one more good jump to know I was on point. When I went in the air the wind stopped all my momentum and I fell into the metal box from about ten feet on my tailbone. I honestly cannot describe that pain to you in any language. When I tried to come back and vault again, I could not physically run the same anymore or jump the same. I'd limp after a few jumps or after sprinting a bit. I loved track and I loved pole vaulting, but after three years it was something I couldn't do the same anymore. That's why I love a journey where real shit befalls characters. Issues that they can't punch their way out of. Circumstances where life doesn't always work out in their favor. I feel stories like that are more relatable.

Boxing is a contact sport different from track, but in any sport, when you can no longer do what you love, that feeling of loss is universal. Especially when it's through no fault of your own but just your body saying, "Nooooope." There's no way to really explain the feeling. You either wonder what could have happened had you not gotten injured, come to terms with what happened, or know that you gave it your all and have no regrets. Listen, I love mangas that tackle fantasy shit, ninja shit, or magic shit, but when it comes to mangas that tackle this sports shit? They hit so differently. No one's life is on the line. The universe isn't in jeopardy. We're just watching a boxing match. The difference is seeing what Ippo as an athlete went through to prepare for his matches as an underdog. Then seeing the preparation he underwent as a champion. There's something about that atmosphere that pulls you in as a reader, especially if you are or used to be an athlete. There's also the question of what happens to an athlete that can't compete anymore. This is where I get invested in storytelling by a writer, because trying to capture that feeling is not an easy feat. Translating that emotion for your readers to really feel that shit takes skill. Morikawa Jouji has utilized his skill in long-form storytelling over the years for this exact turning point for Ippo.

For the time being Ippo has to stop boxing and retires, so he becomes a second (cornerman). We now see him in a coaching role. Through helping others, he sees what he could have done in his own career. The question keeps looming if this new perspective is enough to bring him out of retirement. This feels like more of a journey with a character, as it keeps the development of the character going. Much like the development of an athlete that no longer competes. I love seeing the switch in roles that has to be undertaken as a player in a game now becomes a coach/trainer for someone else. There's also this feeling of life after a sports injury or life after aging out of an athletic career. It's like seeing a famous sports player transition into being a commentator or announcer for the sport they use to do. Again, to me that's such a hard thing to capture but gets done so well.

Hajime no Ippo is truly telling a story for those that gave their body to a sport or a craft and the journey that comes with that. Ippo's injury speaks volumes for those that have gone through something similar or witnessed a favorite athlete of theirs get sidelined by an injury. You can be an injured athlete or a fan of an athlete suffering an injury. There's a feeling between the two that's shared. Capturing this portion of sports is what keeps me so fascinated by the writing. The losses Ippo goes through that we witness feel so heavy, not only emotionally, but seeing the physical toll taken just like in the actual sport of boxing. Being with Ippo as an athlete as he makes his decision to retire for his health is a miraculous journey. We also see hints that he'll be able to come back to the sport as well. This series embodies the roller coaster that sports can take athletes on with victories and crushing defeats. Seeing Ippo lose a boxing match, I instantly get taken back to disappointments at having lost a track meet or not clearing a height in pole vault. Same can be said when I see him standing in victory. At its core, this series is about those that just want to see how far they can go in a sport they love. To me, the physical and mental journey you go through training for your sport is what it takes to be strong. What it means to be strong is how one handles the tribulations to maintain that strength and when that strength is needed to know when to step away.

Do You Have a Moment to Talk About Our Lord and Savior Aloy from *Horizon Zero Dawn*?

WILLIAM EVANS,
aka The Warrior that Vanasha Ghosted

ALL PRAISE TO the Sun God. All hail the changeling, the great blue conversion of the machine. Swordfish/Trinity-hacking, spear-wielding gawd. Have you heard about our Lord and Savior, Aloy? Alpha eff yo Omega. Hair kissed by fire. Moisturized with chillwater. Twisted with metalburn so that shit never come undone. Have you heard the good news? Aloy out here trying to save the tribe, fam. Aloy master strider and quagmire.

I was up in the barber hut, trying to bring back that original human look. Out here doing it for the Gaia culture, nah mean? Sawtooth gonna roll up on the block, like we fuel or some shit. Your boy was lookin' mad thirsty. Naw, fam. Aloy came through like a critical strike, yo. She came through riding sidesaddle on the broadhead, whippin' them three arrows at a time. Oh, a Ravager want to come play too? Aloy got some hardened arrows for that ass, b. Oh, was that your back-mounted cannon? Fuck that. Disc Launcher supposed to mean something to me? Yo, I'm dodging your shit and they still spinning, b, the discs still spinning.

Nah, man, Aloy the truth, the gospel, the stained-glass mosaic and the muthafuckin' sun rays that run through it. The bow and arrow-tip game? Gawdly. I seent her roll out the way of a stalker, pop up, and pull back on two terrablast arrows. *I said she trying to cut about two of them terrablast, fam, cuz that's just what she used to.* Ain't nobody out here fuckin' with the ghost of Legolas, man! Ain't nobody out here trying to see Lara Croft's great-great-great-great-great-great-great-great-great-great-great-great-great-granddaughter in these overgrown streets, man!

I tried to go hunting with Aloy one time, man. I tried to return these machines to the Earth, out here shoulder to shoulder with the deity of the quiver herself. I almost got caught, yo. Corrupted Trampler tried to come for my fade. I'm hittin' this cat with mad hard-edge joints and he like, "Nah, nah." Blockin' that shit like I sent unsolicited nudes or some shit. Aloy yelling from the tall grass like, "Yo, fire arrows, b?" I'm like, "I ain't got none."

I didn't know what was gonna kill me first, that Trampler charging at me or the disappointment in Aloy's face. She pulled back on the bow and let the god flow with fire arrows into the machine's side. And after she saved my life, she didn't ask if I was okay. She didn't check me for scars. She didn't even teach me how to craft the hot nickels myself. She got dead up in my face like, "Boooi, you better get you some Blaze and light these muthafuckas up when you see them in the used-to-be streets. Rost ain't get blown the fuck up so you could be out here shooting flaccid arrows at the corruption, my Nora. You better collect that Blaze. Let that Blaze get down into the joints! YOU DON'T BLAZE, YOU DON'T EAT. YOU DON'T BLAZE, YOU DON'T EAT."

Aloy ain't here for that soft shit, man. I seen her talking to a dude that just lost his sister, drinking his pain away, and she hit him with the "that sounds tragic and all, but I need you to get your shit together cuz machines out here trying to merk you, fam. Machines smell that weakness, they will turn your ass inside out in the tall grass, b." Aloy trying to save civilization, she ain't got time for these non-Noras out here, man. Out here tracking down lost tribesmen like Aragorn. Nah, fuck that, like Darryl, except with some freeze arrows on the bow and if his motorcycle was a Charger machine. You try to ambush Aloy for her spear? You got Aloy fucked up. She walked in and out of the cauldrons, fam, your village ain't got enough Ridge-Wood to bang with Aloy. Get your shards up, fam.

Aloy first of her name, ghost in the Nora shell, one of the best to ever do it, yo. Aloy, aka Kate Bishop with a focus, aka Outkast but not from ATL, aka Elisabet better have my money, aka Thunderjaw ain't got shit on me, is unfuckwithable, man. She put the whole Nora tribe on her back like Samurai Jack, fam. Recognize the sunset hair. Holla at Metal Bourne when you see her in the street. All-Mother be praised, in Aloy's name. Amen.

Two Dope Boys and Movin' Weight with Pusha T's *Daytona*

WILLIAM & OMAR,

aka The D.A.R.E. Kids Ready to Risk It All

[Disclaimer: The album cover that depicts Whitney Houston's bathroom is trash. No qualifier, that shit is despicable. We came to the identification of the cover after this write-up began and perfectly understand if you don't want to eff with the album because of it. I don't think we know how much of this was Kanye's call, Pusha's knowledge of it, or what kind of trash soul it takes to pay $85K for the shock and awe of further perpetuating the narrative of someone that struggled with addiction, but was brilliant and life touching in so many ways. If you good on that, we won't judge you. No offense taken. If you are still enjoying the album, we got the commentary for you.]

I don't care what hood rap, trap rap, rap rap you're listening to, but stop. Just stop. Pusha T dropped his album *Daytona* on the Lord's blessed day of May 25, 2018, and brought back *The Wire* rolled up in Reagan-era economics running for office in *New Jack City*. Yeah, it's that real. *Daytona* goes so hard we had to cut the raw for a taste test before the distribution deal goes through.

214

WILLIAM: I knew, I fuckin' knew, when your boy said, "*I only ever looked up to Sosa / Y'all get a bird, this nigga Oprah,*" we was gettin' that good, vintage *King Push*. That back-to-the-beats-on-the-lunch-table *King Push*. "Still got millions in the ceiling but more like a few hundred K cuz I got some shoes and shit since then" *King Push*. I can't be consoled, fam.

OMAR: I heard that man say, "*Influenced by niggas Straight Outta Compton, the scale never lies / I'm 2.2 incentivized,*" and found myself in the kitchen packing lines of flour off the cutting board and into Ziploc bags. You don't hear me, I'm chopping up Gold Medal all-purpose flour in my drawers 'cause I don't trust myself around my own product. Weird part is, I had a gold chain on the entire time? I don't own a gold chain, man. Push got me thinking I'm C.J. in *San Andreas* doin' work for the Grove, homie.

WILLIAM: Bruh. The fam went away for a long weekend, so the house is empty. I got a Friday off. The sun is shining. I'm out here bumping this shit with the windows down in very white spaces with an empty house and little responsibilities today. This shit felt like 1998 all over again. Right down to that murda/drug flow. I'm out here like, why are none of my long white T-shirts clean? Why don't I own any Adidas anymore? But for real, Pusha got folks out here compromising their morals to get these lyrics off.

OMAR: I'm in the heart of Brooklyn with this album playing. Next thing I know, the ghost of Nino Brown force projected himself next to me, eating a bowl of cereal, talkin' 'bout, "Why this shit so hard?" And Push dropped this in the a.m.? The FCC didn't have a problem with this? He talkin' bricks of cocaine at 8:00 a.m.? Eggs and bacon ain't even finished on the stove, and Push pushin' my plate out the way in order to drop a duffel bag full of money on the table. I . . . I just came here for pancakes, fucked around, and got a court case now.

WILLIAM: This dude done said, "*To all of my young niggas / I am your Ghost and your Rae / This is my Purple Tape.*" I . . . I cried, man. Like Halle Berry winning the Oscar cried. Never has a reference to the drug game and the color of physical multimedia made me so emotional. I was with my boys rockin' the Purple Tape in the old-ass Oldsmobile in the whitest suburb in Central Ohio.

Hearing Pusha say that made me feel like I was the time paradox. I was an anchor to the golden age of problematic rap, and I didn't know I would ever hold such a distinction. And let's be clear, Pusha might be the most problematic fave. This shit is straight up destructive, against every woke instinct in my body and . . . I'm playing it as we speak. Loud! Uncomfortable for my ears loud, b. I done took it back to the rearview mirror shakin' in the car level, fam. That's how serious this is right now.

OMAR: Oh, a problematic fave easily. If Obama called a meeting for rappers, even he would have to say, "*Ahhhhh.* Now, we want to uplift the community, *long pause* you can tell your story but *longer pause* let's be positive. Let's have an influx of art to a higher standard that, *ahhhh*, raises the bar for hip-hop. Let's be better for our future. Except for you, Pusha T. You can, *ahhhhhh*, keep talkin' that dope game shit. We actually need that. I'm sure you do have more to offer, Push . . . but no. I want that, *ahhhh*, dope, Dracos, and dollars on the kitchen counter talk."

WILLIAM: Fam, we keep talkin' about Wakanda as the utopia . . . if I were T'Challa, I might allow some trafficking just so Pusha T can rap about it. I know, I know, but you don't take the brush out of

Picasso's hand, bruh. You gotta let genius be genius, no matter the cost. Whatever it fucking takes.

OMAR: "Evacuate the city, engage all defenses, and get this man some dope money!" As far as I'm concerned, Pusha T is the real Thanos. He wouldn't even need the Infinity Gauntlet. Pusha would just drop this album in order to turn half the universe to dust, plus he'd be ruthless enough to sweep Peter Parker's dust into a Ziploc bag, wrap it in duct tape, dip it in Vaseline, and sell it on the intergalactic streets for an Infinity Stone per ounce.

WILLIAM: Can we talk about "Infrared" real quick? Can we talk about how Pusha, who already gives subzero fucks, found another level of not giving a fuck? *"They ain't even recognize Hov until Annie / so I don't tap dance for the crackers and sing 'Mammy.'"* What in all fucks, man?!?! Not to mention the *"How could you ever right these wrongs / when you don't even write your songs."* Like, we KNOW who he was talking about, but I feel better pretending he talkin' about every-muthafuckin-body.

Pusha write rhymes for dudes that already write and would rather memorize his shit. Pusha write rhymes. I just want to be the Pusha T of TV recaps, man. I just want to write about *Westworld* with the same tenacity that Pusha T talks about interstate trafficking.

OMAR: Dude, I'm ordering food with Pusha T tenacity from now on. It is a must. "Lemme get a ki of fries, an eight ball of lemonade, and three stacks' worth of McRibs." The line that shook me to my core is *"This ain't for the conscious, this is for the mud-made monsters."* Pusha T said, "Don't think piece me, bro," with that line. This is not about well-written analysis or the vicious cycle of violence that continues to engulf the youth. "This is about Black T-shirts . . . and drugs."

Also, can we just appreciate that among all the coke bars Pusha let us know he's pro–sustainable energy? *"White on white that's the tester / Black on black that's the Tesla."* What? Who does that? He talkin' Tony Montana boatload of coke fresh from the pier, then being like, "Oh, my carbon footprint low as fuck, by the way. We been off that fossil fuel shit. It's Earth Day every day when I drop the top." He better have Captain Planet in a Tesla makin' it rain coca leaves in the music video.

WILLIAM: 'Bout fell off my corner with that shit. Left me like Malcolm where X marks my grave. It's wild, right? I did not come to a Pusha T album for content range, but he still droppin' that kind of shit in there? Your boy is a fuckin' weapon, man. You just gotta point him at some shit that needs to be destroyed and let him do his damn thing. I mean, he might leave a crack epidemic in his wake, but whatever you wanted extinguished gonna be fuckin' gone.

OMAR: Yo, I feel like I gotta dye my hair black, change my name to something hard enough for white people to mispronounce but yet still say it's exotic, and head for Mexico, 'cause listening to this album clearly makes me guilty by association. The feds watching and listening through our webcams are petty enough to bust the doors down and try and make the charge stick. In nerd layman's terms tho? Pusha T makes that *Attack on Titan* music that makes you wanna join the Survey Corps so you can see what lies beyond the wall . . . so you can expand your drug ring.

WILLIAM: Every time Pusha drop some new shit, I look at this life in the suburbs with my family and cut lawn and pretty mailbox and be like, "But is this really what I want tho?" I mean, it's a good life, but is this some kingpin shit? But then I remember that Pusha went at Drake on the "Infrared" record. And then I listen to Drake's "Duppy

Freestyle" going back at Pusha and be like, you know what, I'll take my beef in the nerd journalism field. Cuz ain't nobody gonna be talkin' about "Will be talkin' that nerd shit, but I heard he ain't even read a comic book till 2016. Like, Will aiight, but he ain't even top ten on his own site" to a smoothed-out jazz beat. I mean, they *could* do that. Maybe that's what the nerd journalism game been missing. But they better come for me after the holiday. King Push got me way too motivated right now.

Killing Floor: Navigating Real-World Gun Violence as a Hardcore Gamer

WILLIAM EVANS,
aka Luke Cage's Overqualified Intern

HERE IS A simple truth when it comes to me: I think guns are cool. I think guns are cool in the way that I think an electric toothbrush is cool. Or a V-8 engine is cool. I think guns are cool in the way I think it's cool that my daughter looks like both my wife and me or the way that aloe seems to heal everything. To paraphrase Walter White, sometimes it really is about the science, and there is no denying the technological marvel that is the firearm for what it is capable of, regardless of intent or result. That's a huge, unfair *regardless* there, but we'll circle back to that. And as cool as guns are in that modern invention kind of way, it's only half the story. The more nefarious side is that I enjoy what guns can do in the fictional abstract. It isn't really honest to say that I think an AK-47 with a ridiculous high rate of fire is cool and divorce that from the sheer violence of its bullets ripping through something with furious tenacity. So yes, that means that it isn't honest for me to say that I enjoy Rick Grimes spraying automatic vengeance without the people of Terminus being the bullet sponges. Admitting I enjoy watching violent ballistic death as entertainment (example: my many repeat viewings of *John Wick*) doesn't make me a sociopath (I don't think), because it is so wildly enjoyed by others, but it is a bit alarming to say it out loud like that. Even then, that's *watching* gun violence, that's not the act of doing it, so that adds another level between what we would start to consider problematic, right?

Well, what about video games? I game. Hard. I've logged hundreds of hours of *Destiny* and its sequel, *Destiny 2*, a first-person shooter from developer Bungie, famous for the *Halo* franchise. Like most FPS games, you play 85 percent of your time in the game aiming down the sights, killing everything unlucky enough to have hit points and be in your path. Like most shooters, *Destiny* rewards you for being precise. Shoot a Cabal enemy in the head and watch it explode into gas and toxins as its body limply hits the ground, possibly rewarding you with another weapon or more ammo for your current one. It is satisfying and only feeds your hunger to keep doing it. But to be fair, these are aliens you're shooting, a fictional genocide to take part in. It's not like they are human or anything. Not like *you* can do that . . .

The first time I saw a real gun was probably when I was about twelve or thirteen. The first person I remember knowing that lost their life to a bullet was the summer before my fourteenth birthday, though I expect it may have happened before that, but I just didn't know any better and nobody bothered to sully me with the truth. I'd love to say that was the last time I lost a friend to the barrel, but it wasn't and it didn't necessarily slow down as I grew up either, except the number of "eligible" friends for such violence began to narrow itself. Thirty years later, I have collected a small society of men and women that I once spoke with, embraced, played ball with, went to parties with, attended homeroom with, and loved that no longer walk among us, specifically because their bodies were not stronger than the lead that invaded them. Some of them were innocent law-abiding citizens, some of them were less so. For those reasons, I don't own a gun now and never plan to.

Plenty of men like me, family men who feel responsible for their family's protection, have elected to invest in weaponry or carry one themselves, and I get it. Ultimately, it feels like a flawed premise to me when you calculate the number of home invasions compared to the number of accidental shootings in the home, but that's not really the point. For some men and women, a gun makes them *feel* safer, and provided that it doesn't mean that fear spills over to the innocent people (which, sadly, it does all the time), then I could at least see the premise, even if the follow-through is seldom that innocent. I still believe that 80 percent of gun advocate arguments are really just "because I want to," not "because I need to," but I can't always fault the possibility of protecting one's self in its purest intent.

In 2010, a guy I had known for almost ten years was gunned down in front of his family because he got into an argument with a guy at the movies the week prior. Three days after the funeral, I played *Call of Duty: Black Ops* with his younger brother. We spent two hours shooting fifty times more bullets into faceless fictional terrorists than were thrown into his older brother. And we did it in silence, focused and unyielding. Video game killing sometimes isn't always a zero-sum game. Characters appear, you kill them, and they disappear. You stand up from your chair having killed everyone and no one simultaneously. But that doesn't mean that the bodies don't go somewhere.

Is it as easy as saying, "Well, that's fiction"? I tend to think so. I become bothered, actually angered, whenever some young guy goes on a shooting spree and the first thing they do is see what music he listened to and what video games he played. Maybe that started with Columbine and followed many years later by Virginia Tech, where video games became a punching bag for every disturbed and fatally violent kid under thirty-five who became synonymous with tragedy. FPS games and *GTA* are always the first dartboards raised when politicians want to plant their flag with their solution for curbing youth violence (something my Democratic bones still hold firmly against Hillary Rodham to this day). I am old enough to remember when Hillary Clinton introduced a legislative bill in 2005 that sought to limit the sales of Mature video games to minors with this quote: "If you put it just really simply, these violent video games are stealing the innocence of our children." Yeah, I never believed that. The same way that political cartoons didn't "create" the murders in the *Charlie Hebdo* shooting in 2015 but served as their excuse or muse, Rockstar Games doesn't "create" murderers as much as gives every schmoe like myself a playground to run around in with no limits whatsoever. Still, somehow, I believe the rhetoric of people motivates people more than stand-alone media does.

And yet, that doesn't mean I spend time with my daughter showing her around *Grand Theft Auto*'s Liberty City while I mow down civilians in a sports car while spraying a Tec-9 out of the window. There is a judgment there, on myself, to be so wantonly violent in her presence. That doesn't prove a counter to my defense that games aren't a deadly conduit in school shootings or the like, it's just common sense of letting my daughter stumble onto complex subject matters organically or at a time when she can navigate the issues of violence and at her own pace, not at mine. I wouldn't sit her down in front of *Californication* either. Narrowing down video games or most mainstream media as a cause for behaviors that seem extreme or outside of societal norms also ignores mental health and real-world environments, both of which are becoming more prevalent in explaining shooting tragedies.

And yet, it is still hard to ignore just the sheer amount of violence I consume in my media without flinching as some real-world gun deaths cost me sleep. I think about the Gubio massacre in Nigeria that killed eighty-one people in 2020, how men marched into town, killing innocent civilians, and how sick that makes me. There's a level in *Call of Duty: Modern Warfare 2* called "No Russian" where you play as a double agent participating in a terrorist attack in an airport where you and your comrades fill the terminal with M60 rounds. The level was so controversial because you were tasked with killing civilians, and the game actually lets you skip the level if you want to. A friend of mine still gives me grief because I didn't hesitate whatsoever, marching from hall to hall killing and killing.

I think this is where games are going and, to be fair, have been going for a while. There are the BioWare franchises like *Star Wars: Knights of the Old Republic* and *Mass Effect*, where the game responds to your moral choices. The *Dishonored* franchise takes a unique approach, giving you the option to subdue enemies or kill them. But the more killing you do, the more the world changes (for the worse) around you and drastically changes the conclusion of your game. Or the BioWare franchise where you are kind of cartoonishly choosing between saving little abducted girls or *shudder* harvesting them (!?) for more power. But you are at least influencing the world, and the quest for more destructive power has a consequence on the world. Weirdly though, these don't end up being meditations on how the player navigates these worlds as much as foster repeat playthroughs. If you meet a *Mass Effect* fan, they will surely tell you about their experience and also their "Renegade" campaign where they made every demonstrative choice possible just to see what happens.

Perhaps the most interesting games that play with morality are the ones that don't give you a choice. The ones that set you on a path, have you maximize the carnage by design, and then leave you to face the consequences. This is the Naughty Dog approach, or specifically the *Last of Us* franchise. You don't get to make these big moral decisions, but you do have to live with the consequences of your character's actions. Realizing that playing as Joel in the first *Last of Us* game, that I was the Monster at the End of This Book, grounded me more than most games where the decisions were left to me.

On most days, it doesn't matter to me. I'm grown and mature enough to never mix *Payday 2* with my weekly visit to the bank. But I have more days than I used to where it all feels a bit much, and my appetite for gaming has me sideline the shooters for long stretches in favor of strategy games or something lacking combat at all like racing games. Maybe it's just me getting older, maybe there's a cumulative effect. Or maybe how we digest violence, realistic or not, is more complicated than we want to admit. The rise of a present morality in games has helped though. For narrative reasons or for game design choices, having my actions in a video game be given more weight helps me feel less detached from the violence I'm experiencing. Going from kill room to kill room can admittedly be cathartic. We all have long days. We all have days where we kind of just want to burn it down. And I think there are games that can fulfill that task nicely. But I don't think there's anything wrong with asking for more. To look at your virtual body count and reconcile that with the values you hold in reality. And I hope to maintain that. I still want to provide a safe and nonhostile environment for my family. And I still plan to play *Cyberpunk 2077* half a dozen times.

Hamilton and the Case of Historical Fanfics

OMAR HOLMON,
aka Dutty Boukman's Side-Eye

LEMME PAINT THE picture real quick. The year was 2016, I was invited over to watch the Tony Awards with two friends of mine, Cristin and Sarah. These two are performers, writers, and grew up as theater kids. Now, I don't know much about the Tony Awards 'cause ~~I'm a hood nigga~~ I'm a nerd nigga that survived in a hood nigga environment. All I knew was that the Tony Awards are a big deal for actors. I was warned beforehand by them that there was going to be a range of emotions on their part. I came prepared and even brought an apple parfait to show that a dude knows how to be civilized and shit. I learned three things that night. One, apple parfaits don't need to be heated up, you can eat it cold. Two, the Tony Awards are like Source Awards for theater kids. Three, they were happy for all the shows that won, but they really wanted this play called *Hamilton* to take home all the awards and flowers.

As the show came to a close and I'd watched them sing a bunch of songs, Cristin turned to me and said, "Fam, I noticed you not singing along to *Hamilton* tracks." Sarah chimed in with a "Yeah,

I peeped that too. What's good with that? WHAT'S REALLY GOOD WITH THAT?" (Neither of them actually talks like that, this is how I translate tone and intent in my head.) The next like half hour was them telling me I should really check out the *Hamilton* soundtrack ("cast album," if you theater-kid initiated). Let it be known I agreed to do so out of fear from having seen them both throw up theater-kid gang signs the entire night. It felt like I was jumped into the *Hamilton* fandom with the way I listened to that soundtrack for weeks. *Hamilton* tells the story of founding father Alexander Hamilton from his time fighting in the American Revolution and building the government's Treasury department for America, along with his family life. It's a journey, and we meet a lot of other historical figures along the way. Those historical figures are all played by people of color. The play was written and composed by Lin-Manuel Miranda.

Man, I listened to that soundtrack while I was writing, while I was reading, and even when working out. I ain't ever worked out to a play soundtrack before, but there the fuck I was, running three miles listening to Aaron Burr go from R&B crooning to power ballad bravado in his song "Wait for It." I jogged through Queens shouting, *"Life doesn't discriminate / Between the sinners and the saints / It takes and it takes and it takes."* I dunno what y'all call a line like that in your walk of life, but where I'm from that's called muthafucking bars. You know an album is good when you're on Rap Genius's website looking up the lyrics and their meanings. I really enjoyed how Lin-Manuel Miranda weaved in historical events, conversations, and letters to craft the dialogue and music. To this day I still believe Angelica Schuyler's song "Satisfied" cleaned everyone the fuck up on the soundtrack.

Hamilton hit Broadway with the hype of Dr. Dre's *Detox* album or maybe Beyoncé's *Lemonade* album and became the Wrestle-Mania of Broadway. Keeping in mind how Broadway is mad upper echelon. So, *Hamilton*'s success made it inaccessible for most to see with ticket prices in the PS5 range (we talking $500+). With prices that high, the majority of the audience seeing the show were upper-class white folks. It's ironic seeing how the culture of hip-hop and rap are what separates *Hamilton* from the pack. Placing the crown on the musical as the "it" play but then the people part of that very culture that made it a success don't get access to it and aren't the ones reviewing it. In 2016, I knew I was never going to see *Hamilton*. I was content with seeing the musical as a historical fan fiction musical. When I think of *Hamilton* as a historical fanfic, I can enjoy it in that capacity. Which is funny because four years later, in 2020, *Hamilton* became accessible to everyone. Well, everyone with a subscription to Disney+ who was streaming the play on their platform. I remember the internet being excited for this. I, however, was not.

Lemme explain, there's an episode of *Community* called "Intermediate Documentary Filmmaking" where Pierce Hawthorne fakes being on his deathbed to get revenge on his study group for leaving him out of things and making fun of him. Pierce gives Troy Barnes the "gift" of meeting LeVar Burton, who he is a fan of, knowing Troy will freeze up and be unable to interact back with LeVar. In a cutscene we see Troy in a room shouting that he never wanted to meet LeVar Burton in person. He just wanted a photograph because "You can't disappoint a picture! I HATE YOU, PIERCE! *screams*" That's how I felt about seeing *Hamilton*. I am glad those of us who'd have to put up rent money for a *Hamilton* ticket would be able to see it via Disney+, but I was good on it. At the root of the issue, knowing the cast were people of color playing the parts of the founding fathers was fine because I wasn't physically seeing it. Now having the option to, I didn't wanna see people of color humanizing these founding fathers that owned slaves, man. Again, I know this is a historical fanfic, but man, seeing Thomas Jefferson's character moving about, singing and being charming, I knew my initial thought would be "Fuck that dude for life."

At the time *Hamilton* was coming out, I was living in Crown Heights right by the Eastern Parkway. Damn near every day there was a protest happening right in the middle of that parkway. These protests and marches were against police brutality, Black trans women being murdered, Breonna Taylor's death, George Floyd's death, and the death of Black folk from police that didn't make news headlines outside of social media. I could see the protests all from my bedroom window. I'd go to the living room to tell my wife one was happening and see she was already getting dressed and putting her mask on to go outside and join. This was another factor in me not wanting to see people of color cosplaying as these slave-owning hypocrites. I eventually did watch *Hamilton* with a friend on Disney+. It was nice to see how certain scenes played out, the choreography, as well as the set designs. Having seen all that, my initial thought while watching was "Yeah, fuck these founding fathers for life, yo." Alexander Hamilton is shown to be very against slavery in the play, which he was in real life. However, he was also complicit with elements of slavery in order to rise up in politics. He voted in favor of the three-fifths compromise, he married into a slave-owning family in the Schuylers, he bought and sold slaves for his father-in-law, and it's still debatable on if he actually owned slaves. Again, but I know the play is fanfic tho. The truth can only make appearances where it lifts our protagonist Alexander Hamilton up.

If anything, seeing the American Revolution and founding of government portrayed with people of color as founding fathers made me even more enraged at the hypocrisy of the actual American "forefathers" fighting for freedom, liberty, and the very statement that "all men are created equal" while literally owning Black people. I fucking cannot. It's just this reminder that they wanted it to be one way despite all their talk of freedom for the other way.

They kept it the way that benefited them the most. I'm about to get off track, but had this been a musical about the Haitian Revolution, aka a successful uprising of slaves in Haiti against the French colonizers, there woulda been no need for Black and POC folks cosplaying as the founding fathers 'cause everyone in that Haitian Revolution was Black. Americans felt oppressed through taxes and dumped tea. Haitians were oppressed and dropped fucking bodies. I know that can't be done because the colonizers lost, and we'd have to focus on how France crippled Haiti by cutting off its trade with the world and taxing (called the "indemnity tax" at the time) it for its freedom under threat of another invasion. I'm just saying, that's the musical I wanna see getting the upper echelon of Broadway uncomfortable as fuck.

Now, I don't hate *Hamilton* at all. Once again, it's historical fan fiction. I just don't want it to be used as revisionist history for Alexander Hamilton or any of the founding fathers (looking right at you, Thomas Jefferson) because people would rather not have to face the truth to a piece of fiction that they love. I am not here for any "Fuck accountability, we just trying to sing along to the jams" when we could actually enjoy the musical *and* acknowledge that the Hamilton in the Broadway show doesn't give the actual Hamilton a clean slate, because at the end of the day, ya mans Hamilton "has to answer for his [actions and] his words, sir." That's all I'm getting at here. Well, that and . . . *Troy Barnes voice* I TOLD MY FRIEND I NEVER WANTED TO WATCH *HAMILTON*! I JUST WANTED TO LISTEN TO IT BECAUSE YOU CAN'T BE DISAPPOINTED BY BARS!

Graduating to the Grown Folks' Table: I Finally Learned How to Play Spades

OMAR HOLMON,
aka Young Librarian with the Books

WHEN IT'S TIME for the games to come out in a Black household or function, or wherever that atmosphere be so Black, I guarantee you it ain't gon' be Apples to Apples, Parcheesi, or anything from Milton Bradley. The choices will be either Monopoly, Taboo, or Spades. This is the trifecta of games (honorable mention for Uno) in Black culture. Spades sits at the top of the oligarchy. Period. That's a scientific law all Black folk understand. Legend says, if you're able to master all three of these elements, then the experience points on your Black Card unlock a hidden level. I thought I would never achieve that hidden level because I just didn't get how to play Spades. I was okay with that, but apparently my friends weren't. Perhaps the Black planets aligned, 'cause we were in Brooklyn and had just attended Curlfest 2018. I come out my bathroom thinking we're gon' talk. Instead, I see my wife, Tasha, and my friends Bri and Elvis sitting at the living room table with a deck of cards dead center, giving me the intervention look. What part of the come-to-Jesus moment is thissss?

WHY CARD GAMES AREN'T FOR ME:
A FLASHBACK SEQUENCE

It's ok, Black People Who Can't Play Spades. Someone has to make the plates and there's always Uno aka Training Spades. One of you negros talkin bout you feel seen or attacked run and get me two wings, a little bit of mac and cheese and a cold pop.

—Danez Smith

When I was in first grade, my mother and I used to live in Maryland. When my siblings would come to visit, the eldest, Kece (15), would play cards with Mom. Meanwhile, Travis (11) and I would play with our action figures (TMNT all day). You may be wondering why we're having this anime flashback right now 'cause that seems like a nice family moment. That's a hard no. Listen, Travis and I had to make sure we were fed, 'cause when Mom and Kece started playing cards, that loving mother-daughter relationship went out the window. Gradually, voices would get a little higher, cards hit the table a little harder, and then that back-and-forth trash talk would come out. Travis and I would look at each other, look at them, pick up the toys, and walk into the bedroom to keep playing. We didn't want to see how this was gonna turn out. Cracking the bedroom door open, we'd watch them go at it. I'm like, "Come on, Mom, she is a child. *then hears what Kece said back, gasps* That is your mother!" Travis would say, "They can't hear us, man. They're too far gone. We'd have to be holding cards in order to reach 'em." Mom kept a book of all the win-loss records between her and Kece for years. Whenever they got together, that book would come out and it was no-holds-barred.

My guy, that shit had me shook to play any card games. Mom

tried to teach me Spit once and I said, "Look. I've seen how you and Kece get down. I can't do that with you 'cause I know how you get. I'ma keep it strictly Switzerland with you 'cause I want zero problems, Mam."

MEANWHILE, BACK IN THE PRESENT . . .

I just want to reiterate that I didn't mind not knowing how to play Spades. That's a skill tree on the Black Card I was good with not unlocking. I learned Monopoly in South Africa—I don't really have an affinity for it, but I know it. Now when it comes to Taboo, *clenches fist* ask about me. I'd be whupping ass at the function; I'm talking five, seven cards easy. Mom looking at me with pride, like Gai Sensei watching his student Rock Lee bust Gaara's ass in the Chūnin Exams when Rock's leg weights came off, tellin' folk, "I could see he had no aptitude for Spades or Monopoly. So we skipped them and focused solely on Taboo. He is a Taboo specialist that'll lose to no one." The problem with Spades is usually you have to learn by watching, because Black folk don't wanna fuck up their win-loss record partnering with a newbie. Lemme be the first to tell you, the Black Nerd Problems' Slack ain't a safe space for not knowing Spades either. My own people out here exposing me online. It's a lot of pressure, man! "Fine, I'll learn," I told my friends. "Just don't be out here yelling at me." Now, I'll leave the name of the person who agreed to be my training partner anonymous so as not to ruin their win-loss record as they were doing me a favor.

When My Partner and I Win the Practice Round

PARTNER: See?! You got it.

INNER ME: My ass is still not knowing what I'm supposed to see or get. I am not seeing the Matrix's HTML code at any point.

trying to guess the number of books I have

ME: I think I got four books and *upward inflection* a possiblllle?

Me Putting a Spade Down to Start the Round

PARTNER: OMAR! What are you doing?! A hand has to be cut before you can do that!

ME: See?! You're yelling at me! . . . I don't wanna play anymore.

Me Stating That "I-I-I Have Two and Possible?"

I then proceed to win six books and everyone just looks at me

PARTNER: There's thirteen books in total. If you're off then that throws us all off.

ME: Well, no one told me that.

But then something started happening. Fair warning, I'm about to use a bunch of Spades terms without explanation. If ya wanna know what they mean you gotta go through the same struggle to learn the game as I did. As I was saying, my books and possibles became more accurate. My partner was nodding at my moves in pride now. When I saw my partner get cut, I revealed the king of spades to ensure our win and they exploded with excitement. My partner started signaling to me before the next round started: "We got this shit." When we were six turns in, I was screaming with my eyes at them that "we do not have this shit!" After a few more goes, it was evident that I had begun forcing the other team's hand more and more, which then escalated the shit talking from their side right before we grabbed our first win.

And there it was, at last, among all the shit talking and score keeping, I could feel the level up happening. The sudden rush of Blackness doubling and taking over me. Yet, this time it felt different from when I had finally watched *The Wire* (in 2015). I was leveling up, but no longer occupying the same plane of existence. Could this be the hidden level I had heard about? Was there about to be a boss battle? Because I was not prepared for that. As I looked around me, I thought I might have been transported to the ancestral plane. Tables and chairs started appearing. Folks began sitting at them and playing games of Spades and dominoes. Other groups were playing Taboo (I didn't see anyone playing Uno).

There were thousands of tables with all these elder Black folk from different eras: all playing various games, all discussing grown folk business. My god. I realized this was it. I had earned my way to the grown folks' grown folk table.

EPILOGUE

I called my brother and then my sister.

> **ME:** Do you know how to play Spades?
>
> **KECE:** No.
>
> **ME:** Ah, okay. I knew you and Mom played cards. I just learned, and I was curious if you knew how. Travis said ex-cons taught him. Yo, what card game was it that you and Mom would go at it over?
>
> **KECE:** Oh, gin rummy. You remember that?
>
> **ME:** Uhhhh, yeah, man. When I talked to Travis and brought up you and Mom goin' at it over cards, he said, "Yeah . . . I remember that." I could feel his thousand-yard stare in his eyes through the phone.

KECE: *laughing* It was gin rummy. Then it was rummy. As I got older we would include word searches, *Wheel of Fortune* (ten cents a game), and keep score for each game. She wanted to teach me how to play Spades, but it was something about the suits or the books that I didn't get at that age (6). So, it was easier for me to learn gin rummy. I think she didn't teach me Spades because she was so competitive and I woulda beat her. If she was here, she'd say, "I didn't wanna bother [teaching you] 'cause I woulda kicked your ass." She tried to teach me Monopoly when I was about six or seven, but I'd lose and cry and she'd say, "I'm not gonna teach you if you keep crying."

ME: That sounds like her. Hey, I've always wondered. Why would y'all be arguing?

KECE: 'Cause I started winning! I started winning and she'd wanna double-check my cards and count my hand . . . "oh, that doesn't go to this," "oh, that point doesn't count for this game." So I said, "Well, if you're checking my cards, then I'm checking yours." When I got older, you know what she had the nerve to tell me? That sh—

ME: That she let you win. Yeah, I know. She told me that.

KECE: YEAH! You let me win? You. Let. Me. Win? Maaaaaaaaan, please. I'll never forget the first time I beat her. She made it harder and harder to even come close. Which, to her credit, she was doing to make me better. But when I finally whupped her? When I finally whupped her ass? I'll never forget that look in her eye. She looked up and said, "You won," but it was the expression on her face. It was that proud-but-pissed look. Then eventually, she got a book to keep tabs on our scores, wins, and losses over the years. No matter where we were—if I was visiting or we were driving to North Carolina—we always had a deck of cards.

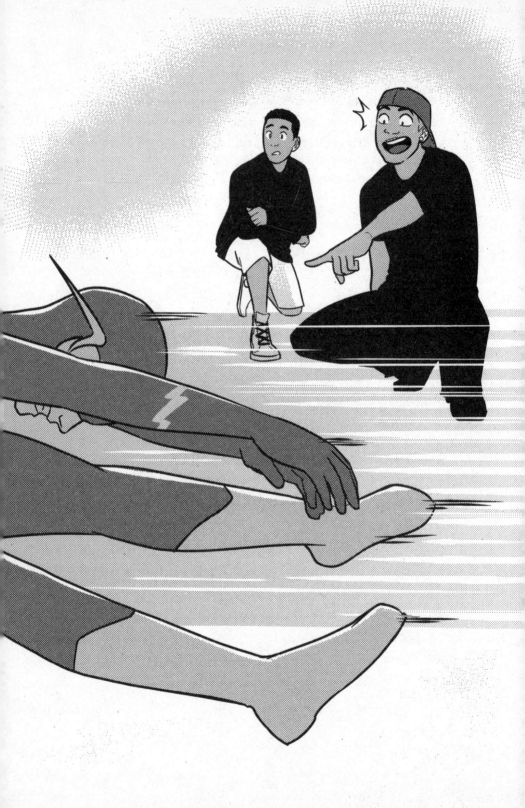

Two Dope Boys and an—
Oh My God, the Flash Got Fucked Up!

OMAR & WILLIAM,

aka Them Dudes Selling White Tees at the Flashpoint

IT'S UNMISTAKABLE THAT *Arrow* on the CW really put on for the live-action hero adaptation (until *Daredevil* came and took that lunch money). *Arrow* walked (hitting those bull's-eyes) so that *The Flash* could run. *The Flash* was light, funny, and didn't take itself too seriously in stark contrast to its predecessor. Compared to Oliver Queen's brooding nature on *Arrow*, Barry Allen was living on high . . . until season two.

In season two we met a villain speedster named Zoom. Not only was Zoom faster than Barry, he apparently didn't get the memo that this was a family show. You can't be on the CW breaking Barry's back, literally putting your hand through my man's spinal cord like that. How you gonna have your hero go from the fastest man alive to being dead from the dick down? He beat the miles per hour out of Barry then proceeded to drag that poor boy through the streets of Central City. Barry's body was flapping in the wind like a white flag of surrender. We still haven't recovered from the PTSD of seeing possibly the most historic beatdown of a superhero in recent history last to this day.

OMAR: Barry Allen needed a ref to throw a flag on the play as well as a kitchen sink. I don't know what the gossip site is in DC Universe. I dunno if they got a Shade Room for all the dirt that happens to superheroes too, but Barry better hope not 'cause I ain't ever seen a hero get their body Earth'd like that since Superman's funeral.

WILLIAM: Yo, the DC version of Shade Room are the comments on Tumblr when the DC Comics' Convergence event was poppin' off. *Convergence* was yet another reboot of the DC Comics continuity, and ya know what, people were tired of that shit. Shit was just savage with no concern for human decency. And that's exactly where Zoom's state of mind was when he was giving Barry the Holy Trinity ass-whuppin'. Dude tried to bury the Scarlet Speedster, then was gonna sit at his tomb three days later just in case he rose again.

OMAR: That highlight reel ain't looking good for our former track hero MVP, man. Barry tried to toss that lightning like it was a *Super Smash Bros.* item and caught the UNO Reverse. How you come out the pocket with Guile's sonic boom and get that shit "return to sender"? Zoom out here cuttin' Barry's lights out like he missed the electric bill payment.

WILLIAM: Barry, my speedster, I hate it had to be you. The lightning is a cool trick and all, but obviously Barry is a novice with that shit, like the first two hours of *Infamous* when you still playing with Cole MacGrath and you haven't unlocked the good powers yet. But can we talk about how Zoom ran around Central City doing press conferences while carrying exhibit A with him everywhere? Cats was probably at home, ordering pizza, heard the doorbell, answered that shit, but instead of getting that large thin-crust cheese, they just got Zoom's demonic ass holding dead-from-the-waist-down Flash.

OMAR: DUUUUUUDE! Why Barry look like an unrolled Fruit by the Foot blowin' in the wind as Zoom was runnin' with him? Barry's body was straight soggy-tortilla-shell limp, looked like a fresh-popped party streamer! Jay Garrick had to be watching that shit from his laptop talkin' 'bout, "And y'all ain't wanna believe me. See? You see? Now you out here lookin' like strained Play-Doh, *eats Dorito* whole body lookin' like khakis with the crease in 'em. These young kids don't wanna fuckin' listen to a damn thing till they get dropped on the blacktop."

WILLIAM: And look, I know shit was scary at the time, when Zoom showed up at the secret lair then kicked in the door waving the limp four limbs of their hero. But the next day, when that muthafucka wakes up . . . how you not lookin' at Barry with pure disgust? Iris gotta be like, "Yeah, after that, ain't no way I'm bearing his children. They gonna ask me how their father ended up in a wheelchair and there's no way I can tell them that someone kneaded his spine like bread dough and made him defecate in his Speed Force draws."

OMAR: I was okay with the ass-whupping until Zoom Taser punched Barry in the spine, making homie's legs turn into spaghetti. I mean damn, ya mans was lookin' like Forrest Gump walkin' with the leg braces! I saw him take that hit and said, "OoOoOOoooo-ughhhh . . . He must have shit himself on that. IT'S OKAY IF YOU SHIT YOURSELF, BARRY!" This is seriously the worst moment of the entire beatdown 'cause it looks like Barry got hit so hard that he ejaculated . . . It's either that or he's trying to hit the high note of a Mariah Carey track. God, that arch in the back, man! Remember that arch?! That's the arch ya moms gets when you were a kid and hit the back of her ankle with a shopping cart.

WILLIAM: Bruh, that's some shit your body ain't supposed to come back from. I feel like Grant Gustin needed at least eighteen months of yoga for that scene. Fam, Flash's body went fuckin' parallel to the earth on that punch. Lookin' like *Sesame Street*, "this episode is presented to you by the letter *C*." Flash is my dude, man, I really don't appreciate Zoom punching him so hard that it turned his body into the shape of a socket wrench.

OMAR: Yo, Oliver Queen (*Arrow*) got his throat hit, stabbed through the abdomen, and kicked off a fucking mountain, and that shit looks like a fucking spa day compared to what Barry went through. Ollie musta watched the news of this shoutin', "I SAID GODDAMN! BARRY! BARRY, SOFTEN THE BLOWS WITH YOUR PRIVI-LEGE! USE YOUR PRIVILEGE OR A WAD OF HUNDREDS TO SOFTEN THE BL— He can't hear me. I'ma get him a walker for Christmas this year."

Zoom out here thinkin' he Z from Zola's story 'cause he trappin' with the Speed Force and Barry in that Jarrett fetal position just wanting a warm glass of milk and an "everything is going to be okay" head pat.

WILLIAM: Yo, if this was Zola's story and Barry wanted to jump (well, fall) off the roof after the shit that Zoom, aka Z, just did, you better let that man meet his maker the way he wants. No judgment from me. I mean, if I were Barry and woke up after that shit, I might have been pissed y'all kept me on life support long enough for me to live through that shit. Barry was basically dead after Zoom gave him the spinal tap. The rest was just parading a corpse.

OMAR: Barry woke up and said, "AWWW FUCK. I'M STILL HERE? Y'ALL AIN'T LET ME GO?" The previews had your boy runnin' on a treadmill but fallin' and shit, still in a wheelchair. Yo, Zoom got in this dude's fucking mind. He gon' need to pull a Korra and meet up with Zaheer to guide his ass back to the Speed Force.

Y'all know damn well the original Flash, Jay Garrick, is Zaheer in this scenario too.

Jay is going to be such a fucking nice guy about it instead of straight entering the room doing the running man (unironically) while singing, "*I told you so,*" which will get remixed into "*I tried to tell your ass,*" then chopped and screwed into "*Buuuuuuuut dooooooooooon'ttt noooooo-boooody wannnna listennn to Jaaaaaay. (Eraaa-eraaa.) Listennnnn, listennnnn to Jay.*"

WILLIAM: See, I disagree. Barry needs to find a way back into the Speed Force and resurrect Earth-1 Harrison "Not Really" Wells instead. That's your Zaheer moment. Also, can we talk about the fact that the beginning of every episode, Barry talkin' about ". . . and I am the fastest man alive"? Muthafucka, we've met two villains who were speedsters and both them bastards were faster than you! Barry 'bout to get sued for slander, but I hope his lawyer has a wheelchair-accessible entrance cuz your boy still got the wind chimes for legs right now.

OMAR: I literally have no words for how he can come back from this next episode. In the intro he needs to be like, "My name is Barry Allen . . . I'ma skip the shit I usually say about being the fastest man alive, because the doctor said my long-term memory should be coming back in about a week but there some shit goin' on I think . . . and I am the only one fast enough to stop it. I am the Batman—I MEAN FLASH! . . . I AM THE FLASH."

Barry going to need Derrick Rose's help to come back from this injury and then get Iyanla or Dr. Drew to help get his emotional shit together, 'cause I guarantee that boy still lyin' in the fetal position as we speak, talkin' 'bout, "Cisco at S.T.A.R. Labs made the suit and all my gear, I really don't want to have the conversation with him about me shitting in it."

WILLIAM: Man, he ain't gotta worry about that conversation because Cisco vibed that suit after they had to cut Barry out of it and saw that nothing but shame and bodily fluids were ahead, so he burned that shit quick. And the intro for the next episode shouldn't even be an intro to *The Flash*. It should be Barry doing a commercial for Depend adult diapers. That shit should be one long infomercial with about twenty minutes of *Flash* content. My faith in humanity needs some breathing room. I can't watch another full hour of *Flash* this soon after the massacre.

Black Nerd Crush Blues: Myra Monkhouse Deserved Way Better

OMAR HOLMON,
aka Adorkable Words of Affirmation

EVERY TIME A Black man says, "Black women don't like nerds," somehow, some way, the universe or the internet will inform him, "You want it to be one way but it's the other way." I can't tell you how over the "Black women didn't like me 'cause I watched *Dragon Ball Z*/I was practicing Bruce Leroy's glow choreography in the mirror" narratives I am. There's this tendency to act as if Black nerd girls are scarce or a rarity if they weren't within your immediate vicinity growing up. Look, I'ma tell you like writer Brittany Williams said it, "Black nerd girls aren't a rarity. We ain't unicorns. We've been here all along." Damn right, and you know who doesn't get enough credit for being at the head of that charge? Myra Monkhouse.

fist over mouth I said, Myra muhfuckin' Monkhouse. How you gonna try to Mel Gibson (in *What Women Want*) Black women with a generalization that they don't fuck with nerdy Black boys (and technically implying they wouldn't mess with nerdy Black girls either—it ain't all about cis, sis) when on January 29, 1993, in sea-

245

WILLIAM EVANS AND OMAR HOLMON

son four, episode fourteen of *Family Matters*, the teen crush game got crushed. The girl-next-door game got changed. Myra Boutros Boutros Monkhouse (say the whole name if you nasty) stepped on the TV screen and *Drake voice* nothing was the same.

First and foremost, let it be known that I'll never claim Urkel as Black nerd king (Dwayne Wayne first of his name the only godfather we acknowledge). I'll admit he was funny (hilarious even), but "is this my nerd king?" No, he ain't have that crown. However, when muhfuckin' Myra Monkhouse stepped on the screen? I wanted him to stop pining after Laura Winslow and win (i.e., not mess this up with Myra). When they first met, Steve casually mentions that the name Myra stems from a seaport in ancient Lycia. Myra says she is aware and notes that the name Steve is derived from the Greek word *Stephanos*, meaning "crown." Yeah, Myra ain't come here to play. She's with the wits, and even after Steve makes a spectacle (read: ass) of himself later that night, Myra is down to wear him down.

> *Y'all lames are corny with that "Black Women don't like nerds" shit.*
>
> —Will Evans

Myra was a Black woman that loved this nerdy lame Steve for the nerdy lame that he was. Don't you sit there and say, "Oh, but that's a TV show, this is real life," as if art don't imitate life, my guy. Representation matters, right? Myra wasn't some damn made-up hobbit or alien. She's a Black woman that fucked with nerds heavy. Also, can we just talk about how fly she was? On the real forget Steve, Myra was THAT chick. Your girl was a nerd through and through. That shit was all up in her alleles.

Nerd boys wanna talk about the perfect pop culture nerd girl to relate to (and then quiz them to "make sure" they're a nerd as if they're a replicant? Host?) and not give academia nerds their due.

Nerd is a spectrum, fam, and all the hues matter. Myra was brilliant, strong, and could code-switch with the best of 'em. That girl-next-door shit was just to navigate through the world, but when that mask came off? Myra. Was. With. The. Shits. You remember the greasy she spoke to Laura Winslow? When she was telling Steve not to fucking change himself into Stefan Urquelle 'cause he was great the way he is? Maaaaaan, this guy Steve out here literally becoming someone he's not for Laura, and Myra stood by this flip-floppin' mofo the entire time. Even after she Kendrick Lamar *"still will take you down right on your mama's couch in Polo socks"*-ed him! Arghh, ya girl got caught in an isosceles love triangle and was still saint-like patient with Steve. You can't tell me Myra Monkhouse ain't deserve better.

I'm a Black nerd and that shit was illegal until like 2003.
—Donald Glover

Don't talk to me about Black women not being here for nerds when Myra Monkhouse was clapping for them to win all day like she was cheering in the crowd. I won't stand for it. I sit down and scoff at that notion. Just 'cause you don't see it doesn't mean it doesn't exist. Just 'cause it ain't within your immediate grasp doesn't mean you're not going to have a wild encounter with one on your Pokémon adventure leaving Pallet Town . . . I'm saying when you get older and leave your familiar surroundings, you'll see there's a whole world out there with different people to meet and greet who will share your interests, be they Black women/men, just try not to be trash upon meeting them 'cause then you were the reason they ain't fuck with you all along.

Myra Boutros Boutros Monkhouse (yeah, I'm nasty) was the beacon of hope that somewhere out there some Black woman (or Black man) gon' fuck with your nerdy Black ass for who the fuck you are. Myra was witty, funny, and adorkably oblivious (when she wanted to be).

As sweet as Myra was, she was way more savage and shady when she felt it was time for the gloves to come off (even if it really wasn't time for 'em to come off). She was on Steve just like he was on Laura Winslow, and son couldn't hack it most of the time. They had Myra being obsessive and possessive of Steve on the show way more into the later seasons, but fuck a load of that, man, nah. Y'all not gonna pigeonhole my girl into a stereotype. The way they had my girl go out, man? On some criminal shit trying to frame Laura Winslow and being three shades away from *Basic Instinct*? I rebuke that ending for Myra. That shit *Dragon Ball GT* to me, I don't count it. Myra Monkhouse still a queen in the Black nerd girl realm as far as I'm concerned.

I say all of that to say this: fuck what you heard, Black women been 'bout the nerd and put some fucking respeck on Myra Boutros Boutros Monkhouse's name, my g. Never forget the most underrated of the teen crush game. Never forget, before Black girl magic, there was Black girl science and ya girl got the Nobel Prize for that shit. The only house I pledge is Monkhouse, muthafuckas. Fuck *Full House*, bring me Monkhouse, muthafuckas. Get you a girl that can play Nina Simone on the Myron Floren Polka Master accordion, muthafuckas. [Editor's note: Omar, how many times you gonna say *muthafuckas*?] Shhhhhhhh! Not while I'm pouring praise to the best nerd girl to ever do it to these muthafuckas.

Pay homage, you serfs. Don't talk to me about Black women not fucking with Black nerd boys/girls/nonbinary gender–conforming, when Myra Monkhouse was standing right there with you with the Viola Davis *Fences* face the entire time. *DJ gunshots* Don't you ever forget who was there for your ass, telling you to do you, every T.G.I. Friday lineup. Myra muhfuckin' Mounkhouse. *Jamaican air horn*

The Push and Pull of Watching
Mad Men while Black

WILLIAM EVANS,
aka Roger Sterling's Uncredited Driver

WHEN I WAS still a teenager nearing my high school graduation, I remember going to (being dragged to) my father's work functions or to dinner at the home of his colleagues. My father is a really smart man—brilliant, really—and was a chemist at, let's say, a really large company. He had ascended into some management hierarchy where the higher he rose, the less people he saw that looked like him. There were times we would be at these large functions with a hundred–plus people and there would be two, maybe three other Black families. My father didn't seem to know them. Years later, I realized they may have been at a different employment level than my father and therefore didn't cross paths with him. It was a reaffirmation that Black folks were still "out of place" in the realm of successful business structures. That was also in the mid-'90s.

I used to watch *Mad Men* with two different minds: "this is a really well put together show that entertains me," and "this is a show that doesn't relate to me in any way, shape, or form, with no interest in doing so." For those that aren't familiar, *Mad Men* is a drama about an advertising firm in New York during the 1960s (mostly). It is a rich and beautiful TV show with a great cast and usually great writing. The costume and set designs are possibly the best in TV history and they often are very true to the times. I guess. As I've stated before in talking about period TV shows, they almost always focus on upper-class white communities. The combo of the time period and the financial class of the people being portrayed often leaves little to no air for people of color to breathe on these shows. But let's be honest, they aren't really making the attempt either.

The two minds that I used to watch *Mad Men* have congealed into one for no other reason than it was on forever. Having debuted in 2007 and not ending until 2015, for me *Mad Men* is the cool uncle that has always said problematic and privileged shit at the family gatherings, but after a while, you have just reached your breaking point and the comments he makes aren't as cute anymore. We got ninety-two episodes of *Mad Men* (which is thirty episodes longer than *Breaking Bad*, FYI), and you barely need two hands to count all the people of color that have appeared on the show. And please name a person of color that held any social station above an elevator operator or a secretary. I used to watch *Mad Men* as appointment TV until I just had my fill of the unapologetic exclusion around season six, when it got relegated to "I'll catch up in the middle of the week" status. By the time season seven began, I had dropped the show altogether.

Well, I am a completionist and eventually finished the show. Spoiler, the inclusion didn't get much better. Let's also be crystal clear about something: this isn't an oversight or omission. The demographic of *Mad Men*, or lack thereof, is completely intentional. The show's creator, Matt Weiner, and his staff have been very deliberate in the story they want to tell and have been pretty unwavering in that approach. Weiner doesn't care about the criticisms of the show's lack of minority representation or impact because POC aren't really part of the story he's interested in telling. *Mad Men* has plenty of "taboo" topics to speak on, like the abuse/treatment of women in its environment or the sexual orientation of some of its characters. There just isn't room for someone of color to be that important on this show. Some critics have praised Weiner for that approach, that he's willing to tell the story he wants regardless of the pressure he receives for it being so myopic. I can't find any Black critics saying that, however.

One of the things that kept me hanging on to *Mad Men* was the progressing timeline at work and thinking that it might lead to more (for lack of a better word) integration in the casting. The fruits of such patience resulted in a couple of Black secretaries to go with the Black maid in Betty's household. Gee, thanks. Except for the aforementioned elevator operator and a pickup guitarist in California, there's been more Black men married to a Kardashian than have been on a show that was on the air for eight years. The criticism that Weiner received in regard to race on the show (that is, outside of the critics who don't simply fall over themselves to praise him) was that Weiner handled race rather clumsily when it did come up.

The JFK episode was one of the best the show produced, as it gripped everyone on the show when it happened (the iconic moment with Loretta, the Drapers' Black maid, sitting next to Betty on the couch while watching TV always burns in my mind). Then came the episode where everyone was at an event when the Dr. King assassination happened and everyone was like, "Ehhhh." And maybe, scarily, that's actually realistic, that these upper-class white folks didn't have much investment for the life of Dr. King (LAWD, because white people LOVE Dr. King Jr., or at least specific quotes of his, now). But what does it really say to a Black viewer to watch all these characters they've spent years with nonchalantly shove off the King assassination? More acutely, does Weiner and his writers have any obligation to a more diverse audience?

Mad Men's dealing with race, as far as a character study, has really said one thing from the show's perspective: white people in the 1960s were horrible. From Roger's blackface to the treatment of the secretaries at SCDP, the racist outburst of Pete, the late Bert Cooper's "I'm not a racist but . . ." dealings, and Peggy's just overall behavior with Black folks (like when she was suspicious that Dawn might steal from her), just about every character has exhibited some sort of racism or racial bias over the show's run.

My problem is that they are rarely running that ideology up against anything substantial. Bert didn't like a Black secretary at the front desk, so she got moved. Pete said horrible things in the office and eventually was made a junior partner. It's one thing to be a showrunner and say, "Look, I'm not afraid to show that these were horrible people for the way they treated people of color," but when it never counts for anything happening, then it becomes very hollow.

One of the cool things about *Mad Men* is that it rarely has characters overtly say, "The year is . . . ," as opposed to having a certain event postmark where the show is. The Nixon broadcast that Draper watches in a midseason premiere put that episode in April of 1970. There are times I wish this show was set in Chicago instead of New York, because by this time, Black businessmen (and a very few women) weren't just a unicorn in the Windy City. It would've been great to see an Arthur G. Gaston avatar appear as the serial entrepreneur with so many businesses that the firm might be interested in. Or the possibility of them trying to woo the inheritors of Annie Malone's estate as the firm tried to expand in cosmetics aimed at Black clients. But none of that imagination existed. Where are the Black folks of consequence in this show? If it wants to make these passing glances concerning race, then why isn't there an antagonist or colleague that is a person of color they can't deal with by simply moving her desk? No start-up business owner looking to get advertising that forces the firm into a quandary of what it stands for and believes in? No company that wants to use a popular athlete to sell its product that forces the firm to reconsider how it does business? No, we don't have anything like that to look back on. Instead, we get Peggy living in a "bad neighborhood" populated by minorities where she gets to play the great comforter to the small, recurring role of Julio, a Latino boy that didn't want to move away. And oh yeah, she owns the building of course. Why else would she be there?

And yet, here I am, talking about *Mad Men*. The show is aimed at me as a lover of good TV in its framework and construction. The show is definitely not aimed at me for any other reason. And I'm sure most think the first reason is the only reason that matters, but when you haven't mattered in media for so long, it becomes a lot harder to ignore for you than it does for people that never had to worry about representation before. It's a show that gets heralded as one of the best of all time—what does it matter if I wasn't invited to watch it or not?

Mario Kart Reveals
Who You Truly Are

OMAR HOLMON,
aka Rainbow Road Rash

Forgiveness is between them and God. It's my job to arrange the meeting.

—John W. Creasy (Denzel Washington),
Man on Fire

THERE ARE VIDEO games that help make you who you are. Case in point? Link from *The Legend of Zelda: Ocarina of Time.* You're with Link every step of the way on his quest as he grows up and saves the land of Hyrule. You're not controlling Link, you're his brother-in-arms from a third-person point of view. Throughout the game, you grow with Link and come to learn about courage, duty, and honor, traits that will help mold you into a productive member of society.

Mario Kart is not that type of game. *Mario Kart* doesn't help make you who you are. *Mario Kart* doesn't give a fuck about duty, honor, or saving anybody. Mercy? What the fuck is mercy? Is that a protein bar? Is that a new five-minute ab workout? Is that a useless update for your smartphone, 'cause it sounds like a useless update for your smartphone? Let me tell you something: there is no mercy in *Mario Kart*. *Mario Kart* doesn't make you a better person. No, *Mario Kart* reveals who you really are. Your true self that just wants to win, that needs to win. It's that same need that the game takes and uses to corrupt your morals and bring the abyss out of you.

You have two choices when that happens. You can recognize that although this game claims to be rated G and family friendly, you should stop playing, because it's all a disguise for the abyss that consumes you with a level of intense competition that slowly brings out the ruthless parts in your soul that you didn't realize existed . . . or you can stare into the abyss and, when it stares back, blow kisses at it. Take a selfie with it. Invite it to brunch for bottomless mimosas because you wanna get comfortable and buddy-buddy with the abyss. You want the abyss to have the spare key to your place because you're ready to take this relationship to the next level, because in *Mario Kart*, it's merk or *get* merked.

I knew this shit from day one on *Mario Kart* . . . and I embraced it. I go out of my way to be a dick to everyone on the sticks in *Mario Kart*. I let you know off the bat, I am not your fucking friend in this game. Once that power switch goes on and PSE&G starts charging us by the minute, I'm on the fucking clock. I'm the muhfucka throwing hands all over the track, and when I say "throwing hands," I don't mean I'm fighting everyone—a group of bananas is called a hand.

Therefore, I'm the asshole literally laying rows of bananas across the track methodically like they're C-4 explosives. THAT'S ME. I'm saving this lightning bolt for when you're in the middle of a jump over a gap. Yeah, THAT'S ME. When that blue shell creeps up on you and takes you out of first place yet again? That wasn't me. I don't get blue shells because I'm the guy already advancing on yo spot up in first place like it's your house and the Slomin's Shield stopped working. That's my SHIT. Words can't describe how good it feels to have a muhfucking green shell in your hand and a racer in front of you unguarded, unaware, just staring at the finish line in front of them. They're thinking it's all good. That they got this. That they're home free. And then they see you Tokyo Drift around the fucking corner bend with the Koopa Troopa choppa loaded up on 'em. They start feelin' like Ricky in *Boyz n the Hood* and they book for that finish line, but we both know how this plays out. We both know how this is going to end. They're yelling out, "No! Not again! Not this time!" and I'm Death's scythe tending the cemetery lawn at 4:00 a.m. on a Sunday morning, quiet, not even giving you the satisfaction of condolences with the sound of my voice as I let the choppa rang out on you . . .

And I don't give a fuck who you are to me. Brother, sister, nephew, uncle, grandpa, significant other, soul mate, love of my life, dude that does my taxes at H&R Block, boss, mailman, landlord, my best friend, Phil, from childhood that I haven't physically seen since the death of my mother back in 2011, and we both laughed and cried on sight of each other together in the street at her funeral . . . Everybody can get it!

deep exhales And you might be reading this chapter thinking, "All right, I get how *Mario Kart* can change you as a person, but surely when you have a family of your own and you're playing with your kids, you'll take it easy on them." No. I won't. I'll be damn sure to pass this savageness down to my children. If my children aren't more ruthless than my wife and I when they play *Mario Kart*, then I have failed as a parent.

ME: What are you doing, why are you holding on to that blue shell?

SON: I— I can't knock Mom out of first place.

WIFE: Don't you put that softness on me, boy. Shoot it!

DAUGHTER: DO IT!

FAMILY DOG: Woooof! [*Translation: "DO IT or pass the sticks!"*]

ME: KILL THE FANBOY SO THE FANDOM CAN LIVE!

SON: AHHHHHHH! *shoots blue shell* I see now. I understand everything.

Lemme put you on fandom real quick and say this: fuck ball. *Mario Kart* is life. If you want to know the true measure of someone, play them in *Mario Kart*. If they act all proper and apologetic when they hit you with an item, don't trust 'em! You can do better. They aren't the one for you. If there isn't some small part of them that feels satisfaction at watching a racer in front of them fall, take a hit, or get knocked out of first place, THEY'RE WEAK! Their whole bloodline is weak and they won't survive the winter.

You know how they say if a person doesn't have books in their place, don't fuck them? Well, if a person can't stay on the track on Rainbow Road in *Mario Kart*, don't fuck them. You'll thank yourself the next morning as you brush your teeth and mockingly quote them in the bathroom mirror saying, "Ugh, do we have to do Rainbow Road again?" The answer is yes, you do. Life is Rainbow Road, homie, you gotta decide how you 'bout to live yours. Because me? I said a fanboy like me? Sheeeeeeeeeit, I live my life 150cc at a time.

Top Five Dead or Alive:
Monica Rambeau (Marvel Comics)

OMAR HOLMON,
aka Supporter and Liaison
of Real Hot Girl Shit

SOMETHING YOU SHOULD know off the riff, one of the most powerful people walking around the Marvel Universe is Monica Rambeau, a dark-skinned woman of color that's been in the hero game for years. Recently she has become more of a household name, leading the latest incarnation of *The Mighty Avengers*. Those in the know know she doesn't take any shit.

Monica Rambeau is somewhere between being the Rihanna and the Jean Grae of Marvel. She strokes no egos, calls you on your shit, and is written with the sharpest of wit/sarcasm (and not in the sassy Black friend way, ever). She has been the leader of the Avengers, has one of the most powerful abilities around (more on that later), and has been rocking her hair natural for years (more on that later too). Monica is one of the best to ever do for women of color in comics when it comes to representation. So let's get more acquainted with Monica Rambeau . . .

What you gon' do when I appear?
W-w-when I premiere?

. . . .

This shit been mine, mine
—Azealia Banks, "212"

Son, Monica Rambeau has tax deductibles on her fux. She gives none. One of the great things about her character is how unapologetic she is about her Blackness and just who the fuck she is. This comes up in the *Marvel Divas* series, where we see her on her downtime with her predominately white hero friends (Firestar, Black Cat, and Hellcat). This is a testament to the way she has been written as, well, again, Monica isn't depicted as the angry Black woman when giving her experiences. Monica is quick-witted, funny, independent, and that friend who will be by your side even when she's annoyed with you. She's a woman of color showing the people around her (as well as the reader) experiences that they may be unaware of—a look behind the veil of what she is going through. That isn't to say she always got the kid gloves on, 'cause Monica doesn't keep it 100, she keeps it 1,000+. Especially when it comes to her home in New Orleans and helping out post-Katrina: "Well, I spent a lot of time there post-K. Cleaning up the mess you white people made." Monica is that friend in the group that tells you like it is. Monica don't do meek, subtle, or quaint. One time when Jim Rhodes was Iron Man, he said to her, "What's happenin', babe?" Monica replied, "Let's make a deal! You call me 'Captain Marvel' instead of 'babe' and I'll call you 'Iron Man' instead of 'Bozo.'" Needless to say that's the last time Iron Man called her "babe."

Beware, 'cause I crush anything I land on
Me here, ain't no mistake, nigga, it was planned on
—Eve, "Let Me Blow Ya Mind"

Listen, Monica is able to tap into the electromagnetic spectrum and become different forms of energy from electricity to gamma rays, cosmic rays to ultraviolet light. Monica must be an anime fan, because when she gets pissed, she'll shout out certain moves. The woman even has her own version of Goku's Spirit Bomb attack. As we've seen in the *Mighty Avengers* comics series, when it comes to Monica and her powers, the question isn't what else can she do, it's what can't she do? She can bend light to make herself look like someone else. Once, the team faced an opponent that could slow down time. Monica, who can be made of light, was able to wreck house because even slowed down the speed of light is still too dope game to handle. The woman is a fucking powerhouse. The best part is that she can assist like John Stockton. We've seen Monica become energy for Captain Marvel (Carol Danvers era) to absorb and disperse at enemies. We then saw her step it the fuck up another notch when she transformed into gamma energy to give She-Hulk a boost. Son, Wolverine and Colossus's fastball special ain't got shit on Monica's legendary team-up skills.

Hairdresser from Milan, that's the monster do
—Nicki Minaj on Kanye West's "Monster"

Ever since her debut, Monica's hair has been all-natural everything. We've seen it go from an Afro to braids to locs and so on and so on. This was a great thing for me to see going through back issues. It is just a reminder that this part of a Black woman's life has been put on fleek in Marvel for years. It's been great seeing different artists tackle this as well, each giving a different interpretation and style on the way she was rocking her hair for the time being. In *Mighty Avengers*, Monica is rocking her hair with a relaxer. This is the first time this has been seen from her character and my initial reaction was totally, "What part of the all-natural everything is this?" I then checked myself, 'cause I'm a dude and a woman's right to change her look is her own, fictional or nonfictional, nah mean? Even as a fan, as tough as it was to see. Since her debut, Monica has always worn her hair natural, so seeing it straight really stood out as a big change. There are also women that do rock that relaxer in the hair as it's easier to manage or just something they like. Doesn't mean they aren't about their natural hair or hate it. It's style . . . This was addressed in *Mighty Avengers* as well by the writer Al Ewing, when a mother tells Monica how much her daughter idolizes her. Monica is flattered until the mom tells her that her daughter seeing Monica with a relaxer in her hair is what finally allowed the daughter to have her hair relaxed. The mom then starts saying, "I always tell her, no one is going to take you seriously with your hair looking like that [natural] and the relaxer only stings for a little bit." As you can imagine, this is über-awkward as fuck for Monica (she can't even hide it on her face) because one, she ain't ever about not rocking her natural hair or shaming it, and two, to her it was just a simple style change, but for the kid it was something more. Monica is stuck in this awkward moment as her teammate Vic taunts her from afar about it. We don't see a resolution, but the scene shows that Ewing acknowledges the concern about the hair change for Monica.

My hormones jumpin' like a disco
—Missy Elliott, "Sock It 2 Me"

When it comes to her love life, Monica is straight up No Flex Zone. We saw her and Jericho Drumm, aka Brother Voodoo (sorcerer supreme), start up a relationship back in *Marvel Divas*. We saw them enjoy a night together, and when Jericho invited her to stay over . . . Monica recounted the story saying, "Yo, I literally flew away. That shit freaked me out." It's hilarious to see Monica, who is so straightforward, be soooo put off by unexpected emotion. She still keeps it one hunna tho, as it isn't a commitment complex, but as she puts it: "I know what I want. And what I want is to move at my pace and not some man's pace."

Come on, man, Monica makes the rules, dude. Seeing her in a relationship with Drumm is hilarious because they are both from the Big Easy and they are both Black. Since Storm and Panther have split, this is the only Black couple I can think of at Marvel. Which kinda says a lot considering how long they've been in the game. The interaction between Monica and Jericho is refreshing to see as a closet peek at a Black rom-com in a Marvel book.

Monica's flirt game gets put on full blast when she meets Dr. Adam Brashear (the Blue Marvel). When testing her powers with Spider-Man monitoring her, she learns to bend her light form to be able to change into different people. She changes into a nude Dr. Brashear. When Adam walks in and sees that, he's taken aback a bit. Spider-Man comments how he could now see how that's weird for him. Meanwhile, all Monica says is "I wanted to get all the detail right." Ya girl got no shame in the thiiiiiirst and I live!

What about your frieeeeeeeeeeeeeeeeends?

—TLC

One of the best things about Monica is how down-to-earth she is. She is always written as the friend you want to hang out with, someone you want to have bail you out and let you know you're fucking up. Monica is written this way when she's with her inner circle of friends as well as when it comes to herself. We've seen her alternate between momma bear and partner in crime, but to me . . . Yo, Monica is the witty one in whatever crew she's in. We done seen her throw shade with the best of 'em. Monica's humor is a big part of what makes her enjoyable as a character, especially when we see that put up against other people in whatever title she is in at the time. As much as she hangs on the sarcastic side, it's a big joy to see her just being outlandish in jest with her peoples when their lives aren't on the line.

When it comes to powerful women of color in Marvel—nah, fuck that, comics in general, y'all gon' start giving my girl Monica Rambeau the respect she deserves. Storm is dope, but she ain't the only one on the pantheon for Black girls killing it in the panel game. Monica is either straight up in your face, making fun of your kicks, or saving your life. I think of the V. Bozeman "Race Jones" lyrics when Monica comes to mind due to how Black and real rap raw she has been presented in terms of issues she faces in her personal life as well as her hero life: *"Black when you stare. Black if you smile. / I was Black back when it wasn't even in style."* That's another big main reason I fucks with Monica. I can't name another character that throws it all out there in her own terms where the reader ain't got a choice but to acknowledge what she's talking about. Again, Monica doesn't keep it 100, she keeps it 1,000+. Every time she hints at it in jest or lays it out occupying whiteness in panels, whenever Monica steps into that limelight it's like she's coming out singing, "I'm Black! Matter of fact I'm Blacker than that."

On Hope, Escapism, and Attrition Discussed Between Black Men

WILLIAM EVANS,
aka Saruman the Black

MY FATHER DOESN'T like *Game of Thrones*. Of course, I knew he wouldn't when he stood in my home and asked to borrow the first season, but I handed him Ned Stark's yet-to-be-severed head in Blu-ray form anyway. As alike as my father and I am, I know his tolerance for violence, gore, and all-out debauchery is a lot lower than mine. And yet, he too had heard about the phenomenon that was *Thrones* and thought he should at least see what the hype was. My father is an Omega-level nerd, so maybe there was some street cred to be lost if he didn't at least try to watch it. By the time season four of *Thrones* had ended, coming off of arguably its best season so far, my father came back to me with season one in hand.

ME: You want season two?
MY POPS: Nope, I'm good.

Apparently my father saw the future and didn't want to be disappointed by the end of the run. Still, I spent a lot of time bolstering my *Game of Thrones* IQ. And that means my overall knowledge base of *Thrones* compares to about 30 percent of what my father knows about Lord of the Rings history. To be fair, the man has been reading, ingesting, reciting, rinse and repeating the books, lore, and movies for longer than I have been alive, so you shouldn't feel sorry for my nerd inferiority to him. But for people my age, Lord of the Rings and *Thrones* share "a" universe, if not "the same" universe. The fantasy and lore, the humans trying to overcome old evil, it's all familiar. But one of the big thematic differences is where Tolkien created a world very independent and unattached to a world we could familiarize with, Martin built his world off one of the most brutal and barbaric time periods within the last 1,500 years.

My father was born in 1951, which means he was a teenager during one of several explosive times to be Black in America. My father never entered the military, even though his older brother went to Vietnam, but that doesn't mean that my father doesn't have some war stories to share. But he doesn't enjoy sharing those. He would rather talk about *The Silmarillion*.

When I was seventeen, I was hanging out with a group of friends from high school. We ended up at a house party with a lot of music, sweat, and liquor. I don't drink alcohol. Never did. Not much moral high ground to it, probably just too much of a control freak to give over that dominion to something else. Well, the party got busted up, maybe ten out of the forty people there were legally allowed to drink, and a lot of us spent the next hour sitting on the curb while the cops decided what to do with us. Two things stood out as I sat there in the grass bathed in the still-flashing lights of the police cruiser: How the hell did I end up being the only Black kid at the party? Why the hell had I constructed a social circle that allowed for the possibility that I ended up as the only Black person at a party? I didn't even give much thought to the fact that I was the only person that spent any time handcuffed that night or that all the cops didn't believe I hadn't drunk anything and wouldn't let me drive my mother's car home while many of my friends did.

My father though, he considered all of this. And he was livid. Ultimately, his lecture to me included responsibility and awareness, but it ended with "If you think you're special out here with all these white people, you'll be real special if you get killed out here too." At the time, I didn't get it and took it as some hyperbolic raving from my out-of-touch parent. But there were a lot of things I didn't get back then.

Another way that LOTR is different from *GOT* is in how one of them really is about escapism with seemingly insurmountable evil being overcome and the other is interested in looking at an alternative to our world with even more brutal mysticism. If you are a man that watched your uncles get beat in the streets even as they came home from war, your heroes assassinated, and your spot on the bus preordained by your skin color, a more brutal version of the world probably isn't how you like to spend your leisure time.

My father grew more and more silent after the string of deaths of Black men at the hands of police that began publicly with Michael Brown and never really ended. I had a hard time understanding why. My father is outspoken and also brilliant, which makes him simultaneously a great conversationalist and annoying if you aren't close to his level on things. But he was saying less as yet another cop was excused in yet another Black person's death and I began to notice. After Tamir Rice was killed in Cleveland, I called my father and we had some very sparse conversation before we began theorizing on the role of fiction in our nonfiction lives. Every once in a while, I get these notions that I can outwit my father into pulling some emotional tether to him. I asked him if we love fantasy and fiction as a means to escape everyday life, but I think I meant, does he use fiction in this way? He answered, "It's not an escape. It's hope. The good guys win and life has value in a fantasy story. It's not about getting away from something. It's about inserting hope into what you can't outrun." See, my father knows when I'm trying to trick him into answering a question about himself, his answer shows me that I've actually tricked myself into believing it's not about me. This is also as direct as he gets these days.

When my father says that he enjoyed how they showed Thorin Oakenshield's descent into madness during the Battle of the Five Armies, what he means is "I can't believe that Charleston cop shot that man in the back." When we argue which movies had the best big battle scenes, we're really talking about how he didn't expect me to watch Black folks killed indiscriminately the way he did over thirty years ago.

The night of the verdict where George Zimmerman was cleared of all charges, I was a mess. I needed to get out of the house, away from everything safe and comfortable, because all of a sudden, it didn't feel that way. It was near midnight, but I called my dad. I didn't expect him to pick up, but he answered like he hadn't been asleep yet either. He listened to me rant for twenty minutes or so without saying much, just letting me rant about my anger. *My* anger. As if he didn't have close to three decades of anger like this ahead of me. He just kept sighing and saying, "Wasn't supposed to be your war."

It sounds like something an elder character in a fantasy novel would say to the young protagonist who is thrust into service ahead of schedule. The difference isn't whether either of those worlds have dragons or not. It's that one of them definitely has a point when things will turn around and work out. I don't dare ask my father if he thinks there's a turn coming in the reality we walk through now.

The week that nine people were killed in the Emanuel African Methodist Episcopal Church, we were both silent: him trying to figure out what to say this time, me still trying to study up on my Tolkien to prepare for the conversation. I've been told that's where you can find hope. Hope by the volumes, if escape isn't a possibility.

Two Dope Boys and a Comic Book: *House of X*

OMAR & WILLIAM,
aka The Two Black Mutants Who
Missed the Mission Cuz of CPT

JONATHAN HICKMAN WOKE up one day and decided to save the X-Men franchise in 2019, and the mutants in the Marvel Universe ain't been the same since. Hickman's *House of X* and *Powers of X* series put the X-Men where the fuck they needed to be. They got their own island of Krakoa, they got their own nation, laws, and politics. But we know Sentinels have been the bane of mutants' existence since the beginning of Marvel space and time. So imagine if humans, led by Dr. Gregor, made a Mother Mold out in space, whose sole purpose is to create next-gen Sentinels that mutants could never counter. I know, fuck humans, right? But before Mother Mold could be finished, the X-Men got wind of this secret space station and sent a strike team to take out the facility before it was completed. Which leads us to Hickman's *House of X* #4 and why it just hits different. Please know that we had to schedule some time in the Danger Room and work this shit out. My mutants, shit might never be the same.

WILLIAM: Nah, man. Naaaaah, man. I wasn't ready. Like, I knew what *could* be coming, but my ass was not ready, my mutant. I don't even know where to begin. Maybe the beginning. Or like, before the beginning, before the tears and shit. What you think the X-Men were listening to in the Blackbird on the way to the Mother Mold, man? I'm guessing Scott "Whatever It Fucking Takes" Summers grabbed the aux cord and put that *Dreams and Nightmares* on as they entered the orbit. Just the thought of that piano playing on their approach got me shook, man.

In a way, this is what Scott's whole fuckin' existence been leading up to, man. Taking a fucking X-Men assault team. Let's not mistake what this was, the gotdamn Navy SEALs of forward-assaulting-ass mutants on a suicide trip. This shit was best/worst-case scenario *Mass Effect 2* going through the Omega 4 Relay. I can't. I done read this issue twice and I still can't.

OMAR: "Push me to the edge, all my X-Men dead!" The foreshadowing for this shit coming down to the Stringer Bell [read: *The Wire*] was Magneto and Professor X an issue ago telling Cyclops that the odds for this mission's success were damn near impossible. Scott's team got sent to stop the Mother Mold from creating Sentinels that would murder mad mutants. Plus if the team does happen to succeed, the Mother Mold is located dumb far in space with no guarantee of making it back alive. Scottie "Five Beams a Day for Three" Summers asked them both, "My mutants, does it need to be done?" Charles Xavier nodded like, "You already know." Scott told them, with utter fucking disgust in his visor at even the thought of his team failing, "Then it will be done." You Marvel Comics fans don't hear me tho. My mutant Cyclops put a blue bandanna on the steering column of the Blackbird jet, looked back at the team seated behind him as they reached orbit, and said, "I'm getting rid of these muthafuckas tomorrow . . . X-Men taking this series in three games."

The mission was supposed to be In-N-Out Burger, baby. They was supposed to order the fade, pull up to the drive-thru window, catch it, then be home in time for *This Is Us*. But these hatin'-ass humans straight blew a whole-ass hole in their hull. Xavier was calling collect via a psychic link to see what's what. They even used the psychic link to project what was happening through a pool of water Storm created. First thing they saw was the Blackbird's paint job all the way fucked up now. You can't blot them bloodstains out. Husk and Angel dead, laid out and folded like ya momma's church crown and Sunday best. Xavier lookin' around like, "This the right channel? Aye, who keeps thinking about *Apollo 13*?! You messing up the link. Oh shit, Jean? This live?! Gaaaaawddayuuuuum!"

WILLIAM: That's when I knew, fam. When they said Angel was dead, I was like sheeeeeiiiiit, Hickman came in like Thor to Thanos except he went for the head the first time. All these muthafuckas might die. How you gonna start the issue that way? Previously on *House of X*: Angel and Husk dead as fuck. I say gawwwwwddayuuuuum. But this X-Men team, man, you hate to see it but they make a mutant proud, man. Nightcrawler's internal plumbing all fucked up and they done stripped Wolverine down to the white adamantium meat.

Speaking of which (and we'll get to the big shit later), but I know folks have been tired of Wolverine's undying ass for the last year. They done killed and rebooted this man more than Spider-Man films in the last decade. Wolverine is an example that cancel culture don't really exist, nah mean? But he earned all the accolades this issue, man. My dude said, "Don't kid yourself, Red, we're playing for blood here." Logan said let them bodies hit the floor and leave that soft shit in the burning Blackbird, fam.

OMAR: Wolverine said, "Just so we're all clear, I'm running up in this Starship *Enterprise* knockoff and stabbing everybody. I'm talking red shirts, blue shirts, yellow shirts, admin roles, everyone in human resources, payroll, legal department, cafeteria workers, maintenance workers, sanitation workers, and IT tech support. I don't give a fuck if it's Take Your Kid to Work Day today either. Snikt. Fucking. Snikt. Feel me?" There's five minutes left on the clock, no time-outs, and two benched players. What you gon' do, Cyclops?! He had the team go for the Phil Jackson full-court press. Nightcrawler teleported them to four different points to fuck up the Mother Mold. Did that shit while his organs were straight cranberry juice. My mutant coughin' up that Ocean Spray and still put 8 points on the board, securing his section on some '88 Isiah Thomas dropping 25 with a sprained ankle. Section 2 closed. Wolverine, *counts bodies he killed* 14 points. Section 4 closed.

We got humans coming for Marvel Girl and Monet who are still stationed on the Blackbird? They tryin' to trap Monet the Empath? Monet the head boss of Bad and Boujee? We just got her back from Generation X. Maaaaan, Monet threw Jean in the escape pod, said, "Keep the channel open while I draw these fouls." Monet took out the Allen Iverson braids when she transformed and made it a Hot Girl Mutant Summer in space where no one could hear these muh-fuckas' knees scream and buckle.

WILLIAM: The Monet exit?!? My gawd. Bury her a fuckin' G. I don't know what to say, Marvel Girl, try harder. Bast. She went straight Blanka on that crew, man. I knew she wasn't gonna survive it, but still, that's the Doc Holliday outro right there . . . unlike Mystique, who got shot out an airlock and is now lookin' like one of the seven hundred ways that the movie *Gravity* could've ended if Sandy B. failed her mission. Remember in *Justice League Unlimited* when they shot Grodd's ass out into space? Well, him and Mystique are neighbors now. Dr. Gregor, head scientist at this Master Mold space station, told Mystique, "Don't let the space freeze you where the good Lord split you." Man, *House of X* came out three days ago and Mystique still drifting through space. She a satellite now, fam. They bouncing DirecTV off her. I feel like we should mention back on Krakoa, where everyone watching Jean emote the terror via the psychic Storm Summer Jam water screen. This was like those Super Bowl parties where the home team blows a 20-point lead. Hank probably burned his X-Men jersey and crying in the shower with a bunch of empty beer cans at his feet.

OMAR: Meanwhile, Dr. Gregor said fuck beta testing and brought Master Mold online early. Whole block heard that advanced 56k modem dial-up get fired up and knew the game was all fucked up now. Charles Xavier heard that Mother Mold computer get the putin and told his children—my fault, his Children of the Atom, his #1 draft pick, his '63 and '75 Dream Team members . . . "Do whatever [the fuck] it takes."

As a former athlete, when your coach says, "Do whatever the fuck it takes"? Your only option is greatness. No excuses. No apologies. Thas it. Scott "Optic Blast Ya Whole Block" Summers was looking out that window thinking nothing but Dido lyrics (*"My tea's gone cold / I'm wondering why I got out of bed at all"*) when the MVP Nightcrawler said, "We can get there" (*"The morning rain clouds up my window / And I can't see at all"*). Wolverine told his mutant, "Ain't no other way, Slim . . ." Scott, forearm against the glass, seeing nothing but red, dead, and a chance at redemption, told his peoples their last marching orders . . . "Go." (*"And even if I could, it'd all be grey / But your picture on my wall / It reminds me that it's not so bad / It's not so bad . . ."*) But it is that bad, Dido, 'cause this is X-Men black ops, baby. SOMEBODY GOTS TO FUCKING GO!

Nightcrawler and Wolverine about to teleport into space in front of a fucking sun to destroy a literal mother of all Sentinels. Ain't no happy endings here. The days of the future done past right here, fam. Right before the quantum leap Wolverine asked Nightcrawler if there's a spot in heaven where thugs get in free and you gotta be a G. Nightcrawler told his mans and dem for the past forty-four years, "I'll have the spliff waiting for you on the other side, my guy." *screams at how fucking good this shit is*

WILLIAM: "The bravest man I know." The fucking respect! Scott is watching Wolverine be turned into a bucket of Popeyes and eulogizing this man in real time. For Scott to say that about Logan . . . nah, man, there are fucking Tetris levels to this. Arrrgghhh. AND WE THOUGHT THAT SHIT WAS OVER. Scott acting like he lost the platoon but won the war. Your boy really thought he was about to find a super-suit in storage and reverse eye blast his way to the escape pod. Humans did all the dirt, but you gotta respect Dr. Gregor's level of savage. Scott tried to tell her that the Mold is a shooting, is just a dead satellite now, so he's worthless as a hostage. Dr. Gregor aimed the pump-action shotgun at his head and was like, "Nah, you just worthless."

We way late on this, but shout-out to the artists Pepe Larraz and Marte Gracia. This whole fuckin' issue slaps in the visuals, but that Dr. Gregor reflection in the mutant formerly known as alive, aka Cyclops? Chef's fucking kiss (translated from "pretty damn great when you need to lead up to a muthafucka getting their head blown off"). And through all that. THROUGH ALL THAT, we're still not done! No X-Men mission is complete until Jean dies. And Jean dying alone at the hands of about four Sentinels in space might have been the most tragic. Fuck, man. Back on Krakoa, Storm dropped that water, then dropped down in the prayer formation cuz that's the only thing she got to whip up now. Some prayer for the souls of them X-Cats.

OMAR: *lifts head from hands* Hickman is . . . Hickman really is, yo. Hickman is giving us *Mutants in the Hood*. Cyclops hit the corner and got that shotty click-clack, bla-ow. All I heard was Cuba Good-ing Jr., yellin', "R̶i̶i̶i̶c̶k̶y̶y̶y̶y̶y̶ Scooooooottieeeee!" I legit don't even have the words. Charles Xavier hit an ill soliloquy in the aftermath when them X-Men got X'd. "Look what they've done . . . what they always do. Look at how this always ends. With fire. With death. And funerals of our children." I dunno about y'all, but I heard that shit in the voice of Danny Glover holding twenty-year-old scotch while staring out into his backyard. Maaaaan, when that X-Men talk start sounding like the Black experience in 'Murica? Wooooooooooo. I mean I'm sure Storm/Bishop given a soliloquy of that effect mad times. Xavier is just saying it out loud now, but I digress.

Look, I don't know what's about to happen, but I do know that we are now in the endgame. All I know is Xavier and Magneto 'bout to go student loans on humanity. They gon' be making mad house calls 'cause there is a debt that must be paid. I need to know how I can show I am a mutant ally 'cause I want no parts of that smoke, bonfire, hell or high water Xavier 'bout to bring. Y'all got a safety pin I can rock? There a form a normie can fill out?! Lemme know.

Blade II Still Has the Most Disrespectful Superhero Fades My Black Ass Has Ever Seen

OMAR HOLMON,
aka **Wesley Snipes's Spotify Playlist Curator**

BLADE IS THE reason superhero movies are the new Spaghetti Western. Tell me I'm wrong, look me in the windows of my soul and tell me differently. *Iron Man* had to get *Blade*'s blessing before ushering in the Marvel Cinematic Universe. *Allen Iverson voice* I mean we talking 'bout *Blade*? *Blaaaaade*? Wesley Snipes's *Blade* series, my vampire? *Blade* was proof that comic book characters could turn in successful film adaptations on the big screen. *Blade II*, however, *wipes tear away* *Blade II* is scientific proof that there's only one way to beat a roomful of henchmen's ass.

I done seen some fight scenes in my day, but a roomful of Edward Cullens getting the stakes beat off 'em? Where they do that at? I ain't ever seen grown-ass vampires get defanged on-screen before. If you've never seen this fight scene it is a must. YouTube it right now. Type in "Blade 2 Final Fight with Reinhardt." I am entirely deadass, do it because we gotta John Madden these highlights *rubs hands together* when I tell you no henchman's ass was safe in *Blade*

WILLIAM EVANS AND OMAR HOLMON

II. Y'all remember the scene, right? Blade was above that pool of blood getting shot at. Then he threw himself off that catwalk into the blood bath bomb below him. In real life, Wesley Snipes then rose up from that pool of red dye #40 and cranberry juice ready for fight choreography. What we saw was Blade rise up from a blood Jacuzzi, get surrounded by the mid-level boss Reinhardt's men, then tell the house DJ, "Yo, put something with some bass on that I can beat these muthafuckas' ass to." I'm not sure why the DJ obliged but whatever, because soon as the Crystal Method's "Name of the Game" came on we got the most detailed mollywhopping fight scene in comic book history to this day.

First and foremost, he gave two dudes a fucking Shawn Michaels Sweet Chin Music superkick. Blade kicked Henchman #2 so hard the windshield of his riot gear helmet said, "Fuck this," and flew out the helmet. I'm just saying, if I'm Henchman #33 and I see Blade channel Shawn Michaels's superkick on Gary (Henchman #2), I'm shopping my résumé out for a new boss. I'm emailing Wilson Fisk, Lex Luthor, Talia al Ghul, or Black Mariah. Blade legit superkicked Henchman #2's face off then went back to Henchman #1, who was already down from a knee to the stomach, regretting all his life choices right as Blade A-Town stomped his face in. That riot headgear must only have +1 defense, 'cause that visor got crushed like a soda can. Blade legit just *American History X*'d a man's facial pattern without a second thought, bruh. Blade gave dude Seth Rollins's Curb Stomp finisher. Blade out here mosh pitting on people's faces then handing out additional Young Bucks–level superkicks! Blade superkicked Henchman #4 so hard gravity forgot which way was right side up for duke. The man turned into a confused twist as that kick sent him into that blood bath.

The next guy (Henchman #6) to get it was a dude that caught the highlight fade of this entire fight. Blade roundhoused this poor man so hard that he went over the rail of the platform they're on doing a gymnastic twisting pass. Yeah, I had to look the move up in order to properly describe it. I'm not even sure that henchman even took gymnastics as a youth, but after the power of that fucking all-around-the-world roundhouse kick? I mean gawtdaaaamn—he still tumbling to his doom as far as we know. For real tho, Blade kicked dude so hard he Fruit Roll Up'd himself. How you kick a man so hard he lands Tony Hawk's 900? Fam went over the rail like a spilled drink. Listen, if you ever get roundhouse kicked so hard that it makes you Simone Biles in the air, you need a new line of work. Security is not for you.

What happens next can only be described as a one-way trip to "fuck outta here." Henchman #8 ran right into a fucking hip toss like he was in the Royal Rumble. How you catch the hip toss into obscurity and get the just for good measure no-look back kick to your face as you down on the ground? If you hip toss a man you can at least look at him before or while kicking him while he's down, right? Pfffft, not Blade. Can we talk about how Blade'll never be a licensed chiropractor?

You see him Jenga Henchman #10's and #11's necks one after the other? Blade caught 'em in Finn Bálor's Sling Blade before finishing 'em off like Billy Bob Thornton in *Sling Blade*. Blade blowing necks and backs out on some Sleepy's box spring mattress. Blade adjusting folk vertebrae like it's an antenna not picking up reception. How he snap into a dude's neck on some Slim Jim shit before UPS overnighting another SUUUUPER-KIIIICK? Blade superkicked Henchman #12 so hard I thought he was one of the paintings on the wall. Dude went into the air like Rick James when Charlie Murphy kicked 'em. Blade making all these nameless dudes working overtime hold all these damn L's. Blade took someone's electric baton and proceeded to nail these dudes with all of Nightwing's combos from *Injustice*, then hit the drum breakdown from Phil Collins's "In the Air Tonight" all over they chest. You on some other shit when you jam a baton in someone's face. Blade plugged that shit in Henchman #23's face like it was a USB port. Dude took a phone charger straight to the face. It's safe to say everybody in this scene probably shit themselves on this fade. However, every hospital bill Blade made these folks have to pay (that their health care won't cover or copay) was nothing compared to the shit he saved up last. To this day it's still the most disrespectful shit I ever seen.

BLADE DEADASS GRABBED HENCHMAN #27, PUT 'EM IN A HEADLOCK, THEN LIFTED HIM IN THE AIR FOR A FUCKING STALLING SUPLEX JUST FOR THE FUCK OF IT. Who fucking suplexes a man just to prove a point in a fight?! Blade held that suplex before coming down with it so it'd hurt more. There must have been a time traveler in the audience, 'cause somebody shouted, "World Star!" at this in 2002 and WorldStarHipHop wasn't founded until 2005. That man's spine got turned into Vermont jam. That man's spine is loose enough to be used for double Dutch jump rope now. That man's spine looking like angel hair pasta with the lobster sauce. That's some fucking sicko shit. Again, your favorite hero could never take disrespect to these heights! Reinhardt got off easy by getting cut in two. If I'm one of the henchmen I'd be pissed about that. Like, "Hey, man, what the fuck, you over here giving us ECW and NJPW pro wrestling finishers for just doing our job. Put Reinhardty's ass in the Coquina Clutch like you did to Gary . . . Gary was Henchman #2; we have names, Blade! You kill the mid-level boss with a slash but I saw you put Jarod in the fucking Boston Crab. He's working this job to buy his kid a bike, man. Don't you just walk away all cool as the music cuts off, Blade! Don't you catch your shades that ya mans Whistler threw to you all dope-like in midair while I'm yelling at you, Blade. What am I supposed to do about my legs, Blade? Huh? My legs lookin' like ramen noodles. Shoulda never gave you niggas a hero film! Ya don't know how to appreciate shit!"

Now we could end this highlight reel right here, with the hero being triumphant and taking a win. *Blade II* don't get down like that. Blade came back for this sequel to give us a WrestleMania-level final boss battle and oh my god did he deliver. Nomak put all of the hands all over Blade. Blade took his L's with the utmost dignity. My man dove after Nomak with the Link Down + A *Smash Bros.* attack and a Van Daminator. Nomak said, "Word? Let's get it, then." Fam, you see Nomak hit the spins moves with his coat before the fake-out by sticking his hand in Blade's face?! Nomak gave 'em Kristi Yamaguchi finesse with the spins before hitting him with that good night right hook. That fake-out may as well have been the "Expose him! EXPOSE HIM!" crossover. Blade got the AND1 Hot Sauce fake-out before that red-eye flight to "Fuck you thought this was?" Blade's face got tsunami waves from the impact, man. How you hit a man so hard his face get ripples on it like ya fist was a skipping stone?

Blade got ahold of Nomak and asked what that health insurance do as he broke his arm with a Kimura lock. Man, Nomak rolled up over the top Blade's head, took his broken arm, and Affordable Care Acted that shit back together like it was nothing. Nomak legit said, "Pop, lock, and drop it," to his arm and was good to go. Dude, Nomak didn't even need Robitussin for that break. Nomak must have had a mom that put the fear of god in 'em if he ever broke something and she had to take 'em to the hospital. Listen, Blade was getting lit the fuck up. I ain't ever seen a hero get his ass kicked like this in his own movie. I seen it happen in their own TV show (the Flash knows what I'm talking about), but in your own movie?! For this long?! Unheard of. Gawtdayum. Blade tried to rush Nomak and Nomak sent Blade's ass out like a bellhop with fucking Usos's superkick. The worst part is the fucking setup for the superkick. He got that Shawn Michaels tuning up the band in the distance Sweet Chin Music superkick. Blade was having a superkick party earlier; he caught a mean one and was like, "Damn, is this what I been doing to people?" Blade hit the elevator so hard it crumpled like the aluminum foil a Nestlé Crunch is wrapped in. Elevator folded in on itself like a politician promising tax cuts for the middle class. Elevator looking like hope post–student loans debits.

Listen, I ain't ever come close to throwing the towel in on a hero getting they ass beat down, but good Yeezus. When Nomak grabbed Blade by the ankles and spun him around? Yo, I ain't ever seen a hero get the *Super Smash Bros.* toss throw in real time. Bruh got caught in the Cesaro Swing. Nomak merry-go-round'd Blade and things were never the same. The swing is bad enough, but Blade's head colliding with a column is that extra insult to injury. Hurts more.

Nomak bounced Blade's head off the wall like a stress ball. Name the last time you saw a villain hammer throw a hero like he was trying to qualify for the Olympics? As if that wasn't bad enough, when Blade landed, Nomak fucking climbed the wall like he was climbing the fucking turnbuckle goin' to the top rope! Nomak jumped off the wall and hit Blade with Kairi Sane elbow, landed, and gave 'em two more elbows of equal force to the first. I let out a Ric Flair "Wooooo" watching this shit. I love Blade, but this is Summer Jam screen worthy right here. This shit needs to be a highlight on ESPN *SportsCenter.* Look at the height! My man took it to gravity to drive home the point.

Do you have any idea how many fucks you have to not give to deliver the fade in the form of a fucking elbow drop? Legend. Nomak is a fucking legendary villain off the strength, off the fucking strength, of these 'bows alone. *standing ovation* I knew this was going to be a good-ass fight when Blade and Nomak rushed each other and just collided. They started swinging on each other, and they both got knocked down to a knee and kept fucking swinging. Yes. Yes. THIS IS HOW YOU FUCKING BEEF! First and foremost, if a hero and villain ain't beefin' like Blade and Nomak, then they fucking failed the hero movie genre. Look at that fight scene segment, man. Don't look at these words, look at that fucking fight scene. That's the definition of beef-on-sight. Dare I say peak beef. Grade-A, grass-fed, and exported-from-Portlandia beef. What Solange's size 7s said to Jay in the elevator beef. What 2008 Kanye said to George W. Bush beef. Stand the test of time beef. "Et tu, Brute?" beef. Judas selling out Jesus beef. Drank thrown in somebody's face so you know it's real beef. Takeout from Arby's beef, my guy.

wipes sweat off forehead It's been sixteen years and no Marvel or DC movie has come close to embarrassing cats on hand-to-hand game like *Blade*. I already got a petition to get these ass-whuppings from Blade in *Blade II* donated to the Smithsonian National Museum of African American History and Culture. I want these fades on the curriculum to be covered for Black History Month in schools. These fades deserve to be studied in a lecture hall for Throwing Hands 101. In the list of things to never forget:

- The Clippers blew a 3-1 lead.
- Megan Thee Stallion is nerd prime minister.
- Fifty-five percent of white women voted for Donald Trump.
- Henrietta Lacks's HeLa cells proved Black women are magic/Highlanders.
- *Blade II* made disrespecting henchmen in a fight scene its own genre of high art.

Chadwick Boseman's Wakanda Salute Is Canon in the History of Black Language

WILLIAM EVANS,
aka Wakanda's Transportation Secretary

WE CATCH IT at about the forty-five-second mark of the second *Black Panther* trailer. Chadwick Boseman, aka T'Challa, aka the Black Panther, is walking through an Afrofuturistic lab where he greets Shuri, the Wakandan princess played by Letitia Wright. The greeting follows the two-beat tradition. The dap is always on the upbeat. The initiator. Anyone can get this step. Even the outsiders. Even the colonizers. The open-hand clap. We're not shaking hands. The fingers angle up toward your recipient's heart, not at their feet. The downbeat is what tells us what the relationship is. If the fingers lock? We cool. A default setting. Maybe we just met. Maybe we ain't as cool as we used to be. But we respect each other enough. And this is fine. Maybe it's a hug. Older heads might pull you in. Now the fists are at the center of our chests. New generation, the hand dap breaks apart before the hug. We clear space. Make room for more. Let nothing hinder this embrace. But *Black Panther* gave us something new.

Chadwick and Letitia were on some other shit. The dap. Then the arms crossed in front of the body. Fists at your shoulders. The sentient form of "you hold me down and I'll hold you down." And we all went, "Oh shit. That's the move." It was so simple. It followed our rhythms. It fit into our arsenal of greetings that say, "I see you, and by doing this, I know I'll be seen."

The clenched fists are perhaps the most important part of the salute. There is a tension between what appears to be an embrace of one's self vs. the fists tight against your shoulders. It is resistance. It is a coiled snake. Don't start none, won't be none. When you make this salute at someone it means "I got you." But also, "if we need to, we ride tonight."

After the bombastic success of *Black Panther*, the actors were everywhere. And as you would expect of the title character, Chadwick was everywhere. It followed the movie-release blueprint, but obviously, something was different. No movie with a predominantly Black cast and a Black director had ever made this much money before. Which is a long way of saying no Black film had ever brought this many white people to the theater. But it was also different because it didn't submit to the white gaze. Chadwick and the team worked on a specific, non-colonized accent. Ruth Carter, the famed costume designer, wove together her own ideas of futuristic design with a reported one hundred samples of clothing from across the African continent and its communities. And so, the guilt of enjoying something with largely Black aesthetics that pandered to white folks didn't exist. So we were all aboard. And we all wanted nothing more than to see the cast talk about their experiences with the film, with each other, and with us after the release.

I usually have a hard time with the way we conflate a character and an artist. When someone exclusively refers to a performer by the name of a character they played, I'm usually quick to state there's a real person under that costume and makeup. But Chadwick loved being Black Panther because we, Black folks, loved him being Black Panther. And nobody did the Wakanda salute more than Chadwick. At the MTV Movie & TV Awards, when he won for best hero and then gave his award to James Shaw, Jr., who had fought off a gunman at a Waffle House. On *The Tonight Show Starring Jimmy Fallon*, when he greeted fans expressing their gratitude toward *Black Panther* and the representation it held. At the Howard commencement ceremony, where he told the graduates about legacy and purpose. At the NBA All-Star Weekend, when he gave Victor Oladipo the Black Panther mask and salute during the dunk contest.

And because the living and breathing internet needs to validate its existence from time to time, the discourse became that Chadwick must be tired of doing the salute. That he looked like he was going through the motions. But then Chadwick again showed us who he was. That he was one of us. On a *Breakfast Club* interview he said, "I'm not gonna tap-dance. It means something. If you give me the salute, I'm gonna give it back." Black folks know what *tap-dance* means. There's a visceral reaction to invoking the action, when it was predicated by a demand. Chadwick was showing a resistance to commodifying the action. The movie was breaking records, the salute wasn't a promotional tool anymore. If it ever was. It was a communication. A language we had become fluent in.

In 2018, about a month after the movie had come out, I had to replace the tires on my car. Probably overdue. I walked into the tire place and handed them my keys. I was the only Black person in the waiting room including the staff that I could see. They told me it would take two hours and so I walked the two miles back home. When I returned two and a half hours later, my car wasn't ready. Actually, they hadn't even started. The man behind the counter wasn't very helpful or empathetic. They got busy, he was saying. What I was seeing were cars that weren't here when I arrived earlier already being done. I was about to argue with this man, pin him down, make him admit he had shoved me to the back of the line. But there was a Black employee, the only one I could see now, who had watched the whole interaction from the mechanics' bay. He came into the store lobby and told the other guy, "I got him." They began to argue for a moment before the Black employee shut it down: "He's been waiting, man, I said I got him. I'll do his car now." And then he looked at me. He shook his head. And then he gave me the Wakanda salute. And I smiled, probably the biggest smile that my body could produce, and I gave him the salute back.

After Chadwick Boseman died at the age of forty-three from cancer, I found myself tagged in different social media posts. They were mostly of me posing with friends at our *Black Panther* premiere party. Arms crossed across our chests, fists burrowed into our shoulders. The pictures are from more than two years ago, and today they mean "hold fast." "Hold tight. We lost another one." I think of the salute as it originated for me before *Black Panther*. We've all seen salutes by the military on TV, whether they were fictional depictions or at a funeral of a former leader lying in state. But I was never in the military, even when so many of the men in my family were. And I still never saw a salute in person. A lot of uniforms but no salutes. And I wouldn't, by function. The salute wasn't intended for me. It was a brotherhood in which I was not a member.

The Wakanda salute is a bitter pill in this way. A simple gesture linking so many of us. An evolution of the nod. The dap from across the room when the distance makes knowing glances too ambivalent. I cross my chest like a sarcophagus in a crowded room and you know what I mean. Any of the dozens of things I may mean. But now, it is no longer just a gift that Chadwick gave us, but an inheritance. Black folks inherit so much, even if it ain't wealth, so much is left for us. And what could be worse than wasting what your ancestors left for you?

Outro

YOU CAN'T SEE it, but the entirety of this outro is taking place in a red 1997 Range Rover that has "Anime Is Life" written on the windshield and the Uchiha Clan's Sharingan painted on the hood of the truck. William is driving, and Omar is leaning out of the window shouting the following:

OMAR: Yeaaaaaaaah, muthafuckas. You wanted that Black subculture nerd shit? Now you got it. You wanted that blerd substance? There's two hundred–plus pages for ya. You wanted everything from Aloy to *The Wire*? Well, there the fuck it is. We done gave it all to you in key of X gon' give it to ya. Are you not entertained?! Are you not satisfied?! Fuck heart and soul, we done went and put all of our AllSpark in this shit for y'all.

WILLIAM: On everything, if you told me ten years ago, "Aye, Will, one day you and Omar gonna go so deep in the nerd shit, you're gonna write a book about it. And muthafuckas gonna be up in Barnes & Noble, Target, or Half Price Books buying that shit," I would've sent you back to the store with that shit like Cube told Regina King in *Boyz n the Hood*. This right here is for all the Black nerds who secretly loved Captain America while being on the board of your school's Black Student Union. This is for the Black nerds who grew up during the zenith of hip-hop but wore a Portishead record out. This is for the Black nerds who identified with every single Black character in *Higher Learning*. The athlete, the nerd, the revolutionary, the teacher. We got you. Just know we got you.

OMAR: All those years of waking up at 6:00 a.m. to catch the *Sailor Moon* and *Iron Man* cartoon block before school, every action figure bought, every pop culture T-shirt, and every combo ever pulled off in a video game was all in preparation to deliver this book for the culture. *takes glasses off and holds them in the air* To all my nearsighted and farsighted fellows, we bequeath this to you. So take it! Take this! Our love (for anime), our anger (over fanfics and webcomics that have gone unfinished), and all of our sorrow (for shows canceled in their prime).

WILLIAM: I remember when my parents asked me who I wanted to be for Halloween one year. And I was like, "Gandalf the Grey!" with all the strength in my chest. And my dad looked at me for a long-ass time and said, "Nah, you want Gandalf the White, when he came back and led everyone to glory." NO, DAD, THE GREY SHIT HIT HARDER. I'm a quest starter, Dad. I am a shepherd, b. Let me liiiiive.

Anyways, Pops was mostly right. Something about sacrificing and coming out shining on the other side just hit different.

Omar and I said the nerd game needed more hip-hop references, more "you only know this shit if you grew up in a Black home, but here's how it relates to X-Men" dialogues. I'm glad y'all took this journey with us. I'm glad y'all invested in some dudes that say *muthafucka* as easily as drawin' breath.

OMAR: Look at how we all connected through nerddom, man. My mother used to read *The Hobbit* to my siblings and me when I was a baby. Ever since the day Mom bought Storm as my first action figure and I found my father's and brother's old comic books, this book was destined to happen. My parents initiated me for this life not knowing it would be taken this far. Not knowing that their boy would say, "Fuck getting a government job or becoming a preacher, what the world really needs is these bars about Scott Summers being an underrated X-Man. What the world really needs is someone to remember all these Black characters in comic book limbo. What the world really needs is to know that *CARS 3* IS AN UNDERRATED PIXAR BANGER!" And I hope that having read this book from Will and I, at some point after finishing a chapter you felt relaxed and comfortable enough to say, "I needed that."

WILLIAM: Shout-out to our parents being the guiding nerddom in our lives, and shout-out to the folks raising nerdy-ass, Black-ass kids today. I know them getting into *Dora the Explorer* lore and fan fiction sounds crazy, but let it happen. I know they want to make You-Tube videos about the origin of those *Marvel: The Hip-Hop Covers* and all their references. ALLOW IT. *John Boyega head nod* Nerd shit can lead to big things, yo. Big things.

Acknowledgments

OMAR: Biggest thank you to my wife/tag-team partner, Natasha, for enduring every good and really bad essay pitch I was working out for this book. To my mom, Isabelle, for taking me to see Meteor Man; my dad, George, for showing me his comic books; and my sister, Kece, and brother, Travis, for taking the time to listen to their little brother rant about pop culture. I've been fortunate enough to meet an array of nerd specialists in their respective fields that I could call friends. I learned how vast the spectrum of nerd truly is from Acting Nerds (Brittany), Comedy Nerds (Josh), Academic Nerds (Christabel), Med School Nerds (Mackenzie), Zombie Apocalypse Nerds (Nicole), Can't-Believe-It's-Not-Hetero Nerds (Malika), Book Nerds (Jordan), Lyricist Nerds (Toney Jackson), Hip-Hop Nerds (Frantz), SneakerHead Nerds (Jive), Wrestling Nerds (Big Mike), Music Nerds (Glynn), Sports Nerds (Elvis, Bri), Poetry Nerds (Cristin), and of course all them Black Nerd Problems Nerds. Much like Deku adjusting to his quirk One For All, y'all have strengthened the foundation for the type of nerdy muhfucka I am.

WILLIAM: First off to my wife, Leah, who displayed superhero patience while this book was being written and for my daughter, Amira, the budding and ultra-fun nerd that she already is and will be. Thank you to my mother, Beverly Ann, and my father, who I named after and was the first Black nerd I came to know. To my sister, who has always kept a constant stream of nerddom flowing between us. Thank you to Carrie "Clipps" McClain, who helped Black Nerd Problems go from some bullshit Omar and I were on to a living, breathing, and accessible community. To Marshall Shorts and Soulo Theory, who helped launch us. To everyone who has and continues to contribute to Black Nerd Problems. Your passion and perspective have pushed me to be better more than you could know. And thank you to our Black Nerd Problems community, for letting Omar and I know that all of those hours, weeks, and years of work—and I mean real-ass work—was not wasted. I'm so happy to share the space with you all.